Ways Of Wisdom

Readings On The Good Life

Edited By Steve Smith

Illustrations By
Linda Powers Leviton

Copyright © 1983 by

University Press of America,™ Inc.

4720 Boston Way
Lanham, MD 20706

3 Henrietta Street
London WC2E 8LU England

Library of Congress Cataloging in Publication Data

Main entry under title:

Ways of wisdom.

Includes bibliographical references.
1. Life—Addresses, essays, lectures. 2. Conduct of
life—Addresses, essays, lectures. I. Smith, Steve,
1939-
BD431.W246   1983   170   83-12444
ISBN 0-8191-3387-6
ISBN 0-8191-3388-4 (pbk. : alk. paper)

To my students

PREFACE

This is a book about living well.

If we are to live good lives, we must learn to live rightly: to treat ourselves and others as we should. But living a good life entails more than living rightly. To live good lives, we must also learn to live well: to make our own lives personally satisfying, rewarding, more fully realized. I believe that the point of living rightly is to make it possible for all of us to live well. If, as the philosopher Hobbes asserted, life without morality and its fruits is "solitary, poor, nasty, brutish and short," then life with morality should be social, rich, delightful, refined and long. The point of morality is the abundant life.

In our hunger to live well, we sometimes abandon our commitment to right behavior, thereby harming ourselves and others. As a result, we may come to think that living well must be abandoned, if we are to live as we should. Morality then seems moralistic, inviting us to be either fanatics or cynics. But morality should enrich our lives, not impoverish them. I believe that living well is not an alternative to living rightly, but is its proper fruit.

Images of living well--personal well-being, and quality of life--are the primary subject-matter of this book. I have sought readings that present compelling pictures of a various ideal ways of life, drawing from major traditions in the West and East. All of the views included here entail moral sensitivity and social responsibility; still, morality is treated not as the primary theme, but as it contributes to living well. In this regard, I have departed from the approach of most current readers in ethics and value theory, which commonly emphasize issues of right and wrong. My aim is not to supplant such approaches but to complement them. Moral issues arise throughout the book in connection with various views of the good life. The book may, in fact, be used as a conceptual laboratory for exploring the relationship between morality and self-interest, between living rightly and living well.

The book develops dialectically: the leading theme of each chapter flows naturally out of the preceding one, with critique selections providing a bridge to the next chapter wherever possible. The sequence of chapter themes is as follows:

–**Chapter I: Encountering Emptiness:** Before positive views of the good life are presented, the need for some such view is forcefully stated, in descriptions of the experience of emptiness and futility. Plato's Apology is a transition piece, an invitation to the search for wisdom.

–**Chapter II: Pleasure:** The first and most obvious answer to the problem of an empty life is to fill it by prudent enjoyment of pleasant things.

–**Chapter III: Detachment:** Life brings, however, not only pleasure but also pain and anxiety. Psychic detachment presents itself as an attractive means to achieve relief and serenity.

–**Chapter IV: Becoming Human:** If detachment from natural desires is regarded as an incomplete way of life, it is natural to move to notions of the development of persons qua human beings.

–**Chapter V: Nature:** A broadened view of personal growth sees it as continuous with growth and change throughout the natural world. The good life is found in affinity with nature.

–**Chapter VI: God:** From identification with nature to identification with God: yet a more exalted object of human aspirations. The chapter addresses generic Western monotheism, those beliefs common to the three major Western theistic traditions; selections are taken from scripture regarded as sacred by all three traditions.

–**Chapter VII: Authentic Existence:** The theme of the death of God introduces atheistic existentialism. The good life is a life of uncompromising honesty, responsibility for creating oneself, and revolt against a meaningless universe.

–**Chapter VIII: Universe:** Not revolt, but loving acceptance of the present moment is the key to happiness. In moments of mystical insight or enlightenment, one awakens to one's unity with all things. Emptiness--the dynamic emptiness of an open, receptive awareness--is not the problem, but the solution.

This arrangement invites a misconception: that each view of the good life is regarded as an improvement upon the previous one, with the final chapter viewed as the most satisfactory. In fact, however, no such comparative evaluation is implied. I regard the various views of the good life presented here not as steps on a ladder but as a string of precious gems, each one of which may reasonably be regarded as the most beautiful of all. The chapter themes might plausibly be organized in a variety of ways; numerous motifs interweave from one complex body of beliefs to the next, permitting many appropriate juxtapositions. Despite the dialectical development described above, each chapter is largely self-contained, permitting the reader to choose a different order of topics without significant loss of intelligibility.

In my brief chapter introductions, I have departed from the ideal of editorial impartiality in favor of advocacy: in each introductory essay I have for pedagogical purposes adopted the view of that chapter, presenting it persuasively rather than merely descriptively. When introducing the critique selections, I return to a more impartial stance.

At the end of each chapter are study questions, organized into three groups: questions for review, questions for reflection, and questions for discussion. The first, questions for review, require a close reading of the chapter materials; they are intended to promote comprehension of key points. The second, questions for reflection, are intended primarily for the private use of the reader, though they can also be used in a group setting to encourage self-disclosure and greater mutual trust. The third, questions for discussion, are open-ended invitations to controversy and argument. Each chapter closes with a limited number of suggestions for further reading on the theme of the chapter.

The flexibility of this book allows its use in a variety of settings: as a primary or supplementary text for courses in ethics and value theory; as a primary or supplementary text for a beginning philosophy course; as one of several texts in courses on the human condition, personal values, perspectives on life and death, the meaning of life, humanistic psychology, and related themes. The book is an exploration of ideas rather than a compendium of techniques; in its focus upon ideals for the conduct of life, the book is concerned primarily with conceptual issues rather than with specific strategies for self-improvement. But where personal and emotional problems are rooted in confusion about larger, life-guiding ideals, the book may be usefully employed in conjunction with various more specific means of personal and spiritual growth.

My own training has been in philosophy, and I like to think of the central inquiry of this book as philosophical. I am aware that some contemporary philosophers dissociate their professional concerns from the kinds of questions asked here. In contrast, my view is that one form of wisdom is the knowledge of how to live rightly and well, and that philosophy, as "love of wisdom," includes the pursuit of such knowledge.

Acknowledgements

I am indebted to many persons for help and support in the creation of this book. My treasured colleagues Steve Davis, Clark Kucheman and John Roth have been generous of their time and moral support; their helpful comments and stalwart encouragement consistently sustained and improved my efforts. My own prose in the book has been subjected to masterful criticism by another colleague, Langdon Elsbree, from whom I have learned more about good writing than from any other person since my college freshman humanities professor. To a dear friend and mentor, Selden Marth, I owe much of my own growth toward the good life, growth that has formed the book in innumerable subtle ways. My wife, Daryl, has been my first and best sounding board, and has helped me through many difficulties with her wise judgment and loving support. Over several years, Pat Padilla has typed and retyped portions of the book, always with impeccable skill and cheerful efficiency. Polly Baker, in addition to lengthy typing of earlier drafts, shouldered the heroic task of putting the book into its final form, responding rapidly and with good humor to my often exacting requests. Finally, for helping me to form the book I am deeply grateful to several generations of students. Years ago, a student's remark that my conventional ethics course, while intellectually stimulating and worthwhile, did not really help him to know how to live, first planted in my mind the seed of a new course that might better meet that need. When I did create such a course, student responses helped me to select readings that I eventually incorporated into the book. Student evaluations helped me to strengthen my editorial introductions. Above all, the remarkable quality of my students' efforts to clarify their own views of the good life confirmed for me the need for a book of this kind, and demonstrated to me the integrity and enduring educational worth of the ancient human quest for a better life.

CONTENTS

GENERAL INTRODUCTION

The good life . . . the very words are inviting. Images come to mind of how our lives might be, if our deepest needs and longings were fulfilled. Yet in awakening our hopes, such images are a reminder of the distance between what is and what might be. When dreams are distant, they may generate ambition, hard work and achievement; but they may also be a source of anguish, only dulled by a dimming of the dreams themselves. Alternatively, if we achieve our goals, we may find them hollow and disillusioning. Put simply: for most of us, our lives are not what we wish they were. Writing in the middle of the nineteenth century, Thoreau declared that "The mass of men lead lives of quiet desperation."[1]* Later in the same century, describing one of his protagonists, Tolstoy wrote "Ivan Ilych's life had been most simple and most ordinary and therefore most terrible."[2] These are harsh judgments; yet they were written by two men with extraordinary powers of observation, empathy and moral insight.

Do Thoreau and Tolstoy overstate the case? While most persons do not lead blissful and idyllic lives, neither do they seem "desperate" nor would one ordinarily describe their existence as "most terrible." While misery and desperation are indeed the lot of far too many persons, surely the more common pattern is one of a more or less adequately satisfying existence, in which the pain one endures is largely balanced by periods of genuine happiness, pleasure and achievement.

When Thoreau wrote of "quiet desperation," however, he did not mean its more visible forms--a prisoner about to be executed, a person missing a bus. He was writing of that hidden desperation which passes for

*See end of each editorial introduction for notes to that introduction. All other notes are at the bottom of each page.

1

resignation, the "making do with one's lot": abandoning dreams, trying to fill up our lives with amusements and diversions, with wealth and status, while inside we are slowly dying. Behind this apparently aimless groping for gratification is, indeed, often a kind of "quiet desperation."

Tolstoy's point is similar. For most of his life Ivan Ilych was self-satisfied, certain of what he wanted, and successful in acquiring the things (social approval, status, wealth, power, the "proper" material goods) which he thought he desired. Only at the end of his life, when he was in great pain and knew that he was dying, did Ivan Ilych realize that he had not been happy after all. Not only had his past life been of little worth to others; it had not even been worthwhile for himself. Thoreau and Tolstoy recognized that what passes for an "adequately satisfying life" is often not adequate at all.

What matters for us here is not, however, a statistical judgment about how many persons live "adequately satisfying lives." What matters is simply the personal fact that for most of us, life falls short of what we would like it to be, and that in moments of quiet reflection we dream and yearn for better things.

The first and primary truth is the fact that we hunger for a better life. But while that is the first truth, it is merely the starting point. We can improve the quality of our lives if we bend our thoughts and efforts toward that improvement. We can grow in many ways: in enjoyment and peace of mind; in self-knowledge and openness; in our capacity to deal effectively with pain, disappointment, anxiety, loneliness, and death; in better relations with other persons and with nature; in deeper and more nourishing insights; and in many other ways.

If our lives fall short of what they might be, it is often because we are unwilling to devote thought and energy to their improvement. Personal growth toward a better life may be discomfiting or painful, and in any case requires much time and effort. We would rather take an easier path, pursuing more immediate attractions. But calling us away from that path are the words of Socrates, the first great Western philosopher. At the trial which led to his conviction and execution, the seventy-year-old Socrates stated his challenge to all whom he met: "Good sir, you are an Athenian, a citizen of the greatest city with the greatest reputation for both wisdom and power; are you not ashamed of your eagerness to possess as much wealth, reputation and honours as possible, while you do not care for nor give thought to wisdom or truth, or the best possible state of your soul?"[3] Socrates' challenge, issued more than two thousand years ago, may be taken as the keynote for this book.

Let us suppose that you, the reader, genuinely accept this challenge. What can you reasonably expect from a careful reading of the various selections which this book contains?

2

First, a note of caution: this is not a series of "recipes" to achieve various desired results. While most of the authors provide some precepts and guidelines for how to achieve the life they advocate, their emphasis is largely upon a description of the desirable life itself. We differ from one another so much, and start from such different places, that no precise map can be given which would tell each of us how to get where we want to go. As with a visit to a travel bureau, one inspects a variety of attractive brochures in order to select a desirable destination, a destination where one may wish to live permanently. But no vehicle is available to take us to the destination we select; we must get there on our own power. What the reader can hope for is a clearer, more compelling picture of where he or she would like to go. Such a picture can be of immense value. As Aristotle remarks, "If, then, there is some end of the things we do, which we desire for its own sake (everything else being desired for the sake of this) . . . clearly this must be the good and the chief good. Will not the knowledge of it, then, have a great influence on life? Shall we not, like archers who have a mark to aim at, be more likely to hit upon what is right?"[4]

The General Concept of the Good Life.

Not every set of precepts and ideals can count as a "theory of the good life." The goal of becoming an expert tennis player, together with a manual which gives techniques for achieving that goal, would not ordinarily be regarded as a "theory of the good life." Nor would a set of prescriptions laying down the "ideal" diet to achieve maximum health ordinarily be regarded as such a theory (though it might well be part of a larger theory which would count as a view of the good life). A "theory of the good life" (as we are using the term here) is more comprehensive; it involves precepts and guidelines about most or all of those aspects of life which affect us deeply and generally. The great historical views of the good life in the East and West give attention to a wide variety of questions, among which the following are perhaps the most important:

1. How shall I treat myself? What is the most accurate and helpful view of my own nature?
2. How shall I relate to other persons? What is the role of interpersonal relations in the good life?
3. How shall I respond to the natural world? What is the significance of nature for the good life?
4. How shall I deal with pain, suffering, guilt, loneliness, fear and other such experiences? And especially: How shall I respond to death?
5. How may I come to feel psychologically or spiritually at home in the universe? How or where may I gain strength, direction, and an uplifting of my spirit?

Not every view of the good life responds to all of these questions. Nor must a view of the good life be limited to responses to these questions. Still, these questions are central to most major historical views of how life should be lived. Any system of beliefs which supplies answers to most of the questions can reasonably qualify as a "theory of the good life." Thus as a preliminary concept of the good life, let us say that the good life is a set of personally fulfilling responses to these questions.

The phrase "personally fulfilling responses" suggests that the content of the good life will vary from person to person. While as humans we have similar needs, we also differ in ways that require different choices. The point is not simply that we begin our inquiry with divergent views of the good life. For even after careful deliberation and an accurate weighing of the alternatives open to us, we can expect that the best choice of a way of life for one person may well differ sharply from the best choice for another. Many variables--one's temperament, one's personal history, one's general living conditions, one's talents and skills, one's age and health--enter into consideration. Some, by virtue of their temperament, will flourish in positions of power and authority, while others will require a quieter, more reflective existence. Highly emotional and impulsive individuals may wish to cultivate tranquility and serenity, whereas overly controlled and rigid persons may benefit from a dose of hedonism. As the conditions of our lives vary, so do our needs. As our needs vary, so also must our decisions as to the best way of life.

We can look at the need for a pluralistic view of the good life in another way. A view of the good life must concern itself in part with the major barriers to a good life: what they are, and how they may be dealt with. These barriers to a good life are at least as varied as the illnesses and disabilities which stand in the way of good physical health. Just as no sensible doctor would prescribe the same treatment for different medical conditions, so we should not prescribe one view of the good life as the panacea for all persons.

But while the best choice of a way of life will vary from person to person, these different versions of the good life may share some general features. If the claims made in the preceding paragraphs are correct, what counts as "the good life" must be relative to specific persons in specific circumstances. Furthermore, for a given person in a given set of circumstances, there may be more than one way of life which might reasonably be chosen. When we speak of the good life, let us therefore think in terms of the indefinite article: a good life. Then we may say that the good life for a specific person in a specific set of circumstances is a way of life which that person would deliberately choose, if he or she were well-informed about all of the major options available, could imaginatively identify with each of them and thus more accurately assess each one, and were choosing freely rather than out of constraint, coercion

4

or fear.[5]

These ideal conditions for a choice of a way of life are seldom if ever met. But they can be approximated in varying degrees. When we are choosing among major options for our lives, more and better understanding of these options is to be preferred over meager, inadequate understanding; and relative freedom to choose is to be preferred to a choice which is made under constraint, coercion or fear. Perhaps the chief value which this book may have for its readers is to enlarge their understanding of the options available to them and thereby enable them to make more intelligent choices. Such understanding should not be limited to abstract intellectual knowledge, but insofar as possible should include a vivid vicarious identification with the various options. An intelligent choice of a way of life requires some capacity for <u>empathy</u>--for imaginative identification with the experiences of others.

Finally, the formulation above for choice of a way of life is written in the subjunctive mood: the good life is one which <u>would</u> be chosen if one were well-informed and free to choose. For a person to be living a genuinely good life, it is not necessary (though it may often be the case) that such a choice ever actually occur. Many persons are fortunate enough to be living an attractive and fulfilling life without ever having deliberately chosen it; others stumble across a good way of life by accident, without comparing it to other options. Our formulation does not require us to hold that all such lives fall short of "the good life." It is sufficient if the individuals in question would choose the lives they now live, under the ideal conditions specified.

Morality and the Good Life

There is an important ambiguity in the phrase "the good life" which we have not yet explored. Suppose we hear someone say of an acquaintance "Fisher is living a good life." The speaker is likely to mean one of two things:

Living well: Fisher is living a personally satisfying, fulfilling life; Fisher has achieved happiness, peace of mind, enjoyment of life, serenity, etc.

Living rightly: Fisher is living an honest, responsible, admirable life; Fisher is decent and fair, a person of good character; Fisher behaves as one should behave.

The primary concern of this book is with the good life in the first of these two meanings: living well. While living rightly is not ignored in the selections included here, it is considered largely in terms of its contribution to the good life in the first sense. Some comments on this focus are called for.

The notion of living rightly is closely linked to the concept of morality, in a specific sense of that term: meeting one's obligations, treating others as one should, and so on. Morality in this specific sense may be seen as a set of rules and guidelines for social behavior: a system of constraints (much of which is usually written into law), which finds its chief rationale in our need to live in a smoothly functioning society governed by mutual restraint and respect. But the term is also used more broadly, to encompass a variety of life-guiding ideals, including conceptions of ideal personal well-being.[6] I believe that moral rules and constraints in the specific sense--living rightly--derive their primary justification from the pursuit of personal well-being or living well. It is because we all strive to improve our lives in various ways, and because these strivings are more likely to succeed in an environment of cooperation rather than conflict, that we need a system of social constraints and principles of behavior which constitutes morality in the specific sense. In the words of Ralph Barton Perry, morality in the specific sense is, properly, "the harmonization of interests for the sake of the interests harmonized."[7] In a society in which no person cared for or respected the desires and interests of any other person, it would be very difficult for most persons to achieve "a good life."

At this point, we should forestall or counter a possible confusion. In contrasting the two senses of "the good life"--living well and living rightly--we are not necessarily contrasting a "selfish" or egoistic concern with an unselfish, socially responsible concern. Maximizing the good life for oneself will probably entail a large measure of moral responsibility and moral sensitivity to other persons. Indeed, perhaps the most pervasive theme in the history of moral philosophy is the view that one cannot achieve a good life for oneself without behaving responsibility and rightly towards others.[8] Living well is not an exclusively selfish, egoistic pursuit.[9] According to most philosophers and nearly all major religious traditions, in fact, the personally fulfilling life is necessarily a life lived in accordance with the highest moral principles, in the specific sense of "morality." All of the views of the good life included here entail a morally responsible regard for the interests of others.

Politics and the Good Life

Some readers will find it odd that a book of readings on the good life contains very little in the way of political philosophy and political thought. Is not the good life for most of us importantly, indeed, crucially dependent upon our political and social setting? Aristotle regarded ethics as a branch of politics and called the latter "the master art."[10] He observed that "it is difficult to get from youth up a right training for virtue if one has not been brought up under right laws."[11] The political conditions of our society affect us so deeply, in so many ways, that it would seem necessary to concentrate upon protecting and improving them if we are to hope for a better life.[12] The conviction that political science is the supreme art for improving the quality of life is central to the views of perhaps most of the greatest social theorists of Western civilization.

Despite the relevance of political conditions to the good life, I believe that a good case can be made for the kind of emphasis which this book of readings exhibits. The chief value issues in political theory-- liberty and responsibility, authority and power, obligation and related notions--concern principles of living rightly, developed for the larger political and social context. Such inquiries are critically important. But if, as Aristotle declared, the state exists "for the sake of a good life,"[13] we also need to understand the quality of successfully lived individual lives--to inquire after human happiness, fulfillment and related notions. Aristotle himself puts such an inquiry at the heart of his ethical and political theory. Through a better understanding of concepts of living well, we may gain clarity about how political and social conditions might best be organized to promote such goods. Further, any fair representation of pieces stating political and social approaches to the betterment of life would have made this text unmanageably large. And a number of the most interesting theories of the good life, including some Eastern views, hold that the good life can be achieved solely through personal transformation. However that may be, my point is not to deny the importance of politics, but to affirm the importance of self-examination and personal growth.

Patterns of Growth

The primary theme of this book is, then, not morality in the sense of interpersonal obligation, and not morality as it develops into the realms of political policy and social utopia. The theme of this book is personal growth toward a better, more satisfying, more successful individual life. Such growth is not easy. As Bertrand Russell writes, a personally good, happy life is not "something that drops into the mouth, like a ripe fruit, by the mere operation of fortunate circumstances,"[14] but must be won through long and often painful searching and effort. The images of the good life presented in the following pages are not only inviting, but also demanding; their achievement requires honesty, self-knowledge and discipline.

In concluding, it may be useful to remember that many of the barriers to the good life arise not out of any absence of long-range vision, but out of a failure of basic day-to-day prudence. For instance: it is difficult to enjoy life if I am always tired and irritable because of insufficient sleep. It is difficult to enjoy life if I am inconsiderate of my physical health in other ways, such as eating poorly or not getting enough exercise. It is difficult to enjoy my contacts with other persons if I behave in offensive and neurotic ways towards them. It is difficult to enjoy myself if I am so overextended and overcommitted that nothing I do is done well. The quality of my life may be greatly improved by attending

7

to such specific and individual problems, either informally or with the help of a professional counselor of some kind.

Nevertheless there can also be great value in a larger, clearer vision of how to conduct my life as a whole. A view of the good life can uplift and sustain me; it can widen my horizons, generate new hopes, provide new pleasures and instill new wisdom. It can free me from many of the burdens of my past. It can provide a direction and rationale for the whole of my existence. For most of us there will be no final resting place this side of death. But we may reasonably hope for a better life than if no effort at self-examination and self-improvement were made. Indeed, we may come to agree with Socrates' claim that the inquiry into the most fundamental truths of human existence is the greatest good of all, and that "the unexamined life is not worth living . . . "[15]

NOTES

1. Henry D. Thoreau, Walden, ed. by J. Lyndon Shanley (Princeton, N. J.: Princeton University Press, 1971), p. 8.

2. Leo Tolstoy, The Death of Ivan Ilych and Other Stories (New York: Signet, New American Library, 1960), p. 104.

3. See this volume, p. 30f.

4. Aristotle, Nicomachean Ethics, translated by W. D. Ross, Book I, Chapt. 2, 1094a 17-24, in Introduction to Aristotle, ed. by Richard McKeon (New York: Random House, 1947), p. 309.

5. Cf. Paul Taylor, Normative Discourse (Englewood Cliffs, N.J.: Prentice Hall, Inc., 1961), pp. 164-175; John Rawls, A Theory of Justice (Cambridge, Mass.: The Belknap Press of Harvard University Press, 1971), pp. 416-424. Cf. also my "Primitive Rationality and Reasons for Being Moral," Bucknell Review, Vol. XXI, Nos. 2-3 (Fall-Winter, 1973), pp. 26-36, for a briefer and more informal version.

6. I have argued this point at greater length in my Satisfaction of Interest and the Concept of Morality (Lewisburg, Pa.: Bucknell University Press, 1974). See esp. pp. 140-144.

7. R. B. Perry, Realms of Value (Cambridge, Mass.: Harvard University Press, 1965), p. 92.

8. For a discussion of this issue, see my "Primitive Rationality and Reasons for Being Moral," in Bucknell Review, Vol. XXI, Nos. 2-3 (Fall-Winter, 1973), pp. 26-36.

9. For a more developed defense of this claim, see my "Ethical Egoism and Value," The Southern Journal of Philosophy, Vol. XII, No. 1 (Spring, 1974), pp. 95-102.

10. Nichomachean Ethics, translated by W. D. Ross, Book I, Chapt. 2 in Introduction to Aristotle, ed. by Richard McKeon (New York: Random House, 1947), p. 309.

11. Ibid., Book X, Chapt. 9, p. 538.

12. Readers who remember the revolutionary youth movement of the 1960s in the United States will recall that precisely this issue--the importance of political reform for the improvement of life--divided many members of the movement against one another. Does one begin "the revolution" by attempting to reform one's society, or attempting to transform oneself?

13. Politics, Book I, Chapt. 2, 1252b29-30; in Introduction to Aristotle, ed. by Richard McKeon (New York: Random House, 1947), p. 555.

14. Bertrand Russell, The Conquest of Happiness (New York: Liveright Publishing Corporation, 1930), p. 232.

15. See this volume, p. 35.

STUDY QUESTIONS FOR GENERAL INTRODUCTION

Questions for Review

1. What did Thoreau mean by the claim that "The mass of men lead lives of quiet desperation"?

2. Why would a manual for improving one's tennis game not count as a "theory of the good life"?

3. What five questions are usually answered by major historical views of the good life?

4. What are the editor's reasons for holding that "the best choice of a way of life for one person may well differ sharply from the best choice for another"?

5. Review the general definition of the good life (pp. 4f) and explain its components.

6. What is the editor's distinction between living rightly and living well? What is his view about the relationship between them?

7. Why are selections from political and social philosophy not included in this anthology?

Questions for Reflection

1. What are my own fondest dreams for the future? How likely is it that if I achieved those dreams, I would be truly happy?

2. How much of my own life could be called "quietly desperate"?

3. How fully do I give myself to the improvement of my own life?

4. To what extent does Socrates' challenge apply to me?

5. In making major choices in my own life, to what extent am I well-informed and free from coercion?

6. In what respects is the life I am now living a genuinely good life? In what respects is it not?

7. Do I see my own attempts to live well as selfish? Why—or why not?

8. To what degree do I frustrate my own efforts to live well, by "a failure of basic day-to-day prudence"?

Questions for Discussion

1. Is it true that "The mass of men lead lives of quiet desperation"?

2. What preliminary answers can be given (subject to later refinement) to the five questions summarized on page 3?

3. Do you agree that no one view of the good life can be correct for all persons? (Clarify what you mean by the phrase "view of the good life.")

4. What is the relationship between living rightly and living well, in your view?

5. What is the role of politics in the good life, in your view?

6. Are value confusions an inevitable part of growing up?

7. How useful is a "view of the good life," in your opinion?

Chapter One:

Encountering
Emptiness

Chapter I: ENCOUNTERING EMPTINESS

Introduction

My life is empty"---Who does not understand the meaning of these words?

We all know of persons who are quite successful by conventional standards, and who experience little pain and much gratification, yet whose lives seem to lack an essential something which would make it all worthwhile. At the core, we say, their lives are empty.

Still, most of us do not have to look to others in order to understand an empty life. For emptiness is something that we have, in varying degrees, experienced in our own lives. There are times when the things that normally sustain us are no longer there, when the heart drops out of effort, when determination weakens and then disappears, when our will deserts us. There are times when we feel that nothing is really worth the effort that we expend upon it: when, literally, nothing matters.

"Nothing matters"--These words conceal an ambiguity. Most commonly, they mean that nothing is felt to have any value or worth. But they can name a deeper, more threatening fact as well. When I encounter emptiness in my life, that emptiness may be experienced as a kind of hole or vacuum in me that I cannot fill up. Like a black hole in outer space, it sucks up my energies, leaving me drained and lifeless. A home is lost, a friend is dead--and a part of myself is simply not there anymore. Here, I have gone beyond the stage of merely "not caring"; here, my emptiness matters deeply to me. Emptiness matters; nothing matters.

When I experience emptiness not simply in some particular part of my life, but deeply within me, at my core--then my distress is profound. At its worst, the experience of emptiness is worse than the most terrible nightmare. It may be a sickening lurch into chaos, or the horror of being drawn inexorably into a dark, bottomless hole. As Michael Novak writes, "The experience of nothingness is an experience beyond the limits of reason. It arises near the borderline of insanity. It is terrifying. It makes all attempts at speaking of purpose, goals, aims, meaning, importance, conformity, harmony, unity--it makes all such attempts seem doubtful and spurious. The person gripped by the experience of nothingness sees nearly everything in reverse image. What other persons call certain, he sees as pretend; what other persons call pragmatic or effective, he sees as a most ironical delusion."[1]

More commonly, however, the experience of emptiness is encountered in milder forms. Perhaps I feel a vague dissatisfaction or sense of unease, as if something is missing. Perhaps I give up, and drift aimlessly. Perhaps I attempt to compensate for an inner lack of purpose by busy, pointless activity. There may be anxious questions, hovering in the background of thought and threatening to disrupt my life. Emptiness generates disorientation and confusion, to which I may respond in various ways. Raths, Harmin and Simon identify eight behavioral symptoms of value confusion:[2] apathy, the inability to care about anything; flightiness, the tendency to jump from one project to another without carrying any one thing through; uncertainty, the inability to make any significant decisions; inconsistency, the disposition to behave in conflicting and contradictory ways; drifting, the tendency to be passively controlled by external circumstances; overconformity, the attempt to find one's identity by thinking and acting like everyone else; overdissent, the effort to define oneself by opposition to everyone and everything; and role playing, the assumption of false poses and identities.

Caught in a value-vacuum, we feel a need to set out upon a new course, to find a fresh foundation for the conduct of our lives. The resulting search is a frequent experience among young people but is by no means confined to them. The search is often an almost involuntary groping in the dark for something new and better; at other times it may involve long, painful deliberation and, finally, a wrenching break with our past. Most often, however, the undertaking of such a search is marked by a more subtle change of direction, though not without inner turmoil. While the search is essentially a psychological and philosophical journey, often it involves physical departure too, as persons leave their homes, work and/or school and strike out to new places, sometimes with no clearer goal than "to find myself."

Whenever and wherever the experience of emptiness occurs, it demands recognition; yet we often refuse to acknowledge it for what it is. Perhaps the most common response is diversionary: we seek to shut our minds to the void within us, and strive to fill up our lives with immediate, apparent goods. The result is what Thoreau called a life of "quiet desperation." The diversionary response to the experience of emptiness is generally no more successful than, say, the attempt to forget the loss of a loved one by drinking heavily or by burying oneself in one's work. The "cure" is ony palliative; the core problem remains. We do not escape emptiness by fleeing from it, but rather by facing it, living through it, and growing beyond it.

Despite their great differences from one another, nearly every historically prominent view of the good life agrees on at least one point: the path to wisdom begins with recognition of my own present state. Before I can begin to grow towards personal fulfillment, I must acknowledge the ways in which my life is now empty. Before I can intelligently seek a cure for my condition, I must come face to face with my illness. The four selections which comprise this chapter, while differing greatly from one another in many ways, share this common insight.

Philosophically, the encounter with emptiness means nihilism, understood as the collapse of all values. In the opening selection of this chapter, Friedrich Nietzsche (1844-1900) trenchantly analyzes the sources of this collapse. Nietzsche identifies three versions or forms of nihilism as a psychological state. The first comes about when I recognize the futility of my aims or goals in life--not only my private goals, but my larger moral ideas such as "the growth of love and harmony." In realizing that my world "aims at nothing," I feel ashamed at having deceived myself and recognize "the long waste of strength."

A second version of nihilism occurs when I can no longer accept my own efforts to interpret the world as a unity, integrated into a meaningful whole. Such efforts were in reality ways to believe in my own value; in doubting them, I doubt myself. The third form of nihilism as a psychological state arises in response to another subterfuge: the effort to gain meaning for this world by creating a fantasy of another world, transcending this one. Belief in a supreme being and an afterlife is such a fantasy, in Nietzsche's view. "But as soon as man finds out how that world is fabricated solely from psychological needs, and how he has absolutely no right to it, the last form of nihilism comes into being"-- disbelief in any other world, and inability to endure this one.

The collapse of values comes about, then, when I no longer can believe in my own devices for reading value into the world. "Briefly: the categories 'aim,' 'unity,' 'being,' which we used to project some value into the world--we pull out again: so the world looks valueless." It should be emphasized that Nietzsche regards nihilism not as a final stopping point for thought, but as a "pathological transitional stage."[3] According to Nietzsche, nihilism occurs as a result of a failure of Christian beliefs;

passage through the experience of nihilism permits a new and sounder affirmation.

Franz Kafka's (1883-1924) brilliant little parable provides a fitting metaphor for the beginning of the psychological journey beyond emptiness to a new and unknown destination. The parable's narrator has become aware that his present state is unsatisfactory and that he must undertake a journey elsewhere. But he is unclear about his goal; indeed, he identifies his destination as simply "Away-From-Here." The narrator recognizes that he is undertaking "a truly immense journey."

Whereas Kafka's narrator is just beginning his quest, the author of Ecclesiastes, identified by scholars as Koheleth,[4] has already traveled many paths in many directions, and has found very little which is worthy of admiration and high regard. Indeed, the skepticism and downright cynicism of the book have caused many readers, both ancient and modern, to wonder how it came to be included within the canon of Scripture.[5] Koheleth's dominant theme is the emptiness and futility of human strivings. While he never doubts the existence and omnipotence of God, Koheleth is skeptical of an afterlife ("Who knows if a man's life-breath does rise upward . . .?") and finds no evidence that God's wisdom and justice are made available to humanity. In fact, quite the opposite seems to be the case: human efforts bear very little worthwhile fruit, and injustice is to be seen everywhere. Even the effort to excel in one's life work is primarily "men's envy of each other." Those who follow the dictates of piety meet the same end--death--as those who do not. Thus, "with justice in human affairs an illusion and truth unattainable,"[6] Koheleth concludes that God must wish us to gather pleasures and enjoy life while we may, for nothing else of worth can be achieved. He closes with an eloquent call to us to take joy in our youth ("How sweet is the light"), for when old age comes it is too late. A leading scholar of the book, Robert Gordis, summarizes the spirit of Ecclesiastes in the following words:

> In the deepest sense, Koheleth is a religious book, because it seeks to grapple with reality. . . This cry of a sensitive spirit wounded by man's cruelty and ignorance, this distilled essence of an honest and courageous mind, striving to penetrate the secret of the universe, yet unwilling to soar on the wings of faith beyond the limits of the knowable, remains one of man's noblest offerings on the altar of truth.[7]

In Plato's Apology we encounter no poetic cynicism, but rather an invitation to pursue wisdom, issued by a man who spent his life in that pursuit. Yet Socrates (469-399 B.C.), for all his skill in philosophical reasoning and all of his years spent in the pursuit of truth, claims no special knowledge for himself. His wisdom, he insists, lies in his recognition of his own ignorance.

16

The scene is a courtroom in Athens in 399 B.C. After years of costly armed struggle with Sparta, resulting in Athenian surrender to Spartan control, an unstable democracy has been reestablished in Athens. But through exposing the ignorance of those around him, Socrates has made many enemies; in addition, one of his pupils, Alcibiades, has behaved badly in the course of a disasterous expedition to conquer Sicily, and another has repudiated the views of his father, Anytus, who has become a spokesman for the prosecution. Socrates, now seventy years old, has been brought to trial on a charge of corrupting the youth of the city and disbelieving in the gods of the state. Socrates' refusal to compromise with his accusers results in conviction and a sentence of death. Within a month, he will be executed by means of a cup of hemlock. In the courtroom is the young Plato (427-347 B.C.), another student and friend of Socrates, who will later record the trial for posterity. Plato's account of the trial, presented here, is generally believed by scholars to be largely accurate. His shock at the treatment of his mentor turned Plato away from an active public career to a lifetime of writing and teaching philosophy; thus, by an ironic turn of justice, Socrates' execution by the Athenian democracy indirectly brought about his immortalization in the Platonic dialogues. Socrates' refusal to compromise his pursuit of wisdom, even in the face of his own death, still serves as a model for those who seek to live life rightly and well.

Nietzsche diagnoses the collapse of value in the experience of nihilism. Kafka's narrator has just become aware of the unsatisfactory nature of his present state, and is beginning a long journey to an undefined destination. Koheleth has already journeyed far and wide, and has found very little of genuine value. Socrates is fully aware of the inadequacy of his knowledge, but is thoroughly committed to the pursuit of wisdom. Each of these figures may help us to see ourselves more clearly and to form a better picture of what we need in order to live a better, more fulfilling life.

NOTES

1. Michael Novak, The Experience of Nothingness (New York: Harper and Row, Harper Colophon Books, 1970). pp. 12f.

2. Raths, Louis E., Merrill Harmin and Sidney B. Simon, Values and Teaching: Working with Values in the Classroom (Columbus, Ohio: Charles E, Merrill Books, Inc., 1966), pp. 5f.

3. Friedrich Nietzsche, The Will to Power, translated by Walter Kaufman and R. J. Hollingdale, ed. by Walter Kaufman (New York: Random House, Vintage, 1967, 1968), p. 14.

4. Following Robert Gordis, in his highly-regarded study, Koheleth: The Man and His World (New York: Bloch Publishing Co., 1955), I treat Ecclesiastes as the work of one author (with the exception of the opening verse of Chapter I and verses 9-14 of Chapter 12). Cf. Gordis, pp. 69-74. Gordis identifies the author as a teacher in one of the Wisdom academies in Jerusalem in the third century B.C., and certainly not Solomon, as is implied by the opening lines. Cf. Gordis, pp. 75-78.

5. Gordis suggests (p. 41) that the book's inclusion is due primarily to its attribution to Solomon, and to its great literary merit.

6. Gordis, p. 113.

7. Gordis, p. 122.

NIHILISM*

By Friedrich Nietzsche

What does nihilism mean?   <u>That the highest values devaluate themselves.</u> The aim is lacking; "why?" finds no answer.

Nihilism as a psychological state will have to be reached, <u>first</u>, when we have sought a "meaning" in all events that is not there: so the seeker eventually becomes discouraged. Nihilism, then, is the recognition of the long <u>waste</u> of strength, the agony of the "in vain," insecurity, the lack of any opportunity to recover and to regain composure--being ashamed in front of oneself, as if one had <u>deceived</u> oneself all too long.-- This meaning could have been: the "fulfillment" of some highest ethical canon in all events, the moral world order; or the growth of love and harmony in the intercourse of beings; or the gradual approximation of a state of universal happiness; or even the development toward a state of universal annihilation--any goal at least constitutes some meaning. What all these notions have in common is that something is to be <u>achieved</u> through the process--and now one realizes that becoming aims at <u>nothing</u> and achieves <u>nothing</u>.--

Nihilism as a psychological state is reached, <u>secondly</u>, when one has posited a totality, a systematization, indeed any organization in all events, and underneath all events, and a soul that longs to admire and revere has wallowed in the idea of some supreme form of domination and administration (--if the soul be that of a logician, complete consistency and real dialectic are quite sufficient to reconcile it to everything). Some sort of unity, some form of "monism": this faith suffices to give man a deep feeling of standing in the context of, and being dependent on, some whole that is infinitely superior to him, and he sees himself as a mode of the deity.-- "The well-being of the universal demands the devotion of the individual"--but behold, there is no such universal! At bottom, man has lost the faith in his own value when no infinitely valuable whole works through him; i.e., he conceived such a whole in order <u>to be able to believe in his own value.</u>

Nihilism as psychological state has yet a <u>third</u> and <u>last</u> form. Given these two insights, that becoming has no goal and that underneath all becoming there is no grand unity in which the individual could immerse himself completely as in an element of supreme value, an escape remains: to pass sentence on this whole world of becoming as a deception and to invent a world beyond it, a <u>true</u> world. But as soon as man finds out how that world is fabricated solely from psychological needs, and how he has absolutely no right to it, the last form of nihilism comes into being: it

*From <u>The Will to Power</u> by Friedrich Nietzsche, translated by Walter Kaufman and R. J. Hollingdale, ed. by Walter Kaufman (New York: Random House, Vintage, 1967, 1968). Reprinted by permission.

includes disbelief in any metaphysical world and forbids itself any belief in a <u>true</u> world. Having reached this standpoint, one grants the reality of becoming as the <u>only</u> reality, forbids oneself every kind of clandestine access to afterworlds and false divinities--but <u>cannot endure this world though one does not want to deny it.</u>

What has happened, at bottom? The feeling of valuelessness was reached with the realizaton that the overall character of existence may not be interpreted by means of the concept of "aim," the concept of "unity," or the concept of "truth." Existence has no goal or end; any comprehensive unity in the plurality of events is lacking: the character of existence is not "true," is <u>false</u>. One simply lacks any reason for convincing oneself that there <u>is</u> a <u>true</u> world. Briefly: the categories "aim," "unity," "being" which we used to project some value into the world--we <u>pull out</u> again; so the world looks <u>valueless</u>.

MY DESTINATION*

by Franz Kafka

I gave orders for my horse to be brought round from the stable. The servant did not understand me. I myself went to the stable, saddled my horse and mounted. In the distance I heard a bugle call, I asked him what this meant. He knew nothing and had heard nothing. At the gate he stopped me, asking: "Where are you riding to, master?" "I don't know," I said, "only away from here, away from here. Always away from here, only by doing so can I reach my destination." "And so you know your destination?" he asked. "Yes," I answered, "didn't I say so? Away-From-Here, that is my destination." "You have no provisions with you," he said. "I need none," I said, "the journey is so long that I must die of hunger if I don't get anything on the way. No provisions can save me. For it is, fortunately, a truly immense journey."

20

ALL IS FUTILE:

EXCERPTS FROM ECCLESIASTES*

The words of Koheleth son of David, king in Jerusalem.   Utter futility!--said Koheleth--Utter futility! All is futile! What real value is there for a man in all the gains he makes beneath the sun?   One generation goes, another comes, but the earth remains the same forever. The sun rises, and the sun sets--and glides back to where it rises. Southward blowing, turning northward, ever turning blows the wind; on its rounds the wind returns. All streams flow into the sea, yet the sea is never full; to the place from which they flow the streams flow back again. All such things are wearisome: no man can ever state them; the eye never has enough of seeing, nor the ear enough of hearing. Only that shall happen which has happened, only that occur which has occurred; there is nothing new beneath the sun! Sometimes there is a phenomenon of which they say, "Look, this one is new!"--it occurred long since, in ages that went by before us. The earlier ones are not remembered; so too those that will occur later will no more be remembered than those that will occur at the very end.

I, Koheleth, was king in Jerusalem over Israel. I set my mind to study and to probe with wisdom all that happens under the sun.--An unhappy business, that, which God gave men to be concerned with! I observed all the happenings beneath the sun, and I found that all is futile and pursuit of wind: a twisted thing that cannot be made straight, a lack that cannot be made good. I said to myself: "Here I have grown richer and wiser than any that ruled before me over Jerusalem, and my mind has zealously absorbed wisdom and learning." And so I set my mind to appraise wisdom and to appraise madness and folly. And I learned--that this too was pursuit of wind: for as wisdom grows, vexation grows; to increase learning is to increase heartache.

I said to myself, "Come, I will treat you to merriment. Taste mirth!" That too, I found, was futile. Of revelry I said, "It's mad!" Of merriment, "What good is that?" I ventured to tempt my flesh with wine and to grasp folly, while letting my mind direct with wisdom, to the end that I might learn which of the two was better for men to practice in their few days of life under heaven. I multiplied my possessions. I built myself houses and I planted vineyards. I laid out gardens and groves, in which I planted every kind of fruit tree. I constructed pools of water, enough to irrigate a forest shooting up with trees. I bought male and female slaves, and I acquired stewards. I also acquired more cattle, both herds and flocks, than all who were before me in Jerusalem. I further

*From The Five Megilloth and the Book of Jonah, translated by H. L. Ginsberg, et. al. (Philadelphia: The Jewish Publication Society of America, 1969) Copyrighted by and used through the courtesy of the Jewish Publication Society of America. Portions reprinted here are 1:1-2:11, 3:9-4:6, 9:1-12, 11:7-12:8.

amassed silver and gold and treasures of kings and provinces; and I got myself male and female singers, as well as the luxuries of commoners-- coffers and coffers of them. Thus, I gained more wealth than anyone before me in Jerusalem. In addition, my wisdom remained with me: I withheld from my eyes nothing they asked for, and denied myself no enjoyment; rather, I got enjoyment out of all my wealth. And that was all I got out of my wealth. Then my thoughts turned to all the fortune my hands had built up, to the wealth I had acquired and won--and oh, it was all futile and pursuit of wind; there was no real value under the sun! . . .

What value, then, can the man of affairs get from what he earns? I have observed the business that God gave man to be concerned with: He brings everything to pass precisely at its time; He also puts eternity in their mind, but without man every guessing, from first to last, all the things that God brings to pass. Thus I realized that the only worth-while thing there is for them is to enjoy themselves and do what is good in their lifetime; also, that whenever a man does eat and drink and get enjoyment out of all his wealth, it is a gift of God. I realized, too, that whatever God has brought to pass will recur evermore: Nothing can be added to it and nothing taken from it--and God has brought to pass that men revere Him. What is occurring occurred long since, and what is to occur occurred long since: and God seeks the pursued. And, indeed, I have observed under the sun: alongside justice there is wickedness, alongside righteousness there is wickedness. I mused: "God will doom both righteous and wicked, for there is a time for every experience and for every happening." So I decided, as regards men, to dissociate them from the divine beings and to face the fact that they are beasts. For in respect of the fate of man and the fate of beast, they have one and the same fate: as the one dies so dies the other, and both have the same life-breath; man has no superiority over beast, since both amount to nothing. Both go to the same place; both came from dust and both return to dust. Who knows if a man's life-breath does rise upward and if a beast's breath does sink down into the earth? I saw that there is nothing better for man than to enjoy his possessions, since that is his portion. For who can enable him to see what will happen afterward?

I further observed all the oppression that goes on under the sun: the tears of the oppressed, with none to comfort them; and the power of their oppressors--with none to comfort them. Then I accounted those who died long since more fortunate than those who are still living; and happier than either are those who have not yet come into being and have never witnessed the miseries that go on under the sun. I have also noted that all labor and skillful enterprise come from men's envy of each other--another futility and pursuit of wind! True, the fool folds his hands together and has to eat his own flesh. But no less truly, better is a handful of gratification than two fistfuls of labor which is pursuit of wind. . . .

For all this I noted, and I ascertained all this: that the actions of even the righteous and the wise are determined by God. Even love! Even hate! Man knows none of these in advance--none! For the same fate is in store for all: for the righteous, and for the wicked; for the good and pure, and for the impure; for him who sacrifices, and for him who does not; for him who is pleasing, and for him who is displeasing: and for him who swears, and for him who shuns oaths. That is the sad thing about all that goes on under the sun: that the same fate is in store for all. (Not only that, but men's hearts are full of sadness, and their minds of madness, while they live; and then--to the dead!) For he who is reckoned among the living has something to look forward to--even a live dog is better than a dead lion--since the living know they will die. But the dead know nothing; they have no more recompense, for even the memory of them has died. Their loves, their hates, their jealousies have long since perished; and they have no more share till the end of time in all that goes on under the sun.

Go, eat your bread in gladness, and drink your wine in joy; for your action was long ago approved by God. Let your clothes always be freshly washed, and your head never lack ointment. Enjoy happiness with a woman you love, all the fleeting days of life that have been granted to you under the sun--all your fleeting days. For that alone is what you can get out of life and out of the means you acquire under the sun. Whatever it is in your power to do, do with all your might. For there is no action, no reasoning, no learning, no wisdom in Sheol where you are going. I have further observed under the sun that the race is not won by the swift, nor the battle by the valiant; nor is bread won by the wise, nor wealth by the intelligent, nor favor by the learned. For the time of mischance comes to all. And a man cannot even know his time. As fishes are enmeshed in a fatal net, and as birds are trapped in a snare, so men are caught at the time of calamity, when it comes upon them without warning. . . .

How sweet is the light, what a delight for the eyes to behold the sun! Even if a man lives many years, let him enjoy himself in all of them, remembering how many the days of darkness are going to be. The only future is nothingness! O youth, enjoy yourself while you are young! Let your heart lead you to enjoyment in the days of your youth. Follow the desires of your heart and the glances of your eyes--but know well that God will call you to account for all such things--and banish care from your mind, and pluck sorrow out of your flesh! For youth and black hair are fleeting. So appreciate your vigor in the days of your youth, before those days of sorrow come and those years arrive of which you will say, "I have no pleasure in them"; before sun and light and moon and stars grow dark, and the clouds come back again after the rain: when the guards of the house become shaky, and the men of valor are bent, and the maids that grind, grown few, are idle, and the ladies that peer through the windows grow dim, and the doors to the street are shut--with the noise of the hand mill growing fainter, and the song of the bird growing feebler, and all the strains of music dying down; when one is afraid of heights and there is terror on the road.--For the almond tree may blossom, the grasshopper be burdened, and the caper bush may bud again; but man sets out for his eternal abode, with mourners all around in the street.--Before the silver cord snaps and the golden bowl crashes, the jar is shattered at the spring, and the jug is smashed at the cistern. And the dust returns to the ground as it was, and the lifebreath returns to God who bestowed it. Utter futility--said Koheleth--all is futile!

APOLOGY*

by Plato

I do not know, gentlemen of the jury, how my accusers affected you; as for me, I was almost carried away in spite of myself, so persuasively did they speak. And yet, hardly anything of what they said is true. Of the many lies they told, one in particular surprised me, namely that you should be careful not to be deceived by an accomplished speaker like me. That they are not ashamed to be immediately proved wrong by the facts, when I show myself not to be an accomplished speaker at all, that I think is most shameless on their part--unless indeed they call an accomplished speaker the man who speaks the truth. If they mean that, I would agree that I am an orator, but not after their manner, for indeed, as I say, practically nothing they said was true. From me you will hear the whole truth, though not, by Zeus, gentlemen, expressed in embroidered and stylized phrases like theirs, but things spoken at random and expressed in the first words that come to mind, for I put my trust in the justice of what I say, and let none of you expect anything else. It would not be fitting at my age, as it might be for a young man, to toy with words when I appear before you.

One thing I do ask and beg of you, gentlemen: if you hear me making my defence in the same kind of language as I am accustomed to use in the market place by the bankers' tables, where many of you have heard me, and elsewhere, do not be surprised or create a disturbance on that account. The position is this: this is my first appearance in a lawcourt, at the age of seventy; I am therefore simply a stranger to the manner of speaking here. Just as if I were really a stranger, you would certainly excuse me if I spoke in that dialect and manner in which I had been brought up, so too my present request seems a just one, for you to pay no attention to my manner of speech--be it better or worse--but to concentrate your attention on whether what I say is just or not, for the excellence of a judge, lies in this, as that of a speaker, in telling the truth.

It is right for me, gentlemen, to defend myself first against the first lying accusations made against me and my first accusers, and then against the later accusations and the later accusers. There have been many who have accused me to you for many years now, and none of their accusations are true. These I fear much more than I fear Anytus and his friends, though they too are formidable. These earlier ones, however, are more so, gentlemen; they got hold of most of you from childhood, persuaded you and accused me quite falsely, saying that there is a man called Socrates, a wise man, a student of all things in the sky and below the earth, who makes the worse argument the strong. Those who spread the rumour,

*Translated by G. M. A. Grube, The Trial and Death of Socrates (Hackett Publishing Co., Inc., 1975). Reprinted by permission of Hackett Publishing Company, Inc., Indianapolis, Indiana. Abridgements are indicated by elipses.

25

gentlemen, are my dangerous accusers, for their hearers believe that those who study these things do not even believe in the gods. Moreover, these accusers were numerous, they have been at it a long time; also, they spoke to you at an age when you would most readily believe them, some of you being children and adolescents, and they won their case by default, as there was no defense.

What is most absurd in all this is that one cannot even know or mention their names unless one of them is a writer of comedies.* Those who maliciously and slanderously persuaded you, those too, who, when persuaded themselves then persuaded others, all those are most difficult to deal with: one cannot bring one of them into court or refute him; one is simply fighting with shadows in making one's defence, and cross-examining when no one answers. I want you to realize too that my accusers are of two kinds: those who have accused me recently, and the old ones I mention; and to think that I must first defend myself against the latter, for you have also heard their accusations first, and to a much greater extent than the most recent.

Very well then. I must surely defend myself and attempt to uproot from your minds in so short a time the slander that has resided there so long. I wish this may happen, if it is in any way better for you and me, and that my defence may be successful, but I think this is very difficult and I am fully aware of how difficult it is. Even so, let the matter proceed as the gods may wish, but I must obey the law and make my defence.

Let us then take up the case from its beginning. What is the accusation from which arose the slander in which Meletus trusted when he wrote out the charge against me? What did they say when they slandered me? I must, as if they were my actual prosecutors, read the affidavit they would have sworn. It goes something like this: Socrates is guilty of wrong doing in that he busies himself studying things in the sky and below the earth; he makes the worse into the stronger argument, and he teaches thse same things to others. You have seen this yourselves in the comedy of Aristophanes, a Socrates swinging about there, saying he was walking on air and talking a lot of other nonsense about things of which I know nothing at all. I do not speak in contempt of such knowledge, if someone is wise in these things--lest Meletus bring more cases against me--but, gentlemen, I have no part in it, and on this point I call upon the majority of you as witnesses. I think it right that all those of you who have heard me conversing, and many of you have, should tell each other if anyone of you has ever heard me discussing such subjects to any extent at all. From this you will learn that the other things said about me by the majority are of the same kind.

*Aristophanes

Not one of them is true. And if you have heard from anyone that I undertake to teach people and charge a fee for it, that is not true either. . .

One of you might perhaps interrupt me and say: "But Socrates, what is your occupation? From where have these slanders come? For surely if you did not busy yourself with something out of the common, all these rumours and talk would not have arisen unless you did something other than most people. Tell us what it is, that we may not speak inadvisedly about you." Anyone who says that seems to be right, and I will try to show you what has caused this reputation and slander. Listen then. Perhaps some of you will think I am jesting, but be sure that all that I shall say is true. What has caused my reputation is none other than a certain kind of wisdom. What kind of wisdom? Human wisdom, perhaps. It may be that I really possess this, while those whom I mentioned just now are wise with a wisdom more than human; else I cannot explain it, for I certainly do not possess it, and whoever says I do is lying and speaks to slander me. Do not create a disturbance, gentlemen, even if you think I am boasting, for the story I shall tell does not originate with me, but I will refer you to a trustworthy source. I shall call upon the god at Delphi as witness to the extent and nature of my wisdom, if it be such. You know Chairephon. He was my friend from youth, and the friend of most of you, as he shared your exile and your return. You surely know the kind of man he was, how impulsive in any course of action. He went to Delphi at one time and ventured to ask the oracle--as I say, gentlemen, do not create a disturbance--he asked if any man was wiser than I, and the Pythian replied that no one was wiser. Chairephon is dead, but his brother will testify to you about this.

Consider that I tell you this because I would inform you about the origin of the slander. When I heard of this reply I asked myself: "Whatever does the god mean? What is his riddle? I am very conscious that I am not wise at all; what then does he mean by saying that I am the wisest? For surely he does not lie; it is not legitimate for him to do so." For a long time I was at a loss; then I very reluctantly turned to some such investigation as this: I went to one of those reputed wise, thinking that there, if anywhere, I could refute the oracle and say to it: "This man is wiser than I, but you said I was." Then, when I examined this man-- there is no need for me to tell you his name, he was one of our public men--my experience was something like this: I thought that he appeared wise to many people and especially to himself, but he was not. I then tried to show him that he thought himself wise, but that he was not. As a result he came to dislike me, and so did many of the bystanders. So I withdrew and thought to myself: "I am wiser than this man; it is likely that neither of us kows anything worthwhile, but he thinks he knows something when he does not, whereas when I do not know, neither do I think I know; so I am likely to be wiser to this small extent, that I do not think I know what I do not know." After this I approached another man,

27

A soul is what defines us as human being.

one of those thought to be wiser than he, and I thought the same thing, and so I came to be disliked both by him and by many others.

After that I proceeded systematically. I realized, to my sorrow and alarm, that I was getting unpopular, but I thought that I must attach the greatest importance to the god's oracle, so I must go to all those who had any reputation for knowledge to examine its meaning. And by the dog, gentlemen of the jury--for I must tell you the truth--I experienced something like this: in my investigation in the service of the god I found that those who had the highest reputation were nearly the most deficient, while those who were thought to be inferior were more knowledgeable. I must give you an account of my journeyings as if they were labours I had undertaken to prove the oracle irrefutable. After the politicans, I went to the poets, the writers of tragedies and dithyrambs and the others, intending in their case to catch myself being more ignorant then they. So I took up those poems with which they seemed to have taken most trouble and asked them what they meant, in order that I might at the same time learn something from them. I am ashamed to tell you the truth, gentlemen, but I must. Almost all the bystanders explained the poems better than their authors could. I soon realized that poets do not compose their poems with knowledge, but by some inborn talent and by inspiration, like seers and prophets who also say many fine things without any understanding of what they say. The poets seemed to me to have had a similar experience. At the same time I saw that, because of their poetry, they thought themselves very wise men in other respects, which they were not. So there again I withdrew, thinking that I had the same advantage over them as I had over the politicians.

Finally I went to the craftsmen, for I was conscious of knowing practically nothing, and I knew that I would find that they had knowledge of many fine things. In this I was not mistaken; they knew things I did not know, and to that extent they were wiser than I. But, gentlemen of the jury, the good craftsmen seemed to me to have the same fault as the poets: each of them, because of his success at his craft, thought himself very wise in other most important pursuits, and this error of theirs overshadowed the wisdom they had, so that I asked myself, on behalf of the oracle, whether I should prefer to be as I am, with neither their wisdom nor their ignorance, or to have both. The answer I gave myself and the oracle was that it was to my advantage to be as I am.

As a result of this investigation, gentlemen of the jury, I acquired much unpopularity, of a kind that is hard to deal with and is a heavy burden; many slanders came from these people and a reputation for wisdom, for in each case the bystanders thought that I myself possessed the wisdom that I proved that my interlocutor did not have. What is probable, gentlemen, is that in fact that god is wise and that his oracular response meant that human wisdom is worth little or nothing, and that when he says this man, Socrates, he is using my name as an example, as if

28

he said: "This man among you, mortals, is wisest who, like Socrates, understands that his wisdom is worthless." So even now I continue this investigation as the gods bade me--and I go around seeking out anyone, citizen or stranger, whom I think wise. Then if I do not think he is, I come to the assistance of the god and show him that he is not wise. Because of this occupation, I do not have the leisure to engage in public affairs to any extent, nor indeed to look after my own, but I live in great poverty because of my service to the god.

Furthermore, the young men who follow me around of their own free will, those who have most leisure, the sons of the very rich, take pleasure in hearing people questioned; they themselves often imitate me and try to question others. I think they find an abundance of men who believe they have some knowledge but know little or nothing. The result is that those whom they question are angry, not with themselves but with me. They say: "That man Socrates is a pestilential fellow who corrupts the young." If one asks them what he does and what he teaches to corrupt them, they are silent, as they do not know, but, so as not to appear at a loss, they mention those accusations that are available against all philosophers, about "things in the sky and things below the earth," about "not believing in the gods" and "making the worse the stronger argument;" they would not want to tell the truth, that they have been proved to lay claim to knowledge when they know nothing. These people are ambitious, violent and numerous; they are continually and convincingly talking about me; they have been filling your ears for a long time with vehement slanders against me. From them Meletus attacked me, and Anytus and Lycon, Meletus being vexed on behalf of the poets, Anytus on behalf of the craftsmen and the politicians, Lycon on behalf of the orators, so that, as I started out by saying, I should be surprised if I could rid you of so much slander in so short a time. That, gentlemen of the jury, is the truth for you. I have hidden or omitted nothing. I know well enough that this very conduct makes me unpopular, and this is proof that what I say is true, that such is the slander against me, and that such are its causes. If you look into this either now or later, this is what you will find.

Let this suffice as a defence against the charges of my earlier accusers. After this I shall try to defend myself against Meletus, that good and patriotic man, as he says he is, and my later accusers. As these are a different lot of accusers, let us again take up their sworn deposition. It goes something like this: Socrates is guilty of corrupting the young and of not believing in the gods in whom the city believes, but in other new divinities. Such is their charge. Let us examine it point by point. . .

I do not think, gentlemen of the jury, that it requires a prolonged defence to prove that I am not guilty of the charges in Meletus' deposition, but this is sufficient. On the other hand, you know that what I said earlier is true, that I am very unpopular with many people. This will be my undoing, if I am undone, not Meletus or Anytus but the slanders and envy of many people. This has destroyed many and will, I think, continue to do so. There is no danger that it will stop at me.

Someone might say: "Are you not ashamed, Socrates, to have followed the kind of occupation that has led to your being now in danger of death?" However, I should be right to reply to him: "You are wrong, sir, if you think that a man who is any good at all should take into account the risk of life or death; he should look to this only in his actions, whether what he does is right or wrong, whether he is acting like a good or a bad man." ... wherever a man has taken a position that he believes to be best, or has been placed by his commander, there he must I think remain and face danger, without a thought for death or anything else, rather than disgrace. It would have been a dreadful way to behave, gentlemen of the jury, if, at Potidaea, Amphipolis and Delium, I had, at the risk of death, like anyone else, remained at my post where those you had elected to command had ordered me, and then, when the god ordered me, as I thought and believed, to live the life of a philosopher, to examine myself and others, I had abandoned my post for fear of death or anything else. That would have been a dreadful thing, and then I might truly have justly been brought here for not believing in the gods, disobeying the oracle, fearing death, and thinking I was wise when I was not. To fear death, gentlemen, is no other than to think oneself wise when one is not, to think one knows what one does not know. No one knows whether death may not be the greatest of all blessings for a man, yet men fear it as if they knew that it is the greatest of evils. And surely it is the most blameworthy ignorance to believe that one knows what one does not know. It is perhaps on this point and in this respect, gentlemen, that I differ from the majority of men, and if I were to claim that I am wiser than anyone in anything, it would be in this, that, as I have no adequate knowledge of things in the underworld, so I do not think I have. I do know, however, that it is wicked and shameful to do wrong, to disobey one's superior, be he god or man. I shall never fear or avoid things of which I do not know, whether they may not be good rather than things that I know to be bad. Even if you acquitted me now and did not believe Anytus, who said to you that either I should not have been brought here in the first place, or that now I am here, you cannot avoid executing me, for if I should be acquitted, your sons would practise the teachings of Socrates and all be thoroughly corrupted. If you said to me in this regard: "Socrates, we do not believe Anytus now; we acquit you, but only on condition that you spend no more time on this investigation and do not practise philosophy, and if you are caught doing so you will die;" if, as I say, you were to acquit me on those terms, I would say to you: "Gentlemen of the jury, I am grateful and I am your friend, but I will obey the god rather than you, and as long as I draw breath and am able, I shall not cease to practise philosophy, to exhort you and to point out to anyone of you whom I happen to meet: Good Sir, you are an Athenian, a citizen of the greatest city with the greatest reputation for both wisdom and power; are you not ashamed of your eagerness to possess as much wealth, reputation and honours as possible, while you do not care for nor give thought to wisdom or truth, or the best possible state of your soul?" Then, if one of you disputes this and says he does care, I shall not let him go at once or leave him, but I shall question him, examine him and test him, and if I do not think he has attained the goodness that he says he has, I shall reproach him because he attaches little importance to the most important things and greater importance to inferior things. I shall treat in this way anyone I happen to meet, young and old, citizen and stranger, and more so the citizens because you are more kindred to me. Be sure that this is what the god orders me to do, and I think there is no greater blessing for the city than my service to the god. For I go around doing nothing but persuading both young and old among you not to care for your body or your wealth in preference to or as strongly as for the best possible state of your soul, as I say to you: "Wealth does not bring about excellence, but excellence brings about wealth and all other public and private blessings for men."

Now if by saying this I corrupt the young, this advice must be harmful, but if anyone says that I give different advice, he is talking nonsense. On this point I would say to you, gentlemen of the jury: "Whether you believe Anytus or not, whether you acquit me or not, do so on the understanding that this is my course of action, even if I am to face death many times." Do not create a disturbance, gentlemen, but abide by my request not to cry out at what I say but to listen, for I think it will be to your advantage to listen, and I am about to say other things at which you will perhaps cry out. By no means do this. Be sure that if you kill the sort of man I say I am, you will harm me more than yourselves. Neither Meletus or Anytus can harm me in any way; he could not harm me, for I do not think it is permitted that a better man be harmed by a worse; cetainly he might kill me, or perhaps banish or disfranchise me, which he and maybe others think to be great harm, but I do not think so. I think he is doing himself much greater harm doing what he is doing now, attempting to have a man executed unjustly. Indeed, gentlemen of the jury, I am far from making a defence now on my own behalf, as might be thought, but on yours, to prevent you from wrong doing by mistreating the god's gift to you by condemning me; for if you kill me you will not easily find another like me. I was attached to this city by the god--though it seems a ridiculous thing to say--as upon a great and noble horse which was somewhat sluggish because of its size and needed to be stirred up by a kind of gadfly. It is to fulfill some such function that the god has placed me in the city. I never cease to rouse everyone of you, to persuade and reproach you all day long and everywhere I find myself in your company.

Another such man will not easily come to be among you, gentlemen, and if you believe me you will spare me. You might easily strike out at me as people do when they are aroused from a doze; if convinced by Anytus you could easily kill me, and then you could sleep on for the rest of your days, unless the god, in his care for you, sent you someone else.

31

That I am the kind of person to be a gift of the god to the city you might realize from the fact that it does not seem like human nature for me to have neglected all my own affairs and to have tolerated this neglect now for so many years while I was always concerned with you, approaching each one of you like a father or an elder brother to persuade you to care for virtue. Now if I profited from this by charging a fee for my advice, there would be some sense to it, but you can see for yourselves that, for all their shameless accusations, my accusers have not been able in their impudence to bring forward a witness to say that I have ever received a fee or ever asked for one. I, on the other hand, have a convincing witness that I speak the truth, my poverty.

It may seem strange that while I go around and give this advice privately and interfere in private affairs, I do not venture to go the assembly and there advise the city. You have heard me give the reason for this in many places. I have a divine sign from the god which Meletus has ridiculed in his deposition. This began when I was a child. It is a voice, and whenever it speaks it turns me away from something I am about to do, but it never encourages me to do anything. This is what has prevented me from taking part in public affairs, and I think it was quite right to prevent me. Be sure, gentlemen of the jury, that if I had long ago attempted to take part in politics, I should have died long ago, and benefitted neither you nor myself. Do not be angry with me for speaking the truth; no man will survive who genuinely opposes you or any other crowd and prevents the occurrence of many unjust and illegal happenings in the city. A man who really fights for justice must lead a private, not a public, life if he is to survive for even a short time. . .

Do you think I would have survived all these years if I were engaged in public affairs and, acting as a good man must, came to the help of justice and considered this the most important thing? For from it, gentlemen of the jury, nor would any other man. Throughout my life, in any public activity I may have engaged in, I am the same man as I am in private life. I have never come to an agreement with anyone to act unjustly, neither with anyone else nor with any one of those they slander me by saying they are my pupils. I have never been anyone's teacher. If anyone, young or old, desire to listen to me when I am talking and dealing with my own concerns, I have never begrudged this to anyone, but I do not converse when I receive a fee and not when I do not. I am equally ready to question the rich and the poor if anyone is willing to answer my questions and listen to what I say. And I cannot justly be held responsible for the good or bad conduct of these people, as I never promised to teach them anything and have not done so. If anyone says that he has learned anything from me, or that he heard anything privately that the others did not hear, be assured that he is not telling the truth.

Why then do some people enjoy spending considerable time in my company? You have heard why, gentlemen of the jury, I have told you the whole truth. They enjoy hearing those being questioned who think they are wise, but are not. And this is not unpleasant. To do this has, as I say, been enjoined upon me by the god, by means of oracles and dreams, and in every other way that a divine manifestation has ever ordered a man to do anything. This is true, gentlemen, and can easily be established.

If I corrupt some young men and have corrupted others, then surely some of them who have grown older and realized that I gave them bad advice when they were young should now themselves come up here to accuse me and avenge themselves. If they were unwilling to do so themselves, then some of their kindred, their fathers or brothers or other relations should recall it now if their family had been harmed by me... You will find quite the contrary, gentlemen. These men are all ready to come to the help of the corruptor, the man who has harmed their kindred, as Meletus and Anytus say. Now those who were corrupted might well have reason to help me, but the uncorrupted, their kindred who are older men, have no reason to help me except the right and proper one, that they know that Meletus is lying and that I am telling the truth.

Very well, gentlemen of the jury. This, and maybe other similar things, is what I have to say in my defence. Perhaps one of you might be angry as he recalls that when he himself stood trial on a less dangerous charge, he begged and implored the jury with many tears, that he brought his children and many of his friends and family into court to arouse as much pity as he could, but that I do none of these things, even though I may seem to be running the ultimate risk. Thinking of this, he might feel resentful and angry and cast his vote in anger. If there is such a one among you--I do not deem there is, but if there is--I think it would be right to say in reply: "My good sir, I too have a household and, in Homer's phrase, I am not born from oak or rock but from men, so that I have a family, indeed three sons, gentlemen of the jury, of whom one is an adolescent while two are children. Nevertheless, I will not beg you to acquit me by bringing them here. Why do I do none of these things? Not through arrogance, gentlemen, nor through lack of respect for you. Whether I am brave in the face of death is another matter, but with regard to my reputation and yours and that of the whole city, it does not seem right to me to do these things, especially at my age and with my reputation. For it is generally believed, whether it be true or false, that in certain respects Socrates is superior to the majority of men. Now if those of you who are considered superior, be it in wisdom or courage or whatever other virtue makes them so, are seen behaving like that, it would be a disgrace. Yet I have often seen them do this sort of thing when standing trial, men who are thought to be somebody, doing amazing things as if they thought it a terrible thing to die, and as if they were to be immortal if you did not execute them. I think these men bring shame upon the city...

Our final goal

33

To concern ourselves with reasoning + learning to reason well.

Quite apart from the question of reputation, gentlemen, I do not think it right to supplicate the jury and to be acquitted because of this. It is not the purpose of a juryman's office to give justice as a favour to whomever seems good to him, but to judge according to law, and this he has sworn to do. We should not accustom you to perjure yourselves, nor should you make a habit of it. This is irreverent conduct for either of us.

Do not deem it right for me, gentlemen of the jury, that I should act towards you in a way that I do not consider to be good or just or pious, especially, by Zeus, as I am being prosecuted by Meletus here for impiety; clearly, if I convinced you by my supplication to do violence to your oath of office, I would be teaching you not to believe in the gods, and my defence would convict me of not believing in them, as my accusers do now, gentlemen of the jury. This is far from being the case, gentlemen, for I do believe in them as none of my accusers do. I leave it to you and the god to judge me in the way that will be best for me and for you.

(The jury now gives its verdict of guilty, and Meletus asks for the penalty of death.)

There are many other reasons for my not being angry with you for convicting me, gentlemen of the jury, and what happened was not unexpected. I am much more surprised at the number of votes cast on each side, for I did not think the decision would be by so few votes but by a great many. As it is, a switch of only thirty votes would have acquitted me. I think myself that I have been cleared on Meletus' charges, and it is clear to all that, if Anytus and Lycon had not joined him in accusing me, he would have been fined a thousand drachmas for not receiving a fifth of the votes.

He assesses the penalty at death. What counter-assessment should I propose to you, gentlemen of the jury? Clearly it should be a penalty I deserve, and what do I deserve to suffer or to pay because I have deliberately not led a quiet life but have neglected what occupies most people: wealth, household affairs, the position of general or public orator or the other offices, the political clubs and factions that exist in the city? I thought myself too honest to survive if I occupied myself with those things. I did not follow that path that would have made me of no use either to you or to myself, but I went to each of you privately and conferred upon him what I say is the greatest benefit, by persuading him not to care for any of his belongings before caring that he himself should be as good and as wise as possible, not to care for the city's possessions more than for the city itself, and to care for other things in the same way. What do I deserve for being such a man? Some good, gentlemen of the jury, if I must truly make an assessment according to my deserts, and something suitable. What is suitable for a benefactor who needs leisure to exhort you? Nothing is more suitable, gentlemen, than for such a man to be fed in the Prytaneum,* much more suitable for him than for anyone of

*A town hall for public entertainment. Olympian victors were celebrated here.

you who has won a victory at Olympia with a pair or a team of horses. The Olympian victor makes you think yourself happy, I make you be happy. Besides, he does not need food, but I do. So if I must make a just assessment of what I deserve, I assess it at this: free meals in the Prytaneum.

When I say this you may think, as when I spoke of appeals to pity and entreaties, that I speak arrogantly, but that is not the case, gentlemen of the jury, rather it is like this: I am convinced that no man willingly does wrong, but I am not convincing you of this, for we have talked together but a short time. If it were the law with us, as it is elsewhere, that a trial for life should not last one but many days, you would be convinced, but now it is not easy to dispel great slanders in a short time. Since I am convinced that I wrong no one, I am not likely to wrong myself, to say that I deserve some evil and to make some such assessment against myself. What should I fear? That I should suffer the penalty Meletus has assessed against me, of which I say I do not know whether it is good or bad? Am I then to choose in preference to this something that I know very well to be an evil and assess the penalty at that? Imprisonment? Why should I live in prison, always subjected to the ruling magistrates? A fine, and imprisonment until I pay it? That would be the same thing for me, as I have no money. Exile? for perhaps you might accept that assessment.

I should have to be inordinately fond of life, gentlemen of the jury, to be so unreasonable as to suppose that other men will easily tolerate my company and conversation when you, my fellow citizens, have been unable to endure them, but found them a burden and resented them so that you are now seeking to get rid of them. Far from it, gentlemen. It would be a fine life at my age to be driven out of one city after another, for I know very well that wherever I go the young men will listen to my talk as they do here. If I drive them away, they will themselves persuade their elders to drive me out; if I do not drive them away, their fathers and relations will drive me out on their behalf.

Perhaps someone might say: But Socrates, if you leave us will you not be able to live quietly, without talking? Now this is the most difficult point on which to convince some of you. If I say that it is impossible for me to keep quiet because that means disobeying the god, you will not believe me and will think I am being ironical. On the other hand, if I say that it is the greatest good for a man to discuss virtue every day and those other things about which you hear me conversing and testing myself and others, for the unexamined life is not worth living for man, you will believe me even less.

What I say is true, gentlemen, but it is not easy to convince you. At the same time, I am not accustomed to think that I deserve any penalty. If I had money, I would assess the penalty at the amount I could pay, for that would not hurt me, but I have none, unless you are willing to set the

35

penalty at the amount I can pay, and perhaps I could pay you one mina of silver. So that is my assessment.

Plato here, gentlemen of the jury, and Crito and Critoboulus and Apollodorus bid me put the penalty at thirty minae, and they will stand surety for the money. Well then, that is my assessment, and they will be sufficient guarantee of payment.

(The jury now votes again and sentences Socrates to death.)

It is for the sake of a short time, gentlemen of the jury, that you will acquire the reputation and the guilt, in the eyes of those who want to denigrate the city, of having killed Socrates, a wise man, for they will say that I am wise even if I am not. If you had waited but a little while, this would have happened of its own accord. You see my age, that I am already advanced in years and close to death. I am saying this not to all of you but to those who condemned me to death, and to these same jurors I say: Perhaps you think that I was convicted for lack of such words as might have convinced you, if I thought I should say or do all I could to avoid my sentence. Far from it. I was convicted because I lacked not words but boldness and shamelessness and the willingness to say to you what you would most gladly have heard from me, lamentations and tears and my saying and doing many things that I say are unworthy of me but that you are accustomed to hear from others. I did not think then that the danger I ran should make me do anything mean, nor do I now regret the nature of my defense. I would much rather die after this kind of defence than live after making the other kind. Neither I nor any other man should, on trial or in war, contrive to avoid death at any cost. Indeed it is often obvious in battle that one could escape death by throwing away one's weapons and by turning to supplicate one's pursuers, and there are many ways to avoid death in every kind of danger if one will venture to do or say anything to avoid it. It is not difficult to avoid death, gentlemen of the jury, it is much more difficult to avoid wickedness, for it runs faster than death. Slow and elderly as I am, I have been caught by the slower pursuer, whereas my accusers, being clever and sharp, have been caught by the quicker, wickedness. I leave you now, condemned to death by you, but they are condemned by truth to wickedness and injustice. So I maintain my assessment, and they maintain theirs. This perhaps had to happen, and I think it is as it should be.

Now I want to prophesy to those who convicted me, for I am at the point when men prophesy most, when they are about to die. I say gentlemen, to those who voted to kill me, that vengeance will come upon you immediately after my death, a vengeance much harder to bear than that which you took in killing me. You did this in the belief that you would avoid giving an account of your life, but I maintain that quite the opposite will happen to you. There will be more people to test you, whom I now held back, but you did not notice it. They will be more difficult to deal with as they will be younger and you will resent them more. You are wrong if you believe that by killing people you will prevent anyone from reproaching you for not living in the right way. To escape such tests is neither possible nor good, but it is best and easiest not to discredit others but to prepare oneself to be as good as possible. With this prophecy to you who convicted me, I part from you.

I should be glad to discuss what has happened with those who voted for my acquittal during the time that the officers of the court are busy and I do not yet have to depart to my death. So, gentlemen, stay with me awhile, for nothing prevents us from talking to each other while it is allowed. To you, as being my friends, I want to show the meaning of what has occurred. A surprising thing has happened to me, judges--you I would rightly call judges. At all previous times my usual mantic sign frequently opposed me, even in small matters, when I was about to do something wrong, but now that, as you can see for yourselves, I was faced with what one might think, and what is generally thought to be, the worst of evils, my divine sign has not opposed me, either when I left home at dawn, or when I came into court, or at any time that I was about to say something during my speech. Yet in other talks it often held me back in the middle of my speaking, but now it has opposed no word or deed of mine. What do I think is the reason for this? I will tell you. What has happened to me may well be a good thing, and those of us who believe death to be an evil are certainly mistaken. I have convincing proof of this, for it is impossible that my customary sign did not oppose me if I was not about to do what was right.

Let us reflect that there is good hope that death is a blessing, for it is one of two things: either the dead are nothing and have no perception of anything, or it is, as we are told, a change for the soul from here to another place. If it is complete lack of perception, like a dreamless sleep, then death would be a great advantage. For I think that if one had to pick out that night during which a man slept soundly and did not dream, put beside it the other nights and days of his life, and then see how many days and nights had been better and more pleasant than that night, not only a private person but the great king would find them easy to count compared with the other days and nights. If death is like this I say it is an advantage, for all eternity would then seem to be no more than a single night. If, on the other hand, death is a change from here to another place, and what we are told is true and all who have died are there, what greater blessing could there be, gentlemen of the jury? If anyone arriving in Hades will have escaped from those who call themselves judges here, and will find those true judges who are said to sit in judgement there, Minos and Radamanthus and Aeacus and Triptolemus and the other demi-gods who have been upright in their own life, would that be a poor kind of change? Again, what would one of you give to keep company with Orpheus and Musaeus, Hesiod and Homer? I am willing to die many times if that is true. It would be a wonderful way for me to spend my time whenever I met Palamedes and Ajax, the son of Telamon, and any other men of old who died through an unjust conviction, to compare my experience with theirs. I think it would be pleasant. Most important, I could spend my time testing and examining people there, as I do here, as to who among them is wise, and who thinks he is, but is not.

What would one not give, gentlemen of the jury, for the opportunity to examine the man who led the great expedition against Troy, or Odysseus, or Sisyphus, and innumerable other men and women one could mention. It would be an extraordinary happiness to talk with them, to keep company with them and examine them. In any case, they would certainly not put one to death for doing so. They are happier there than we are here in other respects, and for the rest of time they are deathless, if indeed what we are told is true.

You too must be of good hope as regards death, gentlemen of the jury, and keep this one truth in mind, that a good man cannot be harmed either in life or in death, and that his affairs are not neglected by the gods. What has happened to me now has not happened of itself, but it is clear to me that it was better for me to die now and to escape from trouble. That is why my divine sign did not oppose me at any point. So I am certainly not angry with those who convicted me, or with my accusers. Of course that was not their purpose when they accused and convicted me, but they thought they were hurting me, and for this they deserve blame. This much I ask from them: when my sons grow up, avenge yourselves by causing them the same kind of grief that I caused you, if you think they care for money or anything else more than they care for virtue, or if they think they are somebody when they are nobody. Reproach them as I reproach you, that they do not care for the right things and think they are worthy when they are not worthy of anything. If you do this, I shall have been justly treated by you, and my sons also.

Now the hour to part has come. I go to die, you go to live. Which of us goes to the better lot is known to no one, except the god.

STUDY QUESTIONS FOR CHAPTER I

Questions for Review:

1. What are the eight behavioral symptoms of value confusion, according to Raths, Harmin and Simon?

2. What are the three forms of nihilism as described by Nietzsche? Reformulate each one in your own words.

3. When asked where he is going, the narrator in "My Destination" gives two somewhat differing answers. What are these answers and how are they different?

4. What are the various ways in which Koheleth has sought for happiness? What are the results, in each case?

5. In what respects are humans like animals, according to Koheleth?

6. Why does Koheleth believe that the dead are more fortunate than the living, and those who have not been born most fortunate of all?

7. What advice does Koheleth give concerning the best conduct of life?

8. What does Socrates say about his own speaking style?

9. What are the accusations brought against Socrates?

10. What did the oracle of Delphi say about Socrates? By what process did Socrates come to agree with the oracle?

11. Why does Socrates reject fear of death?

12. What is Socrates' supreme duty, in his opinion?

13. What does Socrates mean by comparing himself to a gadfly?

14. What are the chief lines of argument that Socrates offers in his own defense?

15. What counter-penalty does Socrates propose for himself?

16. What evidence does Socrates offer at the end of his remarks, that he has defended himself rightly?

17. What reasons does Socrates offer for believing that death may be a great blessing?

18. What request does Socrates make concerning the education of his sons?

Questions for Reflection:

1. Do any of the eight behavioral symptoms of value confusion apply to my own life? If so, which ones?

2. In what ways, if any, have I experienced nihilism, as described by Nietzsche, in my life? How do I deal with such experiences?

3. What might a journey to "Away-From-Here" mean for me? What would I be leaving, and where would I be going?

4. To what degree are the things that I want in my life like the things that Koheleth pursued and achieved?

5. How do I feel about the prospect of my own old age and death?

6. What would I do, if I were faced with the choices before Socrates?

Questions for Discussion

1. Does Nietzsche's description of nihilism apply to the attitude of Koheleth?

2. Do you believe that the experience of emptiness is the most important problem facing humans in their quest for the good life?

3. Do you agree with the editor's claim that "We do not escape emptiness by fleeing from it, but rather by facing it, living through it, and growing beyond it"?

4. Is a "diversionary" response to the experience of emptiness sometimes a good thing? If so, when?

5. Consider the following two contradictory views concerning the value of the search for wisdom:

   "And so I set my mind to appraise wisdom and to appraise madness and folly. And I learned that this too was pursuit of wind: For as wisdom grows, vexation grows; to increase learning is to increase heartache." (Eccesiastes, above, page 21)

   ". . .it is the greatest good for a man to discuss virtue every day and those other things about which you hear me conversing and testing myself and others, for the unexamined life is not worth living. . ." (Apology, above, page 35)

   Which statement do you more nearly agree with? Why?

6. What is the difference between an honest and healthy confrontation with the emptiness in one's life, and a morbid, self-engrossed agonizing over one's problems? How can one distinguish between the two?

SUGGESTIONS FOR FURTHER READING

Anton Chekhov, "A Dull Story," in Ward Six and Other Stories, (New American Library, 1965)

Richard P. Dennis and Edwin P. Moldof, eds., The Search For Meaning, Vol. One (The Great Books Foundation, 1976)

Fyodor Dostoyevsky, Notes From Underground, (New American Library, Signet, 1961)

Doris Lessing, "The Temptation of Jack Orkney," in The Temptation of Jack Orkney and Other Stories, (Knopf, 1972)

Rollo May, Man's Search for Himself, Chaps. 1 and 2 (W. W. Norton, 1953)

Michael Novak, The Experience of Nothingness, (Harper Colophon, 1970)

Leo Tolstoy, "The Death of Ivan Ilych" in The Death of Ivan Ilych and Other Stories, (New American Libary, Signet, 1960) A magnificent story, ideal for use in conjunction with this chapter.

Chapter Two:

Pleasure

Chapter II: PLEASURE

Introduction

Life is to enjoy. If my life is empty, it is because I have lost the ability to appreciate, to have fun, to find pleasure in life. For when I take pleasure in the process of living, my life is rewarding, satisfying, fulfilling. The best answer to the problem of an empty life is to fill it with pleasant, enjoyable activity. The good life consists in the true enjoyment of living--so says the enlightened hedonist.

When someone speaks of pleasure, we are likely to think of such things as the pleasure of playing a game, of eating food food, of making love. But there are other pleasures as well. There is the pleasure of accomplishing a difficult task, or of doing what I know to be right. There is the pleasure of giving, and the pleasure of learning.

Some pleasures are like sunlight that, breaking through the clouds, briefly illuminates the scene and then disappears without a trace. If these were the only pleasures available to us, we may at least be grateful for small favors. But pleasure can be stronger and more lasting, as well. When in the middle of a hard day, I relax upon a park bench and relish the steady warmth of the noon-day sun upon my body, I am meeting a real need. Likewise, when I am lonely and then find my loneliness dispelled by the presence of a loved one, the pleasure I experience is the measure of my recovery into a better state. As enjoyment brightens my life, I become less self-engrossed, and more cheerful, friendly, concerned for others. Pleasure sometimes merely gratifies; but pleasure also often enriches. As sunlight nourishes the green leaf, so pleasures can nourish our genuine needs.

We often think of pleasure as essentially passive. Some pleasures, such as the feeling of warm sunlight upon our bodies, are indeed passively received experiences; but other pleasures are the natural expression of activity, of achievement, of growth. Perhaps we enjoy skiing, or playing tennis, or swimming; perhaps we enjoy gardening, or playing with a child. Perhaps we delight in a difficult task, well performed; or perhaps we exult in the development of new skills, new competencies, new insights. These are the pleasures of doing and becoming; and such pleasures are often the very best moments of our lives.

To live pleasantly means to enjoy life. I may accurately speak of the pleasure of eating good food or of giving a gift to someone whom I love. But I may with equal accuracy say simply that I enjoy doing these things. The original meaning of "to enjoy" is "to be in a joyous state" or "to rejoice." While we commonly distinguish between pleasure or enjoyment, and joy, these concepts retain a closer psychological relationship than we may realize. Their connection is especially apparent when we observe a child who is delighted with a new toy: is the child experiencing pleasure, or joy? We usually reserve the term "joy" for especially intense experience; but we might do well to think of simple, everyday pleasures as small but genuine joys. As a principle for the guidance of life, "Seek pleasure!" may sound crass to our ears; but "Enjoy life!" is surely good and honorable advice.

The pursuit of pleasure has been often slandered in Western thought. A "pleasure seeker," a "hedonist," is pictured as an impulsive, selfish person, one who craves and pursues every immediate gratification, without regard for other persons. But, as deeper thinkers of all ages have known, such a person is less likely to live a pleasant life, overall, than is a more level-headed, prudent and compassionate person. Immediate gratification often brings discomfort or pain in its wake, or interferes with the enjoyment of greater and more lasting pleasures. Here, as elsewhere, it is wise to be guided not only by whims and impulses, but by a longer view ahead. As for our behavior toward others: pleasures gained at their expense often, in the end, hurt us--and them--more deeply than we realize. On this point, the greatest of the ancient Greek hedonists, Epicurus, roundly declared that ". . .it is not possible to live pleasantly without living prudently and honorably and justly, nor again, to live a life of prudence, honor, and justice without living pleasantly. For the virtures are by nature bound up with the pleasant life, and the pleasant life is inseparable from them." If Epicurus is correct, we must exercise responsibility and restraint in order to enjoy life to its fullest.

The enjoyment of life also requires that we know something about ourselves: what we enjoy, what we desire, what we need. Here, again, Epicurus provides guidance. He declares that ". . .of desires some are natural, others vain, and of the natural some are necessary and others merely natural; and of the necessary some are necessary for happiness,

This requires knowledge

others for the repose of the body, and others for very life." We should, therefore, seek first of all to satisfy those desires which are both natural and necessary: the desires for adequate food and drink, the desires for health and growth, the desires for companionship and love, and so on. Natural but unnecessary desires (such as, perhaps, the desire to eat more than we need) should be pursued only cautiously, if at all; and unnatural ("vain") desires should be shunned altogether. Some needs must be met simply in order to live. Certain additional things are necessary for physical comfort and well-being. And some things indeed bring happiness.

For advice in another vein, we may look to the great utilitarian and social reformer, Jeremy Bentham (1748-1832), whose elaborate formula has been called a "hedonic calculus." In determining the best choice of pleasures, he says, we should consider seven matters: (1) How "intense" or profound is the pleasure which is desired? (2) Is the pleasure merely momentary, or does it extend over a significant period of time? (3) How certain is the pleasure to occur, if it is sought? (4) Is the pleasure remote, or readily available? (5) Does the acquisition of the pleasure promise more pleasure as a result? (6) Is the pleasure free from unpleasant consequences? Finally, when we are considering more than one person, (7) To how many persons does the pleasure extend?[21]

The Selections

The opening selections of this chapter present the classical views of Epicurus (341-270 B.C.), as well as more recent formulations by John Stuart Mill (1806-1873) and the contemporary Chinese-American author, Lin Yutang (1895-1976).

The word "Epicurean" has come to suggest to us a person who cultivates exotic tastes and sensuous delights. In this sense of the word, Epicurus--who could be satisfied with a meal of bread and water, and for whom a bit of cheese was a luxury--was certainly no "Epicurean." Our true needs--those desires which are both natural and necessary--are basic and easily satisfied. If we learn to confine our demands to these desires, and enjoy whatever other natural and harmless pleasures come our way, we can be fully satisfied and can achieve true happiness. Epicurus advocates a simple life of restraint and moderation, in which the primary good is "the health of the body and the soul's freedom from disturbance."

A man of unusual generosity, sympathy and responsibility, Epicurus came to be revered with almost religious devotion by his students and disciples.[2] Epicurus was interested in natural science as well, and adopted a form of scientific materialism, built around a theory of atoms, which was largely derived from an earlier Greek natural philosopher, Democritus (ca. 460-370 B.C.). Epicurus saw these scientific views as a needed antidote to the religious superstitions of the day, with their messages of fear and anxiety. Epicurus also recognized that the thought

Epicurous did not believe in a follow on world

45

must be made of matter to be real

of death is a potent source of fear and distress, and argued that this fear and distress is misplaced. Death is, he said, simply the termination of sensation and consciousness, including all unpleasant or painful sensations and thoughts. So long as we are alive and capable of sensation, our death does not exist. When our death occurs, we do not exist. Our death is literally nothing to us. Fear of death is therefore senseless.

In a letter to a disciple and friend, Menoeceus, Epicurus outlines his central thoughts on the good life. A comment on the opening paragraph of this letter is called for here; in it, Epicurus admonishes Menoeceus to study philosophy as a means to happiness. Contemporary readers may wonder why philosophy is accorded this special status by Epicurus. The explanation lies in the ancient Greek meaning of the word "philosophy." The original meaning of "philosophy" is "love of wisdom." Thus a "philosopher" is, literally, a "lover of wisdom." And one central concern of wisdom (sophia) among the ancient Greeks was the knowledge of how to live rightly and well. So understood, philosophy is indeed an appropriate pursuit for one who seeks to live a good life.

In his discussion of qualitative distinctions between pleasures, the British philosopher John Stuart Mill defends the Epicurean claim that happiness--understood as pleasure, and the absence of pain--is the proper goal or end of life. The excerpt reprinted here is taken from Mill's immensely influential book Utilitarianism, in which he develops a version of hedonism as a theory of living rightly: among available options, that action is right which produces the greatest balance of happiness over unhappiness for the greatest number of people. Contrary to Bentham's view that only the quantity of pleasure is relevant in determining the right course of action, Mill argues here that pleasures differ in quality as well, some being higher or more refined than others; thus for beings capable of both, it is often rational to choose a smaller quantity of more refined pleasures over a larger quantity of lower or animal-like pleasures. "It is better to be a human being dissatisfied than a pig satisfied; better to be Socrates dissatisfied than a fool satisfied."

How may one determine which pleasures are "higher" or qualitatively better? Mill's reply is that we must look to those persons who have experienced both, and see which they prefer. The selection from Mill closes with his celebrated argument for the truth of the claim that happiness is desirable as an end of action.

A less austere yet thoroughly civilized statement of hedonism is presented in the selection from Lin Yutang. Born in China and educated in Germany and the United States, Lin Yutang held numerous academic positions, and for a time was associated with United Nations international education efforts. But he gained his greatest recognition through his many books and articles. The hedonism which Lin Yutang advocates here, while certainly not irresponsible, emphasizes a greater variety of sensuous pleasures than does the hedonism of Epicurus or Mill. Yutang disputes Mill's view that pleasures of the "higher faculties" are to be preferred; he says "I am such a materialist that at any time I would prefer pork to poetry, and would waive a piece of philosophy for a piece of filet, brown and crisp and garnished with good sauce." He declares bluntly that "All human happiness is biological happiness." His point is not to deny the existence of pleasures such as the exercise of the mind or spirit, but to assert that even they are ultimately biological in nature. And biological happiness is enjoyment. "I have always assumed," he writes, "that the end of living is the true enjoyment of it." How one should spend one's life is "a practical question, similar to how a man should spend his weekend."

The selection is written in clear and attractive prose, and requires little interpretation here. It will be a rare reader who does not find at least some persuasive points and compelling insights in this discussion of how to live a more enjoyable life.

NOTES

1. For Bentham's original formulation of these seven criteria, see Jeremy Bentham, An Introduction to the Principles of Morals and Legislation, Chapter IV. (Many editions)

2. In 306 B.C. Epicurus established a school in Athens, which came to be called the "Garden of Epicurus" and which gained considerable fame during his lifetime.

EPICURUS TO MENOECEUS*

by Epicurus

Let no one when young delay to study philosophy, nor when he is old grow weary of his study. For no one can come too early or too late to secure the health of his soul. And the man who says that the age for philosophy has either not yet come or has gone by is like the man who says that the age for happiness is not yet come to him, or has passed away. Wherefore both when young and old a man must study philosophy, that as he grows old he may be young in blessings through the grateful recollection of what has been, and that in youth he may be old as well, since he will know no fear of what is to come. We must then meditate on the things that make our happiness, seeing that when that is with us we have all, but when it is absent we do all to win it.

The things which I used unceasingly to commend to you, these do and practice, considering them to be the first principles of the good life. First of all believe that god is a being immortal and blessed, even as the common idea of a god is engraved on men's minds, and do not assign to him anything alien to his immortality or ill-suited to his blessedness: but believe about him everything that can uphold his blessedness and immortality. For gods there are, since the knowledge of them is by clear vision. But they are not such as the many believe them to be: for indeed they do not consistently represent them as they believe them to be. And the impious man is not he who denies the gods of the many, but he who attaches to the gods the beliefs of the many. For the statements of the many about the gods are not conceptions derived from sensation, but false suppositions, according to which the greatest misfortunes befall the wicked and the greatest blessings (the good) by the gift of the gods. For men being accustomed always to their own virtues welcome those like themselves, but regard all that is not of their nature as alien.

Become accustomed to the belief that death is nothing to us. For all good and evil consists in sensation, but death is deprivation of sensation. And therefore a right understanding that death is nothing to us makes the mortality of life enjoyable, not because it adds to it an infinite span of time, but because it takes away the craving for immortality. For there is nothing terrible in life for the man who has truly comprehended that there is nothing terrible in not living. So that the man speaks but idly who says that he fears death not because it will be painful when it comes, but because it is painful in anticipation. For that which gives no trouble when it comes, is but an empty pain in anticipation. So death, the most terrifying of ills, is nothing to us, since so long as we exist, death is not with us; but when death comes, then we do not exist. It does not then

*From Epicurus: The Extant Remains translated by Cyril Bailey (1926). Reprinted by permission of Oxford University Press.

concern either the living or the dead, since for the former it is not, and the latter are no more.

But the many at one moment shun death as the greatest of evils, at another yearn for it as a respite from the evils in life. But the wise man neither seeks to escape life nor fears the cessation of life, for neither does life offend him nor does the absence of life seem to be any evil. And just as with food he does not seek simply the larger share and nothing else, but rather the most pleasant, so he seeks to enjoy not the longest period of time, but the most pleasant.

And he who counsels the young man to live well, but the old man to make a good end, is foolish, not merely because of the desirability of life, but also because it is the same training which teaches to live well and to die well. Yet much worse still is the man who says it is good not to be born, but 'once born make haste to pass the gates of Death'. For if he says this from conviction why does he not pass away out of life? For it is open to him to do so, if he had firmly made up his mind to this. But if he speaks in jest, his words are idle among men who cannot receive them.

We must then bear in mind that the future is neither ours, nor yet wholly not ours, so that we may not altogether expect it as sure to come, nor abandon hope of it, as if it will certainly not come.

We must consider that of desires some are natural, others vain, and of the natural some are necessary and others merely natural; and of the necessary some are necessary for happiness, others for the repose of the body, and others for very life. The right understanding of these facts enables us to refer all choice and avoidance to the health of the body and the soul's freedom from disturbance, since this is the aim of the life of blessedness. For it is to obtain this end that we always act, namely, to avoid pain and fear. And when this is once secured for us, all the tempest of the soul is dispersed, since the living creature has not to wander as though in search of something that is missing, and to look for some other thing by which he can fulfil the good of the soul and the good of the body. For it is then that we have need of pleasure, when we feel pain owing to the absence of pleasure; but when we do not feel pain, we no longer need pleasure. And for this cause we call pleasure the beginning and end of the blessed life. For we recognize pleasure as the first good innate in us, and from pleasure we begin every act of choice and avoidance, and to pleasure we return again, using the feeling as the standard by which we judge every good.

And since pleasure is the first good and natural to us, for this very reason we do not choose every pleasure, but sometimes we pass over many pleasures, when greater discomfort accrues to us as the result of them: and similarly we think many pains better than pleasures, since a greater pleasure comes to us when we have endured pains for a long time. Every pleasure then because of its natural kinship to us is good, yet not every pleasure is to be chosen: even as every pain also is an evil, yet not all are always of a nature to be avoided. Yet by a scale of comparison and by the consideration of advantages and disadvantages we must form our judgement on all these matters. For the good on certain occasions we treat as bad, and conversely the bad as good.

And again independence of desire we think a great good--not that we may at all times enjoy but a few things, but that, if we do not possess many, we may enjoy the few in the genuine persuasion that those have the sweetest pleasure in luxury who least need it, and that all that is natural is easy to be obtained, but that which is superfluous is hard. And so plain savours bring us a pleasure equal to a luxurious diet, when all the pain due to want is removed; and bread and water produce the highest pleasure, when one who needs them puts them to his lips. To grow accustomed therefore to simple and not luxurious diet gives us health to the full, and makes a man alert for the needful employments of life, and when after long intervals we approach luxuries disposes us better towards them, and fits us to be fearless of fortune.

When, therefore, we maintain that pleasure is the end, we do not mean the pleasures of profligates and those that consist in sensuality, as is supposed by some who are either ignorant or disagree with us or do not understand, but freedom from pain in the body and from trouble in the mind. For it is not continuous drinkings and revellings, nor the satisfaction of lusts, nor the enjoyment of fish and other luxuries cf the wealthy table, which produce a pleasant life, but sober reasoning, searching out the motives for all choice and avoidance, and banishing mere opinions, to which are due the greatest disturbance of the spirit.

Of all this the beginning and the greatest good is prudence. Wherefore prudence is a more precious thing even than philosophy: for from prudence are sprung all the other virtues, and it teaches us that it is not possible to live pleasantly without living prudently and honourably and justly, nor, again, to live a life of prudence, honour, and justice without living pleasantly. For the virtues are by nature bound up with the pleasant life, and the pleasant life is inseparable from them. For indeed who, think you, is a better man than he who holds reverent opinions concerning the gods, and is at all times free from fear of death, and has reasoned out the end ordained by nature? He understands that the limit of good things is easy to fulfil and easy to attain, whereas the course of ills is either short in time or slight in pain: he laughs at destiny, whom some have introduced as the mistress of all things. He thinks that with us lies the chief power in determining events, some of which happen by necessity and some by chance, and some are within our control; for while necessity cannot be called to account, he sees that chance is inconstant, but that which is in our control is subject to no master, and to it are naturally attached praise and blame. For, indeed, it were better to follow

51

the myths about the gods than to become a slave to the destiny of the natural philosophers: for the former suggests a hope of placating the gods by worship, whereas the latter involves a necessity which knows no placation. As to chance, he does not regard it as a god as most men do (for in a god's acts there is no disorder), nor as an uncertain cause of all things: for he does not believe that good and evil are given by chance to man for the framing of a blessed life, but that opportunities for great good and great evil are afforded by it. He therefore thinks it better to be unfortunate in reasonable action than to prosper in unreason. For it is better in a man's actions that what is well chosen should fail, rather than that what is ill chosen should be successful owing to chance.

Meditate therefore on these things and things akin to them night and day by yourself, and with a companion like to yourself, and never shall you be disturbed waking or asleep, but you shall live like a god among men. For a man who lives among immortal blessings is not like to a mortal being.

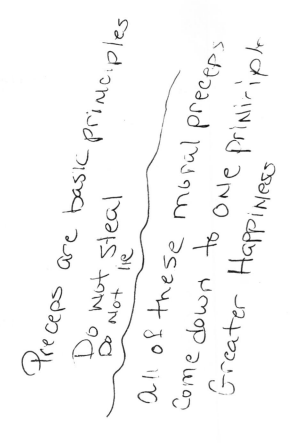

HIGHER AND LOWER PLEASURES*

by John Stuart Mill

The creed which accepts as the foundation of morals, Utility, or the Greatest Happiness Principle, holds that actions are right in proportion as they tend to promote happiness, wrong as they tend to produce the reverse of happiness. By happiness is intended pleasure, and the absence of pain; by unhappiness, pain, and the privation of pleasure. To give a clear view of the moral standard set up by the theory, much more requires to be said; in particular, what things it includes in the ideas of pain and pleasure; and to what extent this is left an open question. But these supplementary explanations do not affect the theory of life on which this theory of morality is grounded--namely, that pleasure, and freedom from pain, are the only things desirable as ends; and that all desirable things (which are as numerous in the utilitarian as in any other scheme) are desirable either for the pleasure inherent in themselves, or as means to the promotion of pleasure and the prevention of pain.

Now, such a theory of life excites in many minds, and among them in some of the most estimable in feeling and purpose, inveterate dislike. To suppose that life has (as they express it) no higher end than pleasure-- no better and nobler object of desire and pursuit--they designate as utterly mean and grovelling; as a doctrine worthy only of swine, to whom the followers of Epicurus were, at a very early period, contemptuously likened; and modern holders of the doctrine are occasionally made the subject of equally polite comparisons by its German, French and English assailants.

When thus attacked, the Epicureans have always answered, that it is not they, but their accusers, who represent human nature in a degrading light; since the accusation supposes human beings to be capable of no pleasures except those of which swine are capable. . . The comparison of the Epicurean life to that of beasts is felt as degrading, precisely because a beast's pleasures do not satisfy a human being's conceptions of happiness. Human beings have faculties more elevated than the animal appetites, and when once made conscious of them, do not regard anything as happiness which does not include their gratification. I do not, indeed, consider the Epicureans to have been by any means faultless in drawing out their scheme of consequences from the utilitarian principle. To do this in any sufficient manner, many Stoic, as well as Christian elements require to be included. But there is no known Epicurean theory of life which does not assign to the pleasures of the intellect, of the feelings and imagination, and of the moral sentiments, a much higher value as pleasures than to those of mere sensation. It must be admitted, however,

*From Utilitarianism. First published in 1861.

53

Utilitarion is the theory of right action

that utilitarian writers in general have placed the superiority of mental over bodily pleasures chiefly in the greater permanency, safety, uncostliness, etc., of the former--that is, in their circumstantial advantages rather than in their intrinsic nature. And on all these points utilitarians have fully proved their case; but they might have taken the other, and, as it may be called, higher ground, with entire consistency. It is quite compatible with the principle of utility to recognise the fact, that some kinds of pleasure are more desirable and more valuable than others. It would be absurd that while, in estimating all other things, quality is considered as well as quantity, the estimation of pleasures should be supposed to depend on quantity alone.

If I am asked, what I mean by difference of quality in pleasures, or what makes one pleasure more valuable than another, merely as a pleasure, except its being greater in amount, there is but one possible answer. Of two pleasures, if there be one to which all or almost all who have experience of both give a decided preference, irrespective of any feeling of moral obligation to prefer it, that is the more desirable pleasure. If one of the two is, by those who are competently acquainted with both, placed so far above the other that they prefer it, even though knowing it to be attended with a greater amount of discontent, and would not resign it for any quantity of the other pleasure which their nature is capable of, we are justified in ascribing to the preferred enjoyment a superiority in quality, so far outweighing quantity as to render it, in comparison, of small account.

Now it is an unquestionable fact that those who are equally acquainted with, and equally capable of appreciating and enjoying, both, do give a most marked preference to the manner of existence which employs their higher faculties. Few human creatures would consent to be changed into any of the lower animals, for a promise of the fullest allowance of a beast's pleasures; no intelligent human being would consent to be a fool, no instructed person would be an ignoramus, no person of feeling and conscience would be selfish and base, even though they should be persuaded that the fool, the dunce, or the rascal is better satisfied with his lot than they are with theirs. They would not resign what they possess more than he, for the most complete satisfaction of all the desires which they have in common with him. If they ever fancy they would, it is only in cases of unhappiness so extreme, that to escape from it they would exchange their lot for almost any other, however undesirable in their own eyes. A being of higher faculties requires more to make him happy, is capable probably of more acute suffering, and is certainly accessible to it at more points, than one of an inferior type; but in spite of these liabilities, he can never really wish to sink into what he feels to be a lower grade of existence. We may give what explanation we please of this unwillingness; we may attribute it to pride, a name which is given indiscriminately to some of the most and to some of the least estimable feelings of which mankind are capable; we may refer it to the love of liberty and personal independence, an appeal to which was with the Stoics one of the most effective means for the inculcation of it; to the love of power, or to the love of excitement, both of which do really enter into and contribute to it: but its most appropriate appellation is a sense of dignity, which all human beings possess in one form or other, and in some, though by no means in exact, proportion to their higher faculties, and which is so essential a part of the happiness of those in whom it is strong, that nothing which conflicts with it could be, otherwise than momentarily, an object of desire to them. Whoever supposes that this preference takes place at a sacrifice of happiness--that the superior being, in anything like the equal circumstances, is not happier than the inferior--confounds the two very different ideas, of happiness, and content. It is indisputable that the being whose capacities of enjoyment are low, has the greatest chance of having them fully satisfied; and a highly-endowed being will always feel that any happiness which he can look for, as the world is constituted, is imperfect. But he can learn to bear its imperfections, if they are at all bearable; and they will not make him envy the being who is indeed unconscious of the imperfections, but only because he feels not at all the good which those imperfections qualify. It is better to be a human being dissatisfied than a pig satisfied; better to be Socrates dissatisfied than a fool satisfied. And if the fool, or the pig, is of a different opinion, it is because they only know their own side of the question. The other party to the comparison knows both sides. . .

According to the Greatest Happiness Principle, as above explained, the ultimate end, with reference to and for the sake of which all other things are desirable (whether we are considering our own good or that of other people), is an existence exempt as far as possible from pain, and as rich as possible in enjoyments, both in point of quantity and quality; the test of quality, and the rule for measuring it against quantity, being the preference felt by those who, in their opportunities of experience, to which must be added their habits of self-consciousness and self-observation, are best furnished with the means of comparison. . .

Of What Sort of Proof the Principle of Utility Is Susceptible

It has already been remarked, that questions of ultimate ends do not admit of proof, in the ordinary acceptation of the term. To be incapable of proof by reasoning is common to all first principles; to the first premises of our knowledge, as well as to those of our conduct. But the former, being matters of fact, may be the subject of a direct appeal to the faculties which judge of fact--namely, our senses, and our internal consciousness. Can an appeal be made to the same faculties on questions of practical ends? Or by what other faculty is cognizance taken of them?

Questions about ends are, in other words, questions what things are desirable. The utilitarian doctrine is, that happiness is desirable, and the only thing desirable, as an end; all other things being only desirable as means to that end. What ought to be required of this doctrine--what conditions is it requisite that the doctrine should fulfil--to make good its claim to be believed?

The only proof capable of being given that an object is visible, is that people actually see it. The only proof that a sound is audible, is that people hear it: and so of the other sources of our experience. In like manner, I apprehend, the sole evidence it is possible to produce that anything is desirable, is that people do actually desire it. If the end which the utilitarian doctrine proposes to itself were not, in theory and in practice, acknowledged to be an end, nothing could ever convince any person that it was so. No reason can be given why the general happiness is desirable, except that each person, so far as he believes it to be attainable, desires his own happiness. This, however, being a fact, we have not only all the proof which the case admits of, but all which it is possible to require, that happiness is a good: that each person's happiness is a good to that person, and the general happiness, therefore, a good to the aggregate of all persons. Happiness has made out its title as one of the ends of conduct, and consequently one of the criteria of morality. . .

THE ENJOYMENT OF LIVING*

by Lin Yutang

In what follows I am presenting the Chinese point of view, because I cannot help myself. I am interested only in presenting a view of life and of things as the best and wisest Chinese minds have seen it and expressed it in their folk wisdom and their literature. It is an idle philosophy born of an idle life, evolved in a different age, I am quite aware. But I cannot help feeling that this view of life is essentially true, and since we are alike under the skin, what touches the human heart in one country touches all. . .

It is useless for me to say whether my philosophy is valid or not for the Westerner. To understand Western life, one would have to look at it as a Westerner born, with his own temperament, his bodily attitudes and his own set of nerves. I have no doubt that American nerves can stand a good many things that Chinese nerves cannot stand, and vice versa. It is good that it should be so--that we should all be born different. And yet it is all a question of relativity. I am quite sure that amidst the hustle and bustle of American life, there is a great deal of wistfulness, of the divine desire to lie on a plot of grass under tall beautiful trees of an ideal afternoon and just do nothing. The necessity for such common cries as "Wake up and live" is to me a good sign that a wise portion of American humanity prefer to dream the hours away. The American is after all not as bad as all that. It is only a question whether he will have more or less of that sort of thing, and how he will arrange to make it possible. Perhaps the American is merely ashamed of the word "loafing" in a world where everybody is doing something, but somehow, as sure as I know he is also an animal, he likes sometimes to have his muscles relaxed, to stretch on the sand, or to lie still with one leg comfortably curled up and one arm placed below his head as his pillow. . . The only thing I desire to see is that he be honest about it, and that he proclaim to the world that he likes it when he likes it, that it is not when he is working in the office but when he is lying idly on the sand that his soul utters, "Life is beautiful". . .

Speaking as a Chinese, I do not think that any civilization can be called complete until it has progressed from sophistication to unsophistication, and made a conscious return to simplicity of thinking and living, and I call no man wise until he has made the progress from the wisdom of knowledge to the wisdom of foolishness, and become a laughing philosopher, feeling first life's tragedy and then life's comedy. For we must weep before we can laugh. Out of sadness comes the awakening and out of the awakening comes the laughter of the philosopher, with kindliness and tolerance to boot.

*From Lin Yutang, The Importance of Living (New York: The John Day Co., 1937). Reprinted by permission of Mrs. Lin Yutang.

The world, I believe, is far too serious, and being far too serious, it has need of a wise and merry philosophy. The philosophy of the Chinese art of living can certainly be called the "gay science," if anything can be called by that phrase used by Nietzsche. After all, only a gay philosophy is profound philosophy; the serious philosophies of the West haven't even begun to understand what life is. To me personally, the only function of philosophy is to teach us to take life more lightly and gayly than the average business man does, for no business man who does not retire at fifty, if he can, is in my eyes a philosopher. This is not merely a casual thought, but is a fundamental point of view with me. The world can be made a more peaceful and more reasonable place to live in only when men have imbued themselves in the light gayety of this spirit. The modern man takes life far too seriously, and because he is too serious, the world is full of troubles. We ought, therefore, to take time to examine the origin of that attitude which will make possible a wholehearted enjoyment of this life and a more reasonable, more peaceful and less hot-headed temperament. . .

Earth-Bound

The situation then is this: man wants to live, but he still must live upon this earth. All questions of living in heaven must be brushed aside. Let not the spirit take wings and soar to the abode of the gods and forget the earth. Are we not mortals, condemned to die? The span of life vouchsafed us, threescore and ten, is short enough, if the spirit gets too haughty and wants to live forever, but on the other hand, it is also long enough, if the spirit is a little humble. One can learn such a lot and enjoy such a lot in seventy years, and three generations is a long, long time to see human follies and acquire human wisdom. Anyone who is wise and has lived long enough to witness the changes of fashion and morals and politics through the rise and fall of three generations should be perfectly satisfied to rise from his seat and go away saying, "It was a good show," when the curtain falls.

For we are of the earth, earth-born and earth-bound. There is nothing to be unhappy about the fact that we are, as it were, delivered upon this beautiful earth as its transient guests. Even if it were a dark dungeon, we still would have to make the best of it; it would be ungrateful of us not to do so when we have, instead of a dungeon, such a beautiful earth to live on for a good part of a century. Sometimes we get too ambitious and disdain the humble and yet generous earth. Yet a sentiment for this Mother Earth, a feeling of true affection and attachment, one must have for this temporary abode of our body and spirit, if we are to have a sense of spiritual harmony. . . .

Any good practical philosophy must start out with the recognition of our having a body. It is high time that some among us made the straight admission that we are animals, an admission which is inevitable since the establishment of the basic truth of the Darwinian theory and the great progress of biology, especially bio-chemistry. It was very unfortunate that our teachers and philosophers belonged to the so-called intellectual class, with a characteristic professional pride of intellect. The men of the spirit were as proud of the spirit as the shoemaker is proud of leather. Sometimes even the spirit was not sufficiently remote and abstract and they had to use the words, "essence" or "soul" or "idea," writing them with capital letters to frighten us. The human body was distilled in this scholastic machine into a spirit, and the spirit was further concentrated into a kind of essence, forgetting that even alcoholic drinks must have a "body"--mixed with plain water--if they are to be palatable at all. And we poor laymen were supposed to drink that concentrated quintessence of spirit. This over-emphasis on the spirit was fatal. It made us war with our natural instincts, and my chief criticism is that it made a whole and rounded view of human nature impossible. It proceeded also from an inadequate knowledge of biology and psychology, and of the place of the senses, emotions and, above all, instincts in our life. Man is made of flesh and spirit both, and it should be philosophy's business to see that the mind and body live harmoniously together, that there be a reconciliation between the two.

Spirit and Flesh

The most obvious fact which philosophers refuse to see is that we have got a body. Tired of seeing our mortal imperfections and our savage instincts and impulses, sometimes our preachers wish that we were made like angels, and yet we are at a total loss to imagine what the angels' life would be like. ...I sometimes think that it is an advantage even for angels to have a body with the five senses. If I were to be an angel, I should like to have a school-girl complexion, but how am I going to have a school-girl complexion without a skin? I still should like to drink a glass of tomato juice or iced orange juice, but how am I going to appreciate iced orange juice without having thirst? And how am I going to enjoy food, when I am incapable of hunger? How would an angel paint without pigment, sing without the hearing of sounds, smell the fine morning air without a nose? How would he enjoy the immense satisfaction of scratching an itch, if his skin doesn't itch? And what a terrible loss in the capacity for happiness that would be! Either we have to have bodies and have all our bodily wants satisfied, or else we are pure spirits and have no satisfactions at all. All satisfactions imply want.

I sometimes think what a terrible punishment it would be for a ghost or an angel to have no body, to look at a stream of cool water and have no feet to plunge into it and get a delightful cooling sensation from it, to see a dish of Peking or Long Island duck and have no tongue to taste it, to see crumpets and have no teeth to chew them, to see the beloved faces of our dear ones and have no emotions to feel toward them. Terribly sad it would be if we should one day return to this earth as ghosts and move silently into our children's bedroom, to see a child lying there in bed and have no hands to fondle him and no arms to clasp him, no chest for his warmth to penetrate to, no round hollow between cheek and shoulder for him to nestle against, and no ears to hear his voice. . .

Why do we despise the body, when the flesh itself shows such intelligence? After all, we are endowed with a body, which is a self-nourishing, self-regulating, self-repairing, self-starting and self-reproducing machine, installed at birth and lasting like a good grandfather clock for three-quarters of a century, requiring very little attention. . .

Above all, it has a sense of the rhythm of life, and a sense of time, not only of hours and days, but also of decades; the body regulates its own childhood, puberty and maturity, stops growing when it should no longer grow, and brings forth a wisdom tooth at a time when no one of us ever thought of it. . . It also manufactures specific antidotes against poison, on the whole with amazing success, and it does all these things with absolute silence, without the usual racket of a factory, so that our superfine metaphysician may not be disturbed and is free to think about his spirit or his essence.

Human Life A Poem

I think that, from a biological standpoint, human life almost reads like a poem. It has its own rhythm and beat, its internal cycles of growth and decay. It begins with innocent childhood, followed by awkward adolescence trying awkwardly to adapt itself to mature society, with its young passions and follies, its ideals and ambitions; then it reaches a manhood of intense activities, profiting from experience and learning more about society and human nature; at middle age, there is a slight easing of tension, a mellowing of character like the ripening of fruit or the mellowing of good wine, and the gradual acquiring of a more tolerant, more cynical and at the same time a kindlier view of life; then in the sunset of our life, the endocrine glands decrease their activity, and if we have a true philosophy of old age and have ordered our life pattern according to it, it is for us the age of peace and security and leisure and contentment; finally, life flickers out and one goes into eternal sleep, never to wake up again. One should be able to sense the beauty of this rhythm of life, to appreciate, as we do in grand symphonies, its main theme, its strains of conflict and the final resolution. The movements of these cycles are very much the same in a normal life, but the music must be provided by the individual himself. In some souls, the discordant note becomes harsher and harsher and finally overwhelms or submerges the main melody. Sometimes the discordant note gains so much power that the music can no longer go on, and the individual shoots himself with a pistol or jumps into a river. But that is because his original leit-motif has been hopelessly over-shadowed through the lack of a good self-education. Otherwise the normal human life runs to its normal end in a kind of dignified movement and procession. There are sometimes in many of us too many staccatos or impetuosos, and because the tempo is wrong, the music is not pleasing to the ear; we might have more of the grand rhythm and majestic tempo of the Ganges, flowing slowly and eternally into the sea.

No one can say that a life with childhood, manhood and old age is not a beautiful arrangement; the day has its morning, noon and sunset, and the year has its seasons, and it is good that it is so. There is no good or bad in life, except what is good according to its own season. And if we take this biological view of life and try to live according to the seasons, no one but a conceited fool or an impossible idealist can deny that human life can be lived like a poem. . .

The Problem of Happiness

The enjoyment of life covers many things: the enjoyment of ourselves, of home life, of trees, flowers, clouds, winding rivers and falling cataracts and the myriad things in Nature, and then the enjoyment of poetry, art, contemplation, friendship, conversation, and reading, which are all some form or other of the communion of spirits. There are obvious things like the enjoyment of food, a gay party or family reunion, an outing on a beautiful spring day; and less obvious things like the enjoyment of poetry, art and contemplation. I have found it impossible to call these two classes of enjoyment material and spiritual, first because I do not believe in this distinction, and secondly because I am puzzled whenever I proceed to make this classification. How can I say, when I see a gay picnic party of men and women and old people and children, what part of their pleasures is material and what part spiritual? I see a child romping about on the grass plot, another child making daisy chains, their mother holding a piece of sandwich, the uncle of the family biting a juicy, red apple, the father sprawling on the ground looking at the sailing clouds, and the grandfather holding a pipe in his mouth. Probably somebody is playing a gramophone, and from the distance there come the sound of music and the distant roar of the waves. Which of these pleasures is material and which spiritual? Is it so easy to draw a distinction between the enjoyment of a sandwich and the enjoyment of the surrounding landscape, which we call poetry? Is it possible to regard the enjoyment of music which we call art, as decidedly a higher type of pleasure than the smoking of a pipe, which we call material? This classification between material and spiritual pleasures is therefore confusing, unintelligible and untrue for me. It proceeds, I suspect, from a false philosophy, sharply dividing the spirit from the flesh, and not supported by a closer direct scrutiny of our real pleasures.

Or have I perhaps assumed too much and begged the question of the proper end of human life? I have always assumed that the end of living is the true enjoyment of it. It is so simply because it is so. I rather hesitate at the word "end" or "purpose." Such an end or purpose of life, consisting in its true enjoyment, is not so much a conscious purpose, as a natural attitude toward human life. The word "purpose" suggests too much contriving and endeavor. The question that faces every man born into this world is not what should be his purpose, which he should set about to achieve, but just what to do with life, a life which is given him for a period of on the average fifty or sixty years? The answer that he should order his life so that he can find the greatest happiness in it is more a practical question, similar to that of how a man should spend his weekend, than a metaphysical proposition as to what is the mystic purpose of his life in the scheme of the universe.

On the contrary, I rather think that philosophers who start out to solve the problem of the purpose of life beg the question by assuming that life must have a purpose. This question, so much pushed to the fore among Western thinkers, is undoubtedly given that importance through the influence of theology. I think we assume too much design and purpose altogether. And the very fact that people try to answer this question and quarrel over it and are puzzled by it serves to show it up as quite vain and uncalled for. Had there been a purpose or design in life, it should not have been so puzzling and vague and difficult to find out. . .

The point of dispute is not what is, but what should be, the purpose of human life, and it is therefore a practical, and not a metaphysical question. Into this question of what should be the purpose of human life, every man projects his own conceptions and his own scale of values. It is for this reason that we quarrel over the question, because our scales of values differ from one another. For myself, I am content to be less philosophical and more practical. I should not presume that there must be necessarily a purpose, a meaning of human existence. As Walt Whitman says, "I am sufficient as I am." It is sufficient that I live--and am probably going to live for another few decades--and that human life exists. Viewed that way, the problem becomes amazingly simple and admits of no two answers. What can be the end of human life except the enjoyment of it?. . .

Human Happiness Is Sensuous

All human happiness is biological happiness. That is strictly scientific. At the risk of being misunderstood, I must make it clearer: all human happiness is sensuous happiness. The spiritualists will misunderstand me, I am sure; the spiritualists and materialists must forever misunderstand each other, because they don't talk the same language, or mean by the same word different things. Are we, too, in this problem of securing happiness to be deluded by the spiritualists, and admit that true happiness is only happiness of the spirit? Let us admit it at once and immediately proceed to qualify it by saying that the spirit is a condition of the perfect functioning of the endocrine glands. Happiness for me is largely a matter of digestion. . .

Let us not lose ourselves in the abstract when we talk of happiness, but get down to facts and analyze for ourselves what are the truly happy moments of our life. In this world of ours, happiness is very often negative, the complete absence of sorrow or mortification or bodily ailment. But happiness can also be positive, and then we call it joy. To me, for instance, the truly happy moments are: when I get up in the morning after a night of perfect sleep and sniff the morning air and there is an expansiveness in the lungs, when I feel inclined to inhale deeply and there is a fine sensation of movement around the skin and muscles of the chest, and when, therefore, I am fit for work; or when I hold a pipe in my hand and rest my legs on a chair, and the tobacco burns slowly and evenly; or when I am traveling on a summer day, my throat parched with thirst, and I see a beautiful clear spring, whose very sound makes me happy, and I take off my socks and shoes and dip my feet in the delightful, cool water; or when after a perfect dinner I lounge in an armchair, when there is no one I hate to look at in the company and conversation rambles off at a light pace to an unknown destination, and I am spiritually and physically at peace with the world; or when on a summer afternoon I see black clouds gathering on the horizon and know for certain a July shower is coming in a quarter of an hour, but being ashamed to be seen going out into the rain without an umbrella, I hastily set out to meet the shower halfway across the fields and come home drenched through and through and tell my family that I was simply caught by the rain.

Just as it is impossible for me to say whether I love my children physically or spiritually when I hear their chattering voices or when I see their plump legs, so I am totally unable to distinguish between the joys of the mind and the joys of the flesh. Does anybody ever love a woman spiritually without loving her physically? And is it so easy a matter for a man to analyze and separate the charms of the woman he loves--things like laughter, smiles, a way of tossing one's head, a certain attitude toward things?

How About Mental Pleasures?

Let us take the supposedly higher pleasures of the mind and the spirit, and see to what extent they are vitally connected with our senses, rather than with our intellect. What are those higher spiritual pleasures that we distinguish from those of the lower senses? Are they not parts of the same thing, taking root and ending up in the senses, and inseparable from them? As we go over these higher pleasures of the mind--literature, art, music, religion and philosophy--we see what a minor role the intellect plays in comparison with the senses and feelings. What does a painting do except to give us a landscape or a portrait and recall in us the sensuous pleasures of seeing a real landscape or a beautiful face? And what does

63

literature do except to recreate a picture of life, to give us the atmosphere and color, the fragrant smell of the pastures or the stench of city gutters? We all say that a novel approaches the standard of true literature in proportion as it gives us real people and real emotions. The book which takes us away from this human life, or merely coldly dissects it, is not literature and the more humanly true a book is, the better literature we consider it. What novel ever appeals to a reader if it contains only a cold analysis, if it fails to give us the salt and tang and flavor of life?

As for the other things, poetry is but truth colored with emotion, music is sentiment without words, and religion is but wisdom expressed in fancy. As painting is based on the sense of color and vision, so poetry is based on the sense of sound and tone and rhythm, in addition to its emotional truth. Music is pure sentiment itself, dispensing entirely with the language of words with which alone the intellect can operate. Music can portray for us the sounds of cowbells and fishmarkets and the battlefield; it can portray for us even the delicacy of the flowers, the undulating motion of the waves, or the sweet serenity of the moonlight; but the moment it steps outside the limit of the senses and tries to portray for us a philosophic idea, it must be considered decadent and the product of a decadent world. . .

I can see no other reason for the existence of art and poetry and religion except as they tend to restore in us a freshness of vision and a more emotional glamour and more vital sense of life. For as we grow older in life, our senses become gradually benumbed, our emotions become more callous to suffering and injustice and cruelty, and our vision of life is warped by too much preoccupation with cold, trivial realities. Fortunately, we have a few poets and artists who have not lost that sharpened sensibility, that fine emotional response and that freshness of vision, and whose duties are therefore to be our moral conscience, to hold up a mirror to our blunted vision, to tone up our withered nerves. Art should be a satire and a warning against our paralyzed emotions, our devitalized thinking and our denaturalized living. It teaches us unsophistication in a sophisticated world. It should restore to us health and sanity of living and enable us to recover from the fever and delirium caused by too much mental activity. It should sharpen our senses, re-establish the connection between our reason and our human nature, and assemble the ruined parts of a dislocated life again into a whole, by restoring our original nature. Miserable indeed is a world in which we have knowledge without understanding, criticism without appreciation, beauty without love, truth without passion, righteousness without mercy, and courtesy without a warm heart!

As for philosophy, which is the exercise of the spirit par excellence, the danger is even greater that we lose the feeling of life itself. I can understand that such mental delights include the solution of a long mathematical equation, or the perception of a grand order in the universe. This perception of order is probably the purest of all our mental pleasures and yet I would exchange it for a well prepared meal. In the first place, it is in itself almost a freak, a by-product of our mental occupations, enjoyable because it is gratuitous, but not in any case as imperative for us as other vital processes. That intellectual delight is, after all, similar to the delight of solving a crossword puzzle successfully. In the second place, the philosopher at this moment more often than not is likely to cheat himself, to fall in love with this abstract perfection, and to conceive a greater logical perfection in the world than is really warranted by reality itself. It is as much a false picture of things as when we paint a star with five points—a reduction to formula, an artificial stylizing, an over-simplification. So long as we do not overdo it, this delight in perfection is good, but let us remind ourselves that millions of people can be happy without discovering this simple unity of design. We really can afford to live without it... I am such a materialist that at any time I would prefer pork to poetry, and would waive a piece of philosophy for a piece of filet, brown and crisp and garnished with good sauce.

Only by placing living above thinking can we get away from this heat and re-breathed air of philosophy and recapture some of the freshness and naturalness of true insight of the child. Any true philosopher ought to be ashamed of himself when he sees a child, or even a lion cub in a cage. How perfectly nature has fashioned him with his paws, his muscles, his beautiful coat of fur, his prickling ears, his bright round eyes, his agility and his sense of fun! The philosopher ought to be ashamed that God-made perfection has sometimes become man-made imperfection, ashamed that he wears spectacles, has no appetite, is often distressed in mind and heart, and is entirely unconscious of the fun in life. From this type of philosopher nothing is to be gained, for nothing that he says can be of importance to us. That philosophy alone can be of use to us which joins hands merrily with poetry and establishes for us a truer vision, first of nature and then of human nature.

This Earth The Only Heaven

A sad, poetic touch is added to this intense love of life by the realization that this life we have is essentially mortal. Strange to say, this sad awareness of our mortality makes the Chinese scholar's enjoyment of life all the more keen and intense. For if this earthly existence is all we have, we must try the harder to enjoy it while it lasts. A vague hope of immortality detracts from our wholehearted enjoyment of this earthly existence. As Sir Arthur Keith puts it with a typical Chinese feeling, "For if men believe, as I do, that this present earth is the only heaven, they will strive all the more to make heaven of it"...

Belief in our mortality, the sense that we are eventually going to crack up and be extinguished like the flame of a candle, I say, is a gloriously fine thing. It makes us sober; it makes us a little sad; and many of us it makes poetic. But above all, it makes it possible for us to make up our mind and arrange to live sensibly, truthfully and always with a sense of our own limitations. It gives peace also, because true peace of mind comes from accepting the worst. Psychologically, I think, it means a release of energy. . .

Deprived of immortality, the proposition of living becomes a simple proposition. It is this: that we human beings have a limited span of life to live on this earth, rarely more than seventy years, and that therefore we have to arrange our lives so that we may live as happily as we can under a given set of circumstances. Here we are on Confucian ground. There is something mundane, something terribly earth-bound about it, and man proceeds to work with a dogged commonsense, very much in the spirit of what George Santayana calls "animal faith." With this animal faith, taking life as it is, we made a shrewd guess, without Darwin's aid as to our essential kinship with animals. It made us therefore, cling to life-- the life of the instinct and the life of the senses--on the belief that, as we are all animals, we can be truly happy only when all our normal instincts are satisfied normally. This applies to the enjoyment of life in all its aspects. . .

This feeling of the reality and spirituality of life is helped by Chinese humanism, in fact by the whole Chinese way of thinking and living. Chinese philosophy may be briefly defined as a preoccupation with the knowledge of life rather than the knowledge of truth. Brushing aside all metaphysical speculations as irrelevant to the business of living, and as pale reflections engendered in our intellect, the Chinese philosophers clutch at life itself and ask themselves the one and only eternal question: "How are we to live?" Philosophy in the Western sense seems to the Chinese eminently idle. In its preoccupation with logic, which concerns itself with the method of arrival at knowledge, and epistemology, which poses the question of the possibility of knowledge, it has forgotten to deal with the knowledge of life itself.

CRITIQUE

While hedonism as a way of life has always had great appeal to many persons, it also has never lacked intelligent and influential critics. Perhaps the most common criticism is directed against the hedonist's claim that only pleasure and avoidance of pain have "intrinsic value" (i.e. are worth seeking for their own sakes). The highly influential English analytic philosopher, G. E. Moore, (1973-1958), in the brief excerpt reprinted here, invites us to consider whether other things besides pleasure have intrinsic value. He cites knowledge, love, moral qualities, and a sense of beauty as examples of things which are valuable in themselves, and not simply insofar as they produce pleasure. By implication, a life must contain more than pleasure if it is to be a truly good life. After reading the passage from Moore, each person should ask himself or herself whether it is indeed "self-evident" that hedonism is mistaken on this matter.

The selection from the eminent American pragmatist, John Dewey (1859-1952), criticizes hedonism on moral grounds. Dewey suggests that advocates of hedonism, when they speak of pleasure, have in mind the pleasures of a normal, healthy and morally responsible person. But people who are none of these things often enjoy pleasures which are very different from the pleasures which the hedonist has in mind. Dewey cites the pleasures of a "crafty, unscrupulous man," the pleasures of "the cruel, the dissolute, the malicious person," the pleasure of the person seeking "harsh revenge," the pleasures of the "dishonest, the mean and stingy." Dewey states, "there is no denying that characters we morally condemn get actual pleasure from their lines of conduct." Dewey's criticism is, thus, that there are morally objectionable pleasures, and therefore that the pursuit of pleasure cannot properly guide us to a good life. This claim is, or appears to be, in direct contradiction to Epicurus's assertion that "it is not possible to live pleasantly without living prudently and honorably and justly . . . ." It should be noted that Dewey speaks of what he regards as specifically immoral pleasures, whereas Epicurus speaks of the process of living itself. Readers are invited to consider whether a genuinely pleasant life, overall, can be fashioned around pleasures of the kind which Dewey cites.

PLEASURE IS NOT THE ONLY GOOD*

by G. E. Moore

Our theory asserts, then, that any whole, which contains a greater amount of pleasure, is always intrinsically better than one which contains a smaller amount, no matter what the two may be like in other respects; and that no whole can be intrinsically better than another unless it contains more pleasure. . .

Is this assumption true, then? Is it true that one whole will be intrinsically better than another, whenever and only when it contains more pleasure, no matter what the two may be like in other respects? It seems to me almost impossible that any one, who fully realises the consequences of such a view, can possibly hold that it is true. It involves our saying, for instance, that a world in which absolutely nothing except pleasure existed--no knowledge, no love, no enjoyment of beauty, no moral qualities--must yet be intrinsically better--better worth creating-- provided only the total quantity of pleasure in it were the least bit greater, than one in which all these things existed as well as pleasure. It involves our saying that, even if the total quantity of pleasure in each was exactly equal, yet the fact that all the beings in the one possessed in addition knowledge of many different kinds and a full appreciation of all that was beautiful or worthy of love in their world, whereas none of the beings in the other possessed any of these things, would give us no reason whatever for preferring the former to the latter. It involves our saying that, for instance, the state of mind of a drunkard, when he is intensely pleased with breaking crockery, is just as valuable, in itself--just as well worth having, as that of a man who is fully realising all that is exquisite in the tragedy of King Lear, provided only the mere quantity of pleasure in both cases is the same. Such instances might be multiplied indefinitely, and it seems to me that they constitute a reductio ad absurdum of the view that intrinsic value is always in proportion to quantity of pleasure. Of course, here again, the question is quite incapable of proof either way. And if anybody, after clearly considering the issue, does come to the conclusion that no one kind of enjoyment is ever intrinsically better than another, provided only that the pleasure in both is equally intense, and that, if we could get as much pleasure in the world, without needing to have any knowledge, or any moral qualities, or any sense of beauty, as we can get with them, then all these things would be entirely superfluous, there is no way of proving that he is wrong. But it seems to me almost impossible that anybody, who does really get the question clear, should take such a view; and, if anybody were to, I think it is self-evident that he would be wrong.

*From G. E. Moore, Ethics (New York: Holt, Rinehart and Winston, 1912) pp. 61f, 236-239.

NOT ALL PLEASURES ARE GOOD*

by John Dewey

All of us get some pleasure by performing the acts which are congenial to our dispositions; such acts are, by conception, agreeable; they agree with, suit, our own tendencies. An expert in tennis likes to play tennis; an artist likes to paint pictures; a scientific man to investigate; a philosopher to speculate; a benevolent man to do kindly deeds; a brave man seeks out scenes in which endurance and loyalty may be exercised, etc. In such cases, given a certain structure of character and trend of aptitudes, there is an intrinsic basis for foreseeing pleasures and pains, and we may limit the theory to such consequences, excluding purely accidental ones.

But in modifying the theory in this way we have really set up the man's existing character as the criterion. A crafty, unscrupulous man, will get pleasure out of his sheer wiliness. When he thinks of an act which would bring pain in the experience of a generous frank person, he will find the thought a source of pleasure, and (so by the theory) a good act to perform. The same sort of thing will be true of the cruel, the dissolute, the malicious, person. The pleasures and pains each will foresee will be those which are in accord with his present character. Imagine two men who momentarily are taken by the idea of a harsh revenge upon a man who has inflicted ill treatment. For the moment both of them will get at least a passing pleasure from the image of the other man as overthrown and suffering. But the one who is kind-hearted will soon find himself pained at the thought of the harm the other man is experiencing; the cruel and revengeful person will glow with more and more pleasure the longer he dwells upon the distress of his enemy--if pleasure be a sign of goodness, the act will indeed be good to him.

There is thus a . . . misconception in the theory. Unconsciously, it slips in the criterion of the kind of pleasures which would be enjoyed by a man already good; the sort of pleasures which are taken to be normal. Other things being equal, pleasures are certainly a good to be enjoyed, not an evil to be shunned. But the phrase "other things being equal" covers a good deal of ground. One does not think of the pleasures of the dissolute, the dishonest, the mean and stingy, person, but of the pleasure of esthetic enjoyment, of friendship and good companionship, of knowledge, and so on. But there is no denying that characters we morally condemn get actual pleasure from their lines of conduct. We may think, and quite properly so, that they ought not to, but nevertheless they do. There are certain kinds of happiness which the good man enjoys which the evil-minded man does not--but the reverse is true. And this fact is fatal to the theory that pleasures constitute the good because of which a given object is entitled to be the end of action.

*From John Dewey and James H. Tufts, Ethics (New York: Henry Holt and Co., 1932). Reprinted with the permission of The Center for Dewey Studies, Southern Illinois University at Carbondale.

STUDY QUESTIONS FOR CHAPTER II

Questions for Review:

1. What are the benefits of studying philosophy, according to Epicurus?

2. What are Epicurus's beliefs concerning the gods?

3. What is Epicurus's attitude toward death? How does he justify his views?

4. Summarize Epicurus's division of desires into categories.

5. What is the relation of pain to pleasure, according to Epicurus?

6. Why is it sometimes prudent to pass over pleasures, according to Epicurus?

7. Epicurus writes

    "When, therefore, we maintain that pleasure is the end, we do not mean the pleasures of profligates and those that consist in sensuality, as is supposed by some who are either ignorant or disagree with us or do not understand, but freedom from pain in the body and from trouble in the mind. For it is not continuous drinkings and revellings, nor the satisfaction of lusts, nor the enjoyment of fish and other luxuries of the wealthy table, which produce a pleasant life . . ." Why does Epicurus reject this kind of hedonism?

8. Why does Epicurus praise prudence?

9. What is "the Greatest Happiness Principle," as formulated by Mill?

10. How does Mill define happiness?

11. What is the criticism of hedonism summarized by Mill? What are the chief lines of his reply to that criticism?

12. How may one determine which pleasures are higher or qualitatively better than others, according to Mill?

13. Why are beings who are capable of higher pleasures unwilling to sink to the level of purely animal pleasures, according to Mill?

14. Summarize in your own words Mill's argument that happiness is desirable as an end.

15. What are Lin Yutang's chief criticisms of Western approaches to the conduct of life? What does he propose instead?

16. What is Lin Yutang's attitude toward the human body?

17. Describe in your own words the "poem" of human life as formulated by Lin Yutang.

18. What does Lin Yutang mean by the statement "All human happiness is biological happiness"?

19. What is Lin Yutang's attitude toward human mortality?

20. Hedonistic views of the good life are often skeptical of religious and supernatural claims, preferring to focus upon the quality of life on earth. To what degree does this description fit the views of Epicurus and Lin Yutang? Briefly explain.

21. By what hypothetical device does G. E. Moore attempt to determine the truth or falsity of hedonism? What is his conclusion?

22. Summarize Dewey's objection to hedonism.

Questions for Reflection:

1. How much of my life is governed by the pursuit of pleasure in some form or another?

2. How prudent am I in my pursuit of pleasure?

3. In my own experience, do I find that some pleasures are qualitatively better than others, quite apart from their quantity?

4. Mill writes that "It is better to be a human being dissatisfied than a pig satisfied; better to be Socrates dissatisfied than a fool satisfied." Speaking just for myself, do I agree? If so, why?

5. How much attention do I give to my own body, in my pursuit of pleasure?

6. How do I feel about Lin Yutang's rejection of an afterlife?

7. Lin Yutang urges people to place living above thinking. Which - living or thinking -is more important to me?

Questions for Discussion:

1. Is pleasure the only thing which is intrinsically valuable (valuable for its own sake), while other things have value only as means? Or are there other intrinsically valuable things?

2. Does enlightened hedonism (the intelligent pursuit of a truly pleasant life overall) necessarily entail being moral?

3. Mill holds that the pleasures of the "higher faculties" are qualitatively better; Lin Yutang prefers pork to poetry, and a filet to philosophy. Which point of view do you more nearly agree with, and why?

4. It has been argued by many scholars that in order for Mill to rate some pleasures as qualitatively better than other pleasures, he must tacitly employ some other standard of value than pleasure itself, and that he thus has abandoned hedonistic utilitarianism. Do you agree?

5. The final portion of the excerpt from Mill above, "Of What Sort of Proof the Principle of Utility Is Susceptible," has been criticized as containing two serious, elementary flaws of logic. What might those flaws be?

6. Do you agree with Lin Yutang that "the end of living is the true enjoyment of it"? Or do you believe that to be meaningful, life requires some other purpose?

7. Does hedonism have an adequate response to human problems of pain, suffering, deprivation, and the like?

SUGGESTIONS FOR FURTHER READING

J.C.B. Gosling, Pleasure and Desire: The Case for Hedonism Reviewed (Oxford, 1969) A scholarly philosophical treatment.

John Hospers, Human Conduct: Problems of Ethics, Chapters 3 and 7 (Harcourt Brace Jovanovich, 1961, 1972) Excellent discussions of Epicureanism and hedonism.

Stuart Levey, A Case for Hedonism (Yale, 1946)

Alexander Lowen, M.D., Pleasure: A Creative Approach to Life (Penguin, 1976)

Kenneth McCormack, The Pursuit of Pleasure (Macmillan 1962)

Chapter Three:

Detachment

Chapter III: DETACHMENT

Introduction

Detachment. Release from pain. Release from desire. Relief. Relaxation. Peace. Tranquility. Serenity . . . .These are some of the concepts that we will encounter in this chapter.

We know that life brings not only pleasure, but pain and anxiety as well. And the pleasures that we enjoy are often overshadowed by a larger, harder reality of striving, disappointment, and suffering. Too often we find ourselves caught up in anxiety and hurt, in yearnings and cravings, that banish peace of mind and leave us in turmoil. We need wisdom to deal with these dimensions of life, wisdom that will enable us to approach our day-to-day existence with greater peace of mind, tranquility and serenity. The way of detachment offers one such kind of wisdom.

Each of us has had the experience of craving some particular thing and being sharply disappointed by the failure to get it. Each of us will also understand the freedom and relief which come from being released from that want, that craving, no longer feeling its insistent demands. To some degree, this process of detachment is a normal feature of growth and maturation. Our growth toward maturity is, in part, a matter of ridding ourselves of some of the desires of childhood. The urgent needs of a child--for toys, for candy, for amusements, for something or other right now--are gradually eased in the maturing adult.

Yet the childhood demands are often merely replaced by other needs and cravings as we grow older, and peace of mind still eludes us. But there are persons for whom this is not so. Some persons do achieve a kind of inner stability and psychic equilibrium that enables them to face life calmly, openly and serenely.

We are not speaking here of the feigned calm of a person who claims to be free of desires, but in reality is still dominated by them. And we are not speaking of a person who strains to ignore real pain and anxiety. Persons who have learned the wisdom of detachment do not engage in self-deception or inner struggle, nor have they simply made a part of themselves numb and unfeeling. The detachment which is the central concept in this chapter is something more positive: it is a true psychic release from pain and striving--a release that frees the inner self and enables it to maintain equilibrium and serenity in the midst of outer turmoil.

While complete detachment is very rare, milder instances of detachment are common, so common that we often fail to recognize them. Perhaps I am eager to watch a particular television program but cannot do so. After my disappointment, I realize that in the long run, it matters very little that I cannot see the program, and soon it is forgotten. Perhaps I badly want to buy a particular item but after reconsidering, decide that I don't really need to have it. Whether or not I have the item becomes unimportant.

Nearly all people are capable of some degree of detachment from pain and desire; but the capacity for detachment varies greatly from person to person. While one individual may break into tears or fly into a rage over a seemingly minor matter, another bears great misfortune with equanimity and even tranquility. Regarding tolerance for physical pain, the differences among people are especially obvious. For instance: having a tooth drilled by the dentist is traumatic for some and only a minor nuisance for others. Some of this variation is probably strictly physiological. (Under apparently similar conditions, some persons simply report less pain than others.) But the capacity to deal with pain is a function not only of physiology but also of psychology. Some dental patients refuse all anesthetics and, when nerve endings in their mouth are abused by the dentist's drill, detach themselves from the pain and are not unduly bothered by it. "Detachment" is an apt description here; one is aware that the pain exists, but experiences it as occurring in a portion of the body which is distinct from the self.[1] One dwells in one's thoughts.

Psychic release from physical pain is perhaps the most obvious form of detachment, when detachment is conceived as an ideal way of life. Closely related is release from psychological pain and anxiety. The former kind of detachment often exists without the latter: we know of persons who can live successfully with physical pain, but whose inner emotional lives are full of turmoil and distress. The reverse is also often found. On the other hand a person who is able to conquer both forms of pain reaps major benefits. The first consequence of distancing from pain is relief; the second is relaxation, of body and of mind. A step further, and detachment yields equanimity and peace of mind. Our lives resume a harmonious and comfortable relationship with the world.

Non-attachment

But detachment can occur at a deeper and broader level as well: detachment from objects of desire, or "non-attachment." For much, if not all of the pain which we experience may be seen to be a consequence of the fact that we are desiring creatures, who care--often deeply--about a great many things. Especially strong forms of desire are yearnings and cravings. Yearning implies a felt need or lack, which is experienced as unpleasant. And craving, likewise, suggests an unsatisified hunger. Other desires may not pull at us so strongly; but they nevertheless create their own particular forms of unease. If we can free ourselves from being drawn by our desires, we may experience a deeper freedom and peace of mind. The object of detachment from desire is not to cease all effort, but rather to detach oneself from the felt need which usually motivates the effort. Thus the result is not mere quietude, a cessation of all activity, but rather a disciplined activity which is unattached to its own outcome. A person who has achieved a state of non-attachment continues to perform all necessary and appropriate acts but is neither elated nor disappointed by the results of those acts. The inner condition of the self is no longer controlled by the outcome of its actions, but is sufficient unto itself.

The concept of non-attachment is subtle but quite important. It is prominently found in a number of great historical views of the good life, including especially Buddhism[2] and Hinduism. A familiar example, our feelings about food, may serve to give us a glimpse into the intuitive content of this concept. For most of us, the simple, essential act of eating is largely controlled by insistent desires and cravings. As a result we often eat too much, eat the wrong things, or both. Alternatively, we control and direct our cravings (more or less) by that internal struggle called "exercise of will power." A person who is non-attached with regard to food is, on the other hand, no longer under the sway of craving for various foods. Such a person does not force himself or herself to eat properly, but does so freely and without internal struggle. Another example concerns our feeling aobut how other people view us. Most of us care deeply about the opinions of others and seek by various means to gain their approval. If successful, we feel that our ego is affirmed; if we fail, we feel shame, and perhaps loneliness. But there are persons who act appropriately in interpersonal matters without concerning themselves with the judgment of others. Unconcern for the opinion of others does not necessarily mean a callous disregard for the interests of others but rather, simply, detachment from any felt need to be viewed by others in a particular way.

When I am controlled by my desires, the path of my life resembles the movement of an iron filing which comes variously under the sway of a great number of different and often competing magnetic fields. When I detach myself from my desires, I am transmuted from iron into a different metal which is free from the magnetism of various desired things, and I achieve equilibrium and inner peace. I am no longer dominated by the attractions and repulsions of life, and am able to function appropriately, without compulsion or inner struggle.

Non-attachment has especially important consequences for the phenomenon of anger. Much of anger springs from thwarted desire: we need or wish for a certain outcome, and feel anger and frustration when that outcome is blocked. On the other hand, insofar as we are detached from a desire, we experience no anger when the desire is deflected. Thus, detachment from desire helps free us from the distress of angry, frustrated feelings.

Detachment from desire, or non-attachment, carries us beyond detachment from pain. Descriptions of non-attachment suggest a deep calmness of spirit, a pervasive sense of "rightness" and well-being, and finally a complete tranquility and serenity. In the third selection in this chapter, we are told of an even more exalted state: "the bliss of Nirvana while still living on earth."

Ideals of detachment are often found in religious contexts. Asceticism, which may be defined as the attempt to detach oneself from all worldly things (including the demands of one's body), is usually coupled with a quest for high spiritual goals. (In the Christian and Hindu traditions especially, asceticism in practice has sometimes taken the form of a deliberate mortification of one's body, as a sign of spiritual devotion. Such humiliation of the body is not, however, a necessary feature of detachment.) As for stoicism in the Western tradition: Epictetus makes it clear that the stoicism of ancient Greeks rested in part upon the confidence that the gods are benevolent and powerful, and hence that external events are in good hands.

What sort of person is drawn to ideals of detachment? In this regard, appearances are often deceiving. An "easy-going" person, one who naturally sails through life on an even keel, is not likely to be strongly drawn to detachment. It is those of us who experience too much of such things as yearning, passion, turmoil, anxiety and pain who are more likely to be drawn to this way of life. T.S. Eliot, whose muted, laconic poetry often suggests detachment, observed that ". . .only those who have personality and emotions know what it means to want to escape from these things."[3]

Some form of release from pain and desire is always involved, when detachment is viewed as an ideal way of life. But descriptions of the ideal separation vary. In this chapter, Epictetus (55-135 A.D.) advocates a separation of one's internal state of mind from all external matters. Socrates, as reported by Plato (427-347 B.C.) speaks of freeing the soul from the body. In the selection by Shankara (788-832 A.D.), we find a particularly pure form of detachment, in which a higher self is separated from all forms of desire.

The Selections

In the Western tradition, the most attractive and widely influential version of detachment as a way of life is found in the teachings of the ancient Greek stoics. Stoicism was widely practiced in the Roman empire in the first two centuries A.D. Among its prominent advocates, still widely read and quoted, were a Roman senator, Seneca (4 B.C.-66 A.D.) and a Roman emperor, Marcus Aurelius (121-180 A.D.) But in many ways the most impressive statement of stoic thought is found in the teachings of Epictetus. For much of his life, Epictetus was a slave in the household of a dissolute Roman soldier. Living and working under conditions in which his body literally belonged to another, Epictetus achieved a psychic detachment that made possible a serene life even under the adverse and degrading conditions of slavery. Epictetus became recognized for his intellect and depth of insight, and eventually became a free man. He subsequently established his own school and spent the rest of his life in the company of devoted followers.

The stoicism of Epictetus is based upon a sharp distinction and separation between one's internal state of mind, and external events of all kinds. Epictetus declared that "What disturbs men's minds is not events but their judgment on events." Events as they occur are neither good nor bad in themselves; they become "good" or "bad" by virtue of the attitudes that we adopt towards them. And we can learn to control those attitudes. Things in our power--"thought, impulse, will to get and will to avoid"-- hold the key to happiness and serenity. We can, through right judgment and disciplined thought, learn to detach ourselves from external events, and keep our will "in harmony with nature." The result is a state of mind that remains unaffected by external matters of all kinds, and is calm and serene regardless of this or that turn of events. Things not in our power-- "the body, property, reputation, office, and in a word, everything which is not our down doing"--no longer dominate our outlook on life, and can be handled appropriately, without emotion or distress.

At first sight, stoicism may suggest a doctrine of total withdrawal into the self, and an irresponsible disregard for the external conditions of social life. In practice, however, the advocates of stoicism were remarkable not ony for their restraint, dignity and self-discipline, but also for their high level of individual and political responsibility. Teachers of stoicism regarded the scrupulously honest, responsible Socrates as their mentor, and preached a firm commitment to right judgment and right action which often carried them deeply into public life.

Today, "stoicism" has come to mean primarily a capacity to withstand pain of various kinds. While detachment from pain was indeed an important goal of the ancient Greek stoics, the teachings of Epictetus penetrate beyond pain to its basis in desire itself. Desire--"the will to get and the will to avoid"--is, in the true stoic, no longer attached to external affairs, and therefore is not affected by how they transpire. In its original meaning, therefore, stoicism is not simply an uncommon capacity to live with suffering, but a freedom from the psychological factors that underly suffering.

A second classical philosophical statement of detachment from the Western tradition is found in the selection from Plato's Phaedo. The dialogue is Plato's reconstruction (Plato himself was not present) of a conversation that occurred between Socrates and some of his followers during the final hours of his life, ending with his execution.[4] The primary topic of the dialogue is immortality, and the tone of Socrates' remarks is otherworldly, as he contemplates his own imminent death. In the brief excerpt reprinted here, Socrates argues that philosophy is a practice and preparation for the death of the body; for death is the detachment and separation of the soul from the body, a separation that a true philosopher seeks even while living. The "soul" is identified here with reason or the faculty of knowledge. Freed by death from the demands and limitations of the body, the soul of the genuine philosopher is able at last to soar upward and gain a vision of higher reality, distinct from the fluctuating, imperfect world that is present to our senses. This higher reality is the unchanging, perfect world of the Forms, where the soul of the philosopher finally looks upon such things as absolute justice, beauty and goodness. The philosopher's love of wisdom is satisfied at last.

The passage is significant not only for its insight into one dimension of Plato's own views, but also for the immense influence which it and other similar Platonic writings exercised upon later Western thought, including a large portion of Christian doctrine and teaching. The first truly great Christian theologian, St. Augustine (354-430) drew heavily from Platonism, and distinguished the soul from the body in a way that resembles Plato's distinction. Later forms of Christian asceticism in turn often drew heavily from this dimension of St. Augustine's teachings. Many of the writings of St. Augustine strongly reflect a desire like that described by Plato, a desire to rise above the body to an ecstatic vision of absolute goodness--found, according to Augustine, in communion with God.

The final selection that advocates detachment as a way of life is taken from the writings of Shankara , a major thinker from the Hindu philosophical tradition, sometimes compared in his importance to Thomas Aquinas in Western thought. Shankara formulated the most prominant traditional school of Hindu philosophy, advaita ("without a second") vedanta. According to the central doctrine of this school, all of reality everywhere is in fact One--a completely undifferentiated unity. The apparent plurality and diversity of everyday experience is an illusion. Recognition of the truth of this view of reality occurs in mystical insight; and an essential means to such insight is the practice of detachment.

NOTES

1. This phenomenon closely parallels the reported experiences of some mental patients who have undergone prefrontal lobotomies for relief from severe affective disorders such as chronic deep anxiety. (A prefrontal lobotomy is the drastic surgical procedure of cutting some of the nerve tissue in the brain connecting the frontal lobes of the cortex with the deeper portion of the brain, which includes the seat of emotional responses. This procedure is still not fully understood and is now less frequently performed than at one time. For various reasons, there is widespread opposition among psychiatrists to the procedures.) After a lobotomy, patients often report that while they are still aware of the original source of their anxiety, they are not so bothered by it.

2. The Four Noble Truths of Buddhism (attributed to Buddha himself) have been paraphrased as follows: "(1) life is permeated by suffering or dissatisfaction (dukkha); (2) the origin of suffering lies in craving or grasping (tanha); (3) the cessation of suffering is possible, through the cessation of craving; and (4) the way to the latter is the Noble Eight-fold Path." Ninian Smart, "Buddhism," in The Encyclopedia of Philosophy, Vol. One (New York: Macmillan, 1967), p. 417.

3. From "Tradition and Individual Talent" in The Sacred Wood: Essays on Poetry and Criticism (London: Methuen and Co., 1920, 1928), p. 58.

4. The views expressed in this passage are probably primarily those of Plato himself, rather than the historical Socrates. See Plato's Phaedo, Translated with an Introduction and Commentary by R. Hackforth (Cambridge: Cambridge University Press, 1955), pp. 48f.

THE MANUAL OF EPICTETUS*

Of all existing things some are in our power, and others are not in our power. In our power are thought, impulse, will to get and will to avoid, and, in a word, everything which is our own doing. Things not in our power include the body, property, reputation, office, and, in a word, everything which is not our own doing. Things in our power are by nature free, unhindered, untrammelled; things not in our power are weak, servile, subject to hindrance, dependent on others. Remember then that if you imagine that what is naturally slavish is free, and what is naturally another's is your own, you will be hampered, you will mourn, you will be put to confusion, you will blame gods and men; but if you think that only your own belongs to you, and that what is another's is indeed another's, no one will ever put compulsion or hindrance on you, you will blame none, you will accuse none, you will do nothing against your will, no one will harm you, you will have no enemy, for no harm can touch you.

Aiming then at these high matters, you must remember that to attain them requires more than ordinary effort; you will have to give up some things entirely, and put off others for the moment. And if you would have these also--office and wealth--it may be that you will fail to get them, just because your desire is set on the former, and you will certainly fail to attain those things which alone bring freedom and happiness.

Make it your study then to confront every harsh impression with the words, 'You are but an impression, and not at all what you seem to be'. Then test it by those rules that you possess; and first by this--the chief test of all--'Is it concerned with what is in our power or with what is not in our power?' And if it is concerned with what is not in our power, be ready with the answer that it is nothing to you.

* *

Remember that the will to get promises attainment of what you will, and the will to avoid promises escape from what you avoid; and he who fails to get what he wills is unfortunate, and he who does not escape what he wills to avoid is miserable. If then you try to avoid only what is unnatural in the region within your control, you will escape from all that you avoid; but if you try to avoid disease or death or poverty you will be miserable.

Therefore let your will to avoid have no concern with what is not in man's power; direct it only to things in man's power that are contrary to nature. But for the moment you must utterly remove the will to get; for

*From Epictetus: The Discourses and Manual translated by P. E. Matheson (1916). Reprinted by permission of Oxford University Press. This 'hand-book' of Epictetus' principles was probably compiled by Arrian, and contains an excellent summary of the master's thought.

if you will to get something not in man's power you are bound to be unfortunate; while none of the things in man's power that you could honourably will to get is yet within your reach. Impulse to act and not to act, these are your concern; yet exercise them gently and without strain, and provisionally.

*   *

When anything, from the meanest thing upwards, is attractive or serviceable or an object of affection, remember always to say to yourself, 'What is its nature?' If you are fond of a jug, say you are fond of a jug; then you will not be disturbed if it be broken. If you kiss your child or your wife, say to yourself that you are kissing a human being, for then if death strikes it you will not be disturbed.

*   *

When you are about to take something in hand, remind yourself what manner of thing it is. If you are going to bathe put before your mind what happens in the bath--water pouring over some, others being jostled, some reviling, others stealing; and you will set to work more securely if you say to yourself at one: 'I want to bathe, and I want to keep my will in harmony with nature,' and so in each thing you do; for in this way, if anything turns up to hinder you in your bathing, you will be ready to say, 'I did not want only to bathe, but to keep my will in harmony with nature, and I shall not so keep it, if I lose my temper at what happens'.

*   *

What disturbs men's minds is not events but their judgements on events. For instance, death is nothing dreadful, or else Socrates would have thought it so. No, the only dreadful thing about it is men's judgement that it is dreadful. And so when we are hindered, or disturbed, or distressed, let us never lay the blame on others, but on ourselves, that is, on our own judgements. To accuse others for one's own misfortunes is a sign of want of education; to accuse oneself shows that one's education has begun; to accuse neither oneself nor others shows that one's education is complete.

*   *

Ask not that events should happen as you will, but let your will be that events should happen as they do, and you shall have peace.

*   *

Sickness is a hindrance to the body, but not to the will, unless the will consent. Lameness is a hindrance to the leg, but not to the will. Say this to yourself at each event that happens, for you shall find that though it hinders something else it will not hinder you.

* *

Never say of anything, 'I lost it', but say, 'I gave it back'. Has your child died? It was given back. Has your wife died? She was given back. Has your estate been taken from you? Was not this also given back? But you say, 'He who took it from me is wicked'. What does it matter to you through whom the Giver asked it back? As long as He gives it you, take care of it, but not as your own; treat it as passers-by treat an inn.

* *

It is silly to want your children and your wife and your friends to live forever, for that means that you want what is not in your control to be in your control, and what is not your own to be yours. In the same way if you want your servant to make no mistakes, you are a fool, for you want vice not to be vice but something different. But if you want not to be disappointed in your will to get, you can attain to that.

Exercise yourself then in what lies in your power. Each man's master is the man who has authority over what he wishes or does not wish, to secure the one or to take away the other. Let him then who wishes to be free not wish for anything or avoid anything that depends on others; or else he is bound to be a slave.

* *

Remember that you must behave in life as you would at a banquet. A dish is handed round and comes to you; put out your hand and take it politely. It passes you; do not stop it. It has not reached you; do not be impatient to get it, but wait till your turn comes. Bear yourself thus towards children, wife, office, wealth, and one day you will be worthy to banquet with the gods. But if when they are set before you, you do not take them but despise them, then you shall not ony share the gods' banquet, but shall share their rule. For by so doing Diogenes and Heraclitus and men like them were called divine and deserved the name.

* *

When you see a man shedding tears in sorrow for a child abroad or dead, or for loss of property, beware that you are not carried away by the impression that it is outward ills that make him miserable. Keep this thought by you: 'What distresses him is not the event, for that does not distress another, but his judgement on the event.' Therefore do not hesitate to sympathize with him so far as words go, and if it so chance, even to groan with him; but take heed that you do not also groan in your inner being.

* *

Remember that you are an actor in a play, and the Playwright chooses the manner of it: if he wants it short, it is short; if long, it is long. If he wants you to act a poor man you must act the part with all your powers; and so if your part be a cripple or a magistrate or a plain man. For your business is to act the character that is given you and act it well; the choice of the cast is Another's.

* *

You can be invincible, if you never enter on a contest where victory is not in your power. Beware then that when you see a man raised to honour or great power or high repute you do not let your impression carry you away. For if the reality of good lies in what is in our power, there is no room for envy or jealousy. And you will not wish to be praetor, or prefect or consul, but to be free; and there is but one way to freedom--to despise what is not in our power.

* *

Remember that foul words or blows in themselves are no outrage, but your judgement that they are so. So when any one makes you angry, know that it is your own thought that has angered you. Wherefore make it your first endeavour not to let your impressions carry you away. For if once you gain time and delay, you will find it easier to control yourself.

* *

If you set your desire on philosophy you must at once prepare to meet with ridicule and the jeers of many who will say, 'Here he is again, turned philosopher. Where has he got these proud looks?' Nay, put on no proud looks, but hold fast to what seems best to you, in confidence that God has set you at this post. And remember that if you abide where you are, those who first laugh at you will one day admire you, and that if you give way to them you will get doubly laughed at.

* *

If it ever happen to you to be diverted to things outside, so that you desire to please another, know that you have lost your life's plan. Be content then always to be a philosopher; if you wish to be regarded as one too, show yourself that you are one and you will be able to achieve it.

* *

If any one trused your body to the first man he met, you would be indignant, but yet you trust your mind to the chance comer, and allow it to be disturbed and confounded if he revile you; are you not ashamed to do so?

* *

Lay down for yourself from the first a definite stamp and style of conduct, which you will maintain when you are alone and also in the society of men. Be silent for the most part, or, if you speak, say only what is necessary and in a few words. Talk, but rarely, if occasion calls you, but do not talk of ordinary things--of gladiators, or horse-races, or athletes, or of meats or drinks--these are topics that arise everywhere-- but above all do not talk about men in blame or compliment or comparison. If you can, turn the conversation of your company by your talk to some fitting subject; but if you should chance to be isolated among strangers, be silent. Do not laugh much, nor at many things, nor without restraint.

* *

When you imagine some pleasure, beware that it does not carry you away, like other imaginations. Wait a while, and give yourself pause. Next remember two things: how long you will enjoy the pleasure, and also how long you will afterwards repent and revile yourself. And set on the other side the joy and self-satisfaction you will feel if you refrain. And if the moment seems come to realize it, take heed that you be not overcome by the winning sweetness and attraction of it; set in the other scale the thought how much better is the consciousness of having vanquished it.

* *

When you do a thing because you have determined that it ought to be done, never avoid being seen doing it, even if the opinion of the multitude is going to condemn you. For if your action is wrong, then avoid doing it altogether, but if it is right, why do you fear those who will rebuke you wrongly?

* *

If you try to act a part beyond your powers, you not only disgrace yourself in it, but you neglect the part which you could have filled with success.

* *

As in walking you take care not to tread on a nail or to twist your foot, so take care that you do not harm your Governing Principle. And if we guard this in everything we do, we shall set to work more securely.

*   *

It is a sign of a dull mind to dwell upon the cares of the body, to prolong exercise, eating, drinking, and other bodily functions. These things are to be done by the way; all your attention must be given to the mind.

*   *

When a man speaks evil or does evil to you, remember that he does or says it because he thinks it is fitting for him. It is not possible for him to follow what seems good to you, but only what seems good to him, so that, if his opinion is wrong, he suffers, in that he is the victim of deception. In the same way, if a composite judgement which is true is thought to be false, it is not the judgement that suffers, but the man who is deluded about it. If you act on this principle you will be gentle to him who reviles you, saying to yourself on each occasion, 'He thought it right.'

*   *

Everything has two handles, one by which you can carry it, the other by which you cannot. If your brother wrongs you, do not take it by that handle, the handle of his wrong, for you cannot carry it by that, but rather by the other handle--that he is a brother, brought up with you, and then you will take it by the handle that you can carry by.

*   *

It is illogical to reason thus, 'I am richer than you, therefore I am superior to you', 'I am more eloquent than you, therefore I am superior to you.' It is more logical to reason, 'I am richer than you, therefore my property is superior to yours', 'I am more eloquent than you, therefore my speech is superior to yours.' You are something more than property or speech.

*   *

If a man wash quickly, do not say that he washes badly, but that he washes quickly. If a man drink much wine, do not say that he drinks badly, but that he drinks much. For till you have decided what judgement prompts him, how do you know that he acts badly? If you do as I say, you will assent to your apprehensive impressions and to none other.

*   *

On no occasion call yourself a philosopher, nor talk at large of your principles among the multitude, but act on your principles. For instance, at a banquet do not say how one ought to eat, but eat as you ought.

Remember that Socrates had so completely got rid of the thought of display that when men came and wanted an introduction to philosophers he took them to be introduced; so patient of neglect was he. And if a discussion arise among the multitude on some principle, keep silent for the most part; for you are in great danger of blurting out some undigested thought. And when some one says to you, 'You know nothing', and you do not let it provoke you, then know that you are really on the right road. For sheep do not bring grass to their shepherds and show them how much they have eaten, but they digest their fodder and then produce it in the form of wool and milk. Do the same yourself; instead of displaying your principles to the multitude, show them the results of the principles you have digested.

*   *

The ignorant man's position and character is this: he never looks to himself for benefit or harm, but to the world outside him. The philosopher's position and character is that he always look to himself for benefit and harm.

The signs of one who is making progress are: he blames none, praises none, complains of none, accuses none, never speaks of himself as if he were somebody, or as if he knew anything. And if any one compliments him he laughs in himself at his compliment; and if one blames him, he makes no defence. He goes about like a convalescent, careful not to disturb his constitution on its road to recovery, until it has got firm hold. He has got rid of the will to get, and his will to avoid is directed no longer to what is beyond our power but only to what is in our power and contrary to nature. In all things he exercises his will without strain. If men regard him as foolish or ignorant he pays no heed. In one word, he keeps watch and guard on himself as his own enemy, lying in wait for him.

*   *

Whatever principles you put before you, hold fast to them as laws which it will be impious to transgress. But pay no heed to what any one says to you; for this is something beyond your own control.

*   *

On every occasion we must have these thoughts at hand,

> 'Lead me, O Zeus, and lead me, Destiny,
> Whither ordained is by your decree.
> I'll follow, doubting not, or if with will
> Recreant I falter, I shall follow still.'
> —Cleanthes

89

'Who rightly with necessity complies
In things divine we count him skilled and wise.'
                              -Euripides, Fragment 965

Well, Crito, if this be the gods' will, so be it.'
                              -Plato, Crito, 43d

Anytus and Meletus have power to put me to death,
but not to harm me.'
                              -Plato, Apology, 30c

THE TRUE PHILOSOPHER PRACTICES DYING*

by Plato

'Ordinary people seem not to realize that those who really apply themselves in the right way to philosophy are directly and of their own accord preparing themselves for dying and death. If this is true, and they have actually been looking forward to death all their lives, it would of course be absurd to be troubled when the thing comes for which they have so long been preparing and looking forward.'

Simmias laughed and said 'Upon my word, Socrates, you have made me laugh, though I was not at all in the mood for it. I am sure that if they heard what you said, most people would think--and our fellow-countrymen would heartily agree--that it was a very good hit at the philosophers to say that they are half dead already, and that they, the normal people, are quite aware that death would serve the philosophers right.'

'And they would be quite correct, Simmias; except in thinking that they are "quite aware". They are not at all aware in what sense true philosophers are half dead, or in what sense they deserve death, or what sort of death they deserve. But let us dismiss them and talk among ourselves. Do we believe that there is such a thing as death?'

'Most certainly," said Simmias, taking up the role of answering.

'Is it simply the release of the soul from the body? Is death nothing more or less than this, the separate condition of the body by itself when it is released from the soul, and the separate condition by itself of the soul when released from the body? Is death anything else than this?'

'No, just that.'

'Well then, my boy, see whether you agree with me; I fancy that this will help us to find out the answer to our problem. Do you think that it is right for a philosopher to concern himself with the so-called pleasures connected with food and drink?'

'Certainly not, Socrates,' said Simmias.

'What about sexual pleasures?'

'No, not at all.'

'And what about the other attentions that we pay to our bodies? do you think that a philosopher attaches any importance to them? I mean

*From Plato, Phaedo, in The Last Days of Socrates, trans. Hugh Tredennick (Penguin Classics, Revised edition, 1969), pp. 107-113. Copyright (c) Hugh Tredennick, 1954, 1959, 1969. Reprinted by permission of Penguin Books Ltd.

things like providing himself with smart clothes and shoes and other bodily ornaments; do you think that he values them or despises them--in so far as there is not real necessity for him to go in for that sort of thing?'

'I think the true philosopher despises them,' he said.

'Then it is your opinion in general that a man of this kind is not concerned with the body, but keeps his attention directed as much as he can away from it and towards the soul?'

'Yes, it is.'

'So it is clear first of all in the case of physical pleasures that the philosopher frees his soul from association with the body (so far as is possible) to a greater extent than other men?'

'It seems so.'

'And most people think, do they not, Simmias, that a man who finds no pleasure and takes no part in these things does not deserve to live, and that anyone who thinks nothing of physical pleasures has one foot in the grave?'

'That is perfectly true.'

'Now take the acquisition of knowledge; is the body a hindrance or not, if one takes it into partnership to share an investigation? What I mean is this: is there any certainty in human sight and hearing, or is it true, as the poets are always dinning into our ears, that we neither hear nor see anything accurately? Yet if these senses are not clear and accurate, the rest can hardly be so, because they are all inferior to the first two. Don't you agree?'

'Certainly.'

'Then when is it that the soul attains to truth? When it tries to investigate anything with the help of the body, it is obviously led astray.'

'Quite so.'

'Is it not in the course of reflection, if at all, that the soul gets a clear view of facts?'

'Yes.'

'Surely the soul can best reflect when it is free of all distractions such as hearing or sight or pain or pleasure of any kind--that is, when it ignores the body and becomes as far as possible independent, avoiding all physical contacts and associations as much as it can, in its search for reality.'

'That is so.'

'Then here too--in despising the body and avoiding it, and endeavouring to become independent--the philosopher's soul is ahead of all the rest.'

'It seems so.'

'Here are some more questions, Simmias. Do we recognize such a thing as absolute uprightness?'

'Indeed we do.'

'And absolute beauty and goodness too?'

'Of course.'

'Have you ever seen any of these things with your eyes?'

'Certainly not,' said he.

'Well, have you ever apprehended them with any other bodily sense? By "them" I mean not only absolute tallness or health or strength, but the real nature of any given thing--what it actually is. Is it through the body that we get the truest perception of them? Isn't it true that in any inquiry you are likely to attain more nearly to knowledge of your object in proportion to the care and accuracy with which you have prepared yourself to understand that object in itself?'

'Certainly.'

'Don't you think that the person who is likely to succeed in this attempt most perfectly is the one who approaches each object, as far as possible, with the unaided intellect, without taking account of any sense of sight in his thinking, or dragging any other sense into his reckoning--the man who pursues the truth by applying his pure and unadulterated thought to the pure and unadulterated object, cutting himself off as much as possible from his eyes and ears and virtually all the rest of his body, as an impediment which by its presence prevents the soul from attaining to truth and clear thinking? Is not this the person, Simmias, who will reach the goal of reality, if anybody can?'

'What you say is absolutely true, Socrates,' said Simmias.

'All these considerations,' said Socrates, 'must surely prompt serious philosophers to review the position in some such way as this. "It looks as though this were a bypath leading to the right track. So long as we keep to the body and our soul is contaminated with this imperfection, there is no chance of our ever attaining satisfactorily to our object, which we assert to be Truth. In the first place, the body provides us with innumerable distractions in the pursuit of our necessary sustenance; and any diseases which attack us hinder our quest for reality. Besides, the body fills us with loves and desires and fears and all sorts of fancies and a great deal of nonsense, with the result that we literally never get an opportunity to think at all about anything. Wars and revolutions and battles are due simply and solely to the body and its desires. All wars are undertaken for the acquisition of wealth; and the reason why we have to acquire wealth is the body, because we are slaves in its service. That is why, on all these accounts, we have so little time for philosophy. Worst of all, if we do obtain any leisure from the body's claims and turn to some line of inquiry, the body intrudes once more into our investigations, interrupting, disturbing, distracting, and preventing us from getting a glimpse of the truth. We are in fact convinced that if we are ever to have pure knowledge of anything, we must get rid of the body and contemplate things by themselves with the soul by itself. It seems, to judge from the argument, that the wisdom which we desire and upon which we profess to have set our hearts will be attainable only when we are dead, and not in our lifetime. If no pure knowledge is possible in the company of the body, then either it is totally impossible to acquire knowledge, or it is only possible after death, because it is only then that the soul will be separate and independent of the body. It seems that so long as we are alive, we shall continue closest to knowledge if we avoid as much as we can all contact and association with the body, except when they are absolutely necessary; and instead of allowing ourselves to become infected with its nature, purify ourselves from it until God himself gives us deliverance. In this way, by keeping ourselves uncontaminated by the follies of the body, we shall probably reach the company of others like ourselves and gain direct knowledge of all that is pure and uncontaminated—that is, presumably, of Truth. For one who is not pure himself to attain to the realm of purity would no doubt be a breach of universal justice." Something to this effect, Simmias, is what I imagine all real lovers of learning must think themselves and say to one another; don't you agree with me?'

'Most emphatically, Socrates.'

'Very well, then,' said Socrates; 'if this is true, there is good reason for anyone who reaches the end of this journey which lies before me to hope that there, if anywhere, he will attain the object to which all our efforts have been directed during my past life. So this journey which is now ordained for me carries a happy prospect for any other man also who believes that his mind has been prepared by purification.'

'It does indeed,' said Simmias.

'And purification, as we saw some time ago in our discussion, consists in separating the soul as much as possible from the body, and accustoming it to withdraw from all contact with the body and concentrate itself by itself; and to have its dwelling, so far as it can, both now and in the future, alone by itself, freed from the shackles of the body. Does not that follow?'

'Yes, it does,' said Simmias.

'Is not what we call death a freeing and separation of soul from body?'

'Certainly,' he said.

'And the desire to free the soul is found chiefly, or rather only, in the true philosopher; in fact the philosopher's occupation consists precisely in the freeing and separation of soul from body. Isn't that so?'

'Apparently.'

'Well then, as I said at the beginning, if a man has trained himself throughout his life to live in a state as close as possible to death, would it not be ridiculous for him to be distressed when death comes to him?'

'It would, of course.'

'Then it is a fact, Simmias, that true philosophers make dying their profession, and that to them of all men death is least alarming. Look at it in this way. If they are thoroughly dissatisfied with the body, and long to have their souls independent of it, when this happens would it not be entirely unreasonable to be frightened and distressed? Would they not naturally be glad to set out for the place where there is a prospect of attaining the object of their lifelong desire, which is Wisdom; and of escaping from an unwelcome association? Surely there are many who have chosen of their own free will to follow dead lovers and wives and sons to the next world, in the hope of seeing and meeting there the persons whom they loved. If this is so, will a true lover of wisdom who has firmly grasped this same conviction--that he will never attain to wisdom worthy of the name elsewhere than in the next world--will he be grieved at dying? Will he not be glad to make that journey? We must suppose so, my dear boy; that is, if he is a real philosopher; because then he will be of the firm belief that he will never find wisdom in all its purity in any other place. If this is so, would it not be quite unreasonable (as I said just now) for such a man to be afraid of death?'

'It would, indeed.'

95

LIBERATION THROUGH RENUNCIATION*

by Shankara

Listen attentively, O prudent one, to what I say. By listening, you shall certainly be liberated from the bonds of the world.

Of the steps to liberation, the first is declared to be complete detachment from all things which are noneternal. Then comes the practice of tranquillity, self-control, and forebearance. And then the entire giving-up of all actions which are done from personal, selfish desire.

Then the disciple must hear the truth of the Atman,[1] and reflect on it, and meditate upon it constantly, without pause, for a long time. Thus the wise man reaches that highest state, in which consciousness of subject and object is dissolved away and the infinite unitary consciousness alone remains--and he knows the bliss of Nirvana while still living on earth.

Now I shall explain discrimination between the Atman and the non-Atman, which you must learn. Listen carefully; then realize the truth of it within your own soul.

What the seers call the gross body is made up of these substances--marrow, bone, fat, flesh, blood, skin, and epidermis. It consists of legs, thighs, chest, arms, feet, back, head, and other parts. It is known to be the root of that delusion of "I" and "mine".

The subtle elements are ether, air, fire, water and earth. Portions of each of these, compounded together, compose the gross body.

Sound, touch, sight, taste and smell--these five essences of the elements are what we experience. They exist in order to be experienced by the individual man.

Those deluded beings who are tied to the objects they experience by the strong cord of desire, so hard to break, remain subject to birth and death. They travel upward or downward, impelled by their own karma,[2] that inescapable law.

The deer, the elephant, the moth, the fish and the bee--each of these goes to its death under the fascination of one single sense out of the

---

*From Shankara's Crest Jewel of Discrimination, translated by Swami Prabhavananda and Christopher Isherwood. Vedanta Press Edition, pp. 42-45. By permission of the copyright owner, Vedanta Society of Southern California.

1. Atman: the highest Self or Soul, transcending and encompassing all apparently finite things and ultimately identical with Brahman, the impersonal absolute World-soul. SAS

2. Karma conveys a view of moral causation according to which my present actons control my own future, for good or ill. SAS

five. What, then, must be the fate that awaits a man who is under the fascination of all five senses?

The objects experienced by the senses are even stronger in their evil effects than the poison of the cobra. Poison kills only when it is absorbed into the body, but these objects destroy us merely by being seen with the eyes.

Only he who is free from the horrible trap of craving for sense-enjoyment, so hard to renounce, is ready for liberation--and no other, even though he may be schooled in the six systems of philosophy.

So-called seekers for liberation, who lack the true spirit of renunciation, try, nevertheless, to cross the ocean of this world. The shark of craving catches them by the throat, and drags them violently from the course, and they are drowned mid-way.

He who has killed the shark of sense-craving with the sword of true dispassion, crosses the ocean of this world without meeting any obstacle.

Know that that deluded man who walks the dreadful path of sense-craving, moves nearer to this run with every step. And know this to be true also--that he who walks the path indicated by his teacher, who is his truest well-wisher, and by his own better judgment, reaps the highest fruit of the knoweldge of Brahman.

If you really desire liberation, hold the objects of sense-enjoyment at a distance, like poison; and keep drinking in with delight such virtues as contentment, compassion, forgiveness, straightforwardness, tranquillity and self-control, as if they were nectar.

A man should be continually occupied in trying to free himself from the bondage of ignorance, which is without beginning. He who neglects this duty and is passionately absorbed in feeding the cravings of the body, commits suicide thereby. For the body is merely a vehicle of experience for the human spirit.

He who tries to find the Atman by feeding the cravings of the body, is trying to cross a river by grasping a crocodile, mistaking it for a log.

Attachment to body, objects and persons is considered fatal to a seeker for liberation. He who has completely overcome attachment is ready for the state of liberation.

Kill this deadly attachment to body, wife, children and others. The seers who have overcome it go to that high dwelling-place of Vishnu,[3] the all-pervading.

3. Vishnu, one manifestation of the Hindu trinity, Brahma-Vishnu-Shiva; the principle of conservation, maintenance, or stability. SAS

This body, which is made up of skin, flesh, blood, arteries, veins, fat, marrow and bone, is full of waste matter and filth. It deserves our contempt.

CRITIQUE

The charge most often leveled against detachment as a way of life is that it is, in some respect or another, unnatural and contrary to life itself. In the first critique, Friedrich Nietzsche (1844-1900) directs his remarks primarily to asceticism in the Western religious tradition. Asceticism, says Nietzsche, springs from the morbid, pathological condition of much of human existence. For humans are "the most precarious, the most profoundly sick of all the sick beasts of the earth." Asceticism arises as a kind of "stop-gap" remedy for sickness and suffering; the denial or suspension of natural desires is a protective device against the suffering which such desires often bring in their wake. "Life employs asceticism in its desperate struggle against death." But while asceticism serves to preserve life, its thrust is essentially negative, a turning of life against itself. Asceticism is "a will to nothingness, a revulsion from life, a rebellion against the principal conditions of living."

In a compact piece of analysis, Sigmund Freud (1856-1939) offers a similar line of explanation. All humans naturally seek happiness, which is "the satisfaction of instincts." But reality is more likely to frustrate human desires than to gratify them. To be happy is hard; "unhappiness is much less difficult to experience." Detachment from desire is a defense against unhappiness and pain; in its extreme form, it is "killing off the instincts." While some protection from suffering is secured thereby, the vividness of experience is also blunted, resulting in "an undeniable diminution in the potentialities of enjoyment."

Is detachment in fact a kind of suppression or stifling of feelings, in which we seek comfort by insulating ourselves from our natural experiences? Is what is called detachment simply a form of denial? Or is genuine detachment a quite different response, a healthy and useful way of dealing with emotions? In an engaging, personal essay, the contemporary clinical psychologist, David Van Nuys (1940-   ) explores these questions, focussing especially upon constructive responses to one's own anger. Van Nuys distinguishes between two styles of dealing with anger, detachment and "ventilation"; according to the latter, the healthy response to anger and other powerful emotions is to release them freely and expressively, rather than "bottling them up." Van Nuys traces the two views to sources in humanistic and transpersonal psychology, and concludes with some practical suggestions for determining which response, ventilation or detachment, is appropriate in a specific situation. In particular, Van Nuys suggests that denial which masquerades as detachment is unhealthy and unhelpful--a refusal to acknowledge and deal with what one is.

SICKNESS AND ASCETICISM*

by Friedrich Nietzsche

The kind of inner split we have found in the ascetic, who pits "life against life," is nonsense, not only in psychological terms, but also physiologically speaking. Such a split can only be apparent; it must be a kind of provisional expression, a formula, an adaptation, a psychological misunderstanding of something for which terms have been lacking to designate its true nature. A mere stopgap to fill a hiatus in human understanding. Let me state what I consider to be the actual situation. The ascetic ideal arises from the protective and curative instinct of a life that is degenerating and yet fighting tooth and nail for its preservation. It points to a partial physiological blocking and exhaustion, against which the deepest vital instincts, still intact, are battling doggedly and resourcefully. The ascetic ideal is one of their weapons. The situation, then, is exactly the opposite from what the worshipers of that ideal believe it to be. Life employs asceticism in its desperate struggle against death; the ascetic ideal is a dodge for the preservation of life. The ubiquitousness and power of that ideal, especially wherever men have adopted civilized forms of life, should impress upon us one great, palpable fact: the persistent morbidity of civilized man, his biological struggle against death, or to put it more exactly, against taedium vitae, exhaustion, the longing for "the end." The ascetic priest is an incarnation of the wish to be different, to be elsewhere; he is that wish, raised to its highest power, its most passionate intensity. And it is precisely the intensity of his wishing that forges the fetter binding him to this earth. At the same time he becomes an instrument for bettering the human condition, since by this intensity he is enabled to maintain in life the vast flock of defeated, disgruntled sufferers and self-tormentors, whom he leads instinctively like a shepherd. In other words, the ascetic priest, seemingly life's enemy and great negator, is in truth one of the major conserving and affirmative forces. . . . But what about the sources of man's morbidity? For certainly man is sicker, less secure, less stable, less firmly anchored than any other animal; he is the sick animal. But has he not also been more daring, more defiant, more inventive than all the other animals together?--man, the great experimenter on himself, eternally unsatisifed, vying with the gods, the beasts, and with nature for final supremacy; man, unconquered to this day, still unrealized, so agitated by his own teeming energy that his future digs like spurs into the flesh of every present moment. . . . How could such a brave and resourceful animal but be the most precarious, the most profoundly sick of all the sick beasts of the earth?

Until the advent of the ascetic ideal, man, the animal man, had no meaning at all on this earth. His existence was aimless; the question,

*Excerpt from The Birth of Tragedy and the Genealogy of Morals, by Friedrich Nietzsche, translated by Francis Golffing. Copyright (c) 1956 by Doubleday & Company, Inc. Reprinted by permission of the publisher.

"Why is there such a thing as man?" could not have been answered; man willed neither himself nor the world. Behind every great human destiny there rang, like a refrain, an even greater "In vain!" Man knew that something was lacking; a great vacuum surrounded him. He did not know how to justify, to explain, to affirm himself. His own meaning was an unsolved problem and made him suffer. He also suffered in other respects, being altogether an ailing animal, yet what bothered him was not his suffering but his inability to answer the question "What is the meaning of my trouble?" Man, the most courageous animal, and the most inured to trouble, does not deny suffering per se: he wants it, he seeks it out, provided that it can be given a meaning. Finally the ascetic ideal arose to give it meaning--its only meaning, so far. But any meaning is better than none and, in fact, the ascetic ideal has been the best stopgap that ever existed. Suffering had been interpreted, the door to all suicidal nihilism slammed shut. No doubt that interpretation brought new suffering in its wake, deeper, more inward, more poisonous suffering: it placed all suffering under the perspective of guilt. . . . All the same, man had saved himself, he had achieved a meaning, he was no longer a leaf in the wind, a plaything of circumstance, of "crass causality": he was not able to will something--no matter the object or the instrument of his willing; the will itself had been saved. We can no longer conceal from ourselves what exactly it is that this whole process of willing, inspired by the ascetic ideal, signifies--this hatred of humanity, of animality, of inert matter; this loathing of the senses, of reason even; this fear of beauty and happiness; this longing to escape from illusion, change, becoming, death, and from longing itself. It signifies, let us have the courage to face it, a will to nothingness, a revulsion from life, a rebellion against the principal conditions of living. And yet, despite everything, it is and remains a will. Let me repeat, now that I have reached the end, what I said at the beginning: man would sooner have the void for his purpose than be void of purpose. . . .

ON THE AVOIDANCE OF PAIN*

by Sigmund Freud

We will . . . turn to the . . . question of what men themselves show by their behaviour to be the purpose and intention of their lives. What do they demand of life and wish to achieve in it? The answer to this can hardly be in doubt. They strive after happiness; they want to become happy and to remain so. This endeavour has two sides, a positive and a negative aim. It aims, on the one hand, at an absence of pain and unpleasure, and, on the other, at the experiencing of strong feeling of pleasure. In its narrower sense the word 'happiness' only relates to the last. In conformity with this dichotomy in his aims, man's activity develops in two directions, according as it seeks to realize--in the main, or even exclusively--the one or the other of these aims.

As we see, what decides the purpose of life is simply the programme of the pleasure principle. This principle dominates the operation of the mental apparatus from the start. There can be no doubt about its efficacy, and yet its programme is at loggerheads with the whole world, with the macrocosm as much as with the microcosm. There is no possibility at all of its being carried through; all the regulations of the universe run counter to it. One feels inclined to say that the intention that man should be 'happy' is not included in the plan of 'Creation'. What we call happiness in the strictest sense comes from the (preferably sudden) satisfaction of needs which have been dammed up to a high degree, and it is from its nature only possible as an episodic phenomenon. When any situation that is desired by the pleasure principle is prolonged, it only produces a feeling of mild contentment. We are so made that we can derive intense enjoyment only from a contrast and very little from a state of things. Thus our possibilities of happiness are already restricted by our constitution. Unhappiness is much less difficult to experience. We are threatened with suffering from three directions: from our own body, which is doomed to decay and dissolution and which cannot even do without pain and anxiety as warning signals; from the external world, which may rage against us with overwhelming and merciless forces of destruction; and finally from our relations to other men. The suffering which comes from this last source is perhaps more painful to us than any other. We tend to regard it as a kind of gratuitous addition, although it cannot be any less fatefully inevitable than the suffering which comes from elsewhere.

It is no wonder if, under the pressure of these possibilities of suffering, men are accustomed to moderate their claims to happiness-- just as the pleasure principle itself, indeed, under the influence of the external world, changed into the more modest reality principle--, if a man

*Reprinted from Civilization and Its Discontents by Sigmund Freud, translated and edited by James Strachey. With the permission of W. W. Norton & Company, Inc. Copyright (c) 1961 by James Strachey.

thinks himself happy merely to have escaped unhappiness or to have survived his suffering, and if in general the task of avoiding suffering pushes that of obtaining pleasure into the background. Reflection shows that the accomplishment of this task can be attempted along very different paths; and all these paths have been recommended by the various schools of worldly wisdom and put into practice by men. An unrestricted satisfaction of every need presents itself as the most enticing method of conducting one's life, but it means putting enjoyment before caution, and soon brings its own punishment. The other methods, in which avoidance of unpleasure is the main purpose, are differentiated according to the source of unpleasure to which their attention is chiefly turned. Some of these methods are extreme and some moderate; some are one-sided and some attack the problem simultaneously at several points. Against the suffering which may come upon one from human relationships the readiest safeguard is voluntary isolation, keeping oneself aloof from other people. The happiness which can be achieved along this path is, as we see, the happiness of quietness. Against the dreaded external world one can only defend oneself by some kind of turning away from it, if one intends to solve the task by oneself. There is, indeed, another and better path: that of becoming a member of the human community, and, with the help of a technique guided by science, going over to the attack against nature and subjecting her to the human will. Then one is working with all for the good of all. But the most interesting methods of averting suffering are those which seek to influence our own organism. In the last analysis, all suffering is nothing else than sensation; it only exists in so far as we feel it, and we only feel it in consequence of certain ways in which our organism is regulated.

The crudest, but also the most effective among these methods of influence is the chemical one--intoxication. I do not think that anyone completely understands its mechanism, but it is a fact that there are foreign substances which, when present in the blood or tissues, directly cause us pleasurable sensations; and they also so alter the conditions governing our sensibility that we become incapable of receiving unpleasurable impulses. The two effects not ony occur simultaneously, but seem to be intimately bound up with each other. But there must be substances in the chemistry of our own bodies which have similar effects, for we know at least one pathological state, mania, in which a condition similar to intoxication arises without the administration of any intoxicating drug. Besides this, our normal mental life exhibits oscillations between a comparatively easy liberation of pleasure and a comparatively difficult one, parallel with which there goes a diminished or an increased receptivity to unpleasure. It is greatly to be regretted that this toxic side of mental processes has so far escaped scientific examination. The service rendered by intoxicating media in the struggle for happiness and in keeping misery at a distance is so highly prized as a benefit that individuals and peoples alike have given them an established place in the economics of their libido. We owe to such media not merely the immediate yield of pleasure, but also a greatly desired degree of independence from the external world. For one knows that, with the help of this 'drowner of cares' one can at any time withdraw from the pressure of reality and find refuge in a world of one's own with better conditions of sensibility. As is well known, it is precisely this property of intoxicants which also determines their danger and their injuriousness. They are responsible, in certain circumstances, for the useless waste of a large quota of energy which might have been employed for the improvement of the human lot.

The complicated structure of our mental apparatus admits, however, of a whole number of other influences. Just as a satisfaction of instinct spells happiness for us, so severe suffering is caused us if the external world lets us starve, if it refuses to sate our needs. One may therefore hope to be freed from a part of one's sufferings by influencing the instinctual impulses. This type of defence against suffering is no longer brought to bear on the sensory apparatus; it seeks to master the internal sources of our needs. The extreme form of this is brought about by killing off the instincts, as is prescribed by the worldly wisdom of the East and practised by Yoga. If it succeeds, then the subject has, it is true, given up all other activities as well--he has sacrificed his life; and, by another path, he has once more only achieved the happiness of quietness. We follow the same path when our aims are less extreme and we merely attempt to control our instinctual life. In that case, the controlling elements are the higher psychical agencies, which have subjected themselves to the reality principle. Here the aim of satisfaction is not by any means relinquished; but a certain amount of protection against suffering is secured, in that non-satisfaction is not so painfully felt in the case of instincts kept in dependence as in the case of uninhibited ones. As against this, there is an undeniable diminution in the potentialities of enjoyment. The feeling of happiness derived from the satisfaction of a wild instinctual impulse untamed by the ego is incomparably more intense than that derived from sating an instinct that has been tamed. The irresistibility of perverse instincts, and perhaps the attraction in general of forbidden things finds an economic explanation here.

DEALING WITH ANGER: DETACHMENT OR DENIAL?*

by David Van Nuys

The question has to do with anger and how to deal with it. Work it out in fantasy, express it directly and immediately through words, count to 10, pound pillows, scream, sublimate or meditate? These and other solutions are advocated within the loose conglomeration of individuals groping towards growth that we call the Human Potential Movement.

I once was quite active in leading encounter groups. As hostilities inevitably surfaced, I encouraged others to arm wrestle, bad mouth, all-out wrestle or pulverize the floor with a plastic bat. Naturally, I had to model such methods of dealing with one's anger and I got to be pretty good at this in groups. Sometimes, group members were initially terrified by my more flamboyant outbursts. I learned that game well. After all, the rules of the group encouraged such behavior. And, it was supported by a "plumbing" model of emotional release that implies that the pipes will burst without frequent flushing.

Yet, outside of groups, I think I remained the usually soft-spoken, mild-mannered and, at times, retiring person that I usually am. The fact is that in real life, I'm pretty easygoing and don't often get angry.

Another Way

As I suspect has happened for many others, this phase of my life dropped out after a bit, and I found myself drawn to the practice of yoga and other esoteric disciplines. During this next phase, I was exposed to various readings and passing gurus advocating detachment--not only from anger but from other emotional extremes and desires, as well. It sounded right and good, but I was troubled by what (with my clinical training) I often perceived as covert, unowned hostility in many of these people and their followers, sometimes thinly masked by what looked like a spiritual one-upmanship game. Was this detachment or was it, in fact, denial? Is detachment a real possibility or another fiction of the yearning heart?

Upon coming to California, I found that a great many of my students were straining toward their detachment by dressing in white, eating brown rice, avoiding "heavy vibes" and generally keeping "mellow." I was even foolhardy enough to attempt a class on group facilitation with such a group in which I tried some of the old strategies for encouraging people to get their "garbage" out. They insisted there was no garbage, but it sure looked like pollution to me. I was in the devastating position of being the only one who saw the emperor as having no clothes.

Actually, this split between acting out and detachment is more than a personal one. What we have is a head-on collision between Neo-Reichian psychology and what has been called the emerging "fourth force," transpersonal psychology.

Transpersonal psychology is an outgrowth of humanistic psychology, which was called the "third force," underlining its challenge to Freudian psychology. Transpersonal psychology reclaims as legitimate, ground that has been mostly abandoned and shunned by academic psychology--the entire realm of our spirituality.

This idea of nonattachment to anger, then, is but one tender shoot of the growing transpersonal movement, which in its turn has been greatly influenced by Eastern mysticism.

Lead Soldiers

So we have both nonattachment and catharsis advanced as ideals for dealing with anger. Both sides have interesting facts to marshal for their support. Facts in psychology these days, however, appear more and more to me like little lead soldiers set up to be knocked over by other little lead soldiers. The game can be played over and over again, with the tide of ferocious battle as often turning one way as the next. . . .

I've given the matter a lot of thought and I've tried to watch myself closely. I believe I am beginning to get some clarity on the issue.

Denial Sign

So, here is the distinction. It holds for me and I am going to risk a generalization. When your guts are churning; your breathing is short; your voice is getting clipped, or loud, or unusually soft; or you're getting obliquely sarcastic, but doing your damndest to suppress it; that is not detachment. That's denial. And I don't think denial is healthy, intrapsychically or interpersonally. Whether or not you need to scream or pound pillows at that point, I don't know. But I do think it is important to own your anger and deal with it in some way.

Detachment, on the other hand, has to do with taking a broader (or, perhaps, higher) point of view. I had a friend who frequently used to say, "Hell, it ain't no big thing." And when he would say that, I would have to stop for a split second, examine whatever he was referring to in perspective and then admit in my mind-body wholeness that, in the overall picture, he was right. It ain't no big thing. That's detachment.

I don't believe we need to react to every little slight with an outburst of anger to keep our insides clean. I believe we can and must learn to know what's going on in our insides. I believe we can also learn to

106

overlook. I believe we can evolve personally, if not collectively, toward a broader awareness in which more and more we can truly say, "It ain't no big thing," and just let it slip by. I think that must be what the mystics mean by detachment—letting go of it, completely. But evolution is slow, and if you or I rush into a holy man's robes too fast, pretending to let go while secretly holding on—that's denial.

I think both concepts—denial and detachment—are useful and we should strive to get as clear with them as we can.

STUDY QUESTIONS FOR CHAPTER III

Questions for Review:

1. Summarize the notion of non-attachment.

2. What things are in our power, and what things are not, according to Epictetus?

3. What does Epictetus mean by saying that "the reality of good lies in what is in our power"?

4. What does Epictetus mean by the statement "What disturbs men's minds is not events but their judgements on events"?

5. What is the point of Epictetus' advice to "behave in life as you would at a banquet"?

6. Summarize Epictetus' advice as to "a definite stamp and style of conduct."

7. What does Epictetus mean by the statement that "everything has two handles, one by which you can carry it, the other by which you cannot"?

8. How are the ignorant person and the philosopher different, according to Epictetus?

9. What does Plato mean by the statement that "true philosophers make dying their profession"?

10. How does the body interfere with the pursuit of truth, according to Plato?

11. Why is death a hopeful prospect, according to Plato?

12. What does Shankara mean by "sense-craving"?

13. What is Shankara's attitude toward the body?

14. How does the ascetic ideal arise, according to Nietzsche?

15. What is it about humans that makes them "the most precarious, the most profoundly sick of all the sick beasts of the earth" according to Nietzsche?

16. What does Nietzsche mean by the claim that asceticism is "a will to nothingness, a revulsion from life"?

17. What do humans through their behavior show to be "the purpose and intention of their lives" according to Freud? What are the chief components of this purpose?

18. Why is it that life cannot be continuously happy in the usual sense of that word, according to Freud?

19. What are the three sources of unhappiness, according to Freud?

20. Why does the pursuit of pleasure become transformed into the avoidance of pain, according to Freud?

21. Summarize Freud's account of "the worldly wisdom of the East...practiced by Yoga."

22. What is the effect of controlling "our instinctual life" upon our capacity to enjoy life, according to Freud?

23. What is Van Nuys' distinction between ventilation and detachment as ways of dealing with anger?

24. How can one distinguish between detachment and denial, according to Van Nuys?

Questions for Reflection:

1. In what respects do I now practice detachment in my life? In what areas of my life would I like to practice more--or less--detachment than I now do?

2. When I do not detach myself from pain and suffering, how do I deal with it instead?

3. How do I feel about Plato's advice to "practice dying"?

4. When I experience anger, do I deal with it more commonly by ventilation, detachment, or denial?

Questions for Discussion:

1. When is detachment desirable? When is it undesirable?

2. Is detachment really a form of escapism? Clarify your terms.

3. Is it possible to detach oneself from pain, but not from pleasure?

4. Do persons who seek detachment cut themselves off from a full and rich experience of life?

5. Do you agree with Epictetus that "the reality of good lies in what is in our power"?

6. Do you agree with Epictetus that "What disturbs men's minds is not events but their judgements on events"?

7. Is rejection of one's bodily nature an essential part of detachment, in your opinion?

8. Is detachment actually a kind of denial, after all?

9. On balance, are ideals of detachment a satisfactory account of the good life, in your opinion?

SUGGESTIONS FOR FURTHER READING

The Bhagavad Gita. This most revered and celebrated text of Hinduism is available in many editions and translations.

John Hospers, Human Conduct: Problems of Ethics, Chapter 4 (Harcourt Brace Jovanovich, 1961, 1972) Good discussion of stoicism.

Ken Keyes, Jr., Handbook to Higher Consciousness (Living Love Center, 1972, 1975) A popular treatment that describes attachment as "addiction."

W. J. Oates, ed., The Stoic and Epicurean Philosophers (Modern Library 1957)

John Rist, ed., The Stoics (University of California Press, 1978)

Shankara, Shankara's Crest-Jewel of Discrimination, trans. by Swami Prabhavananda and Christopher Isherwood (Vedanta 1947)

Ways of Wisdom

Chapter
Four:

Becoming Human

Chapter IV: BECOMING HUMAN

Introduction

I will become what I am. For I am not wholly myself; I have not become the person I am capable of becoming. Within me is a person wanting to emerge, a potential seeking to become real. The good life for me lies in expressing what I am, in growing as a person, in becoming more fully myself.

Becoming human is more than a matter of learning to cope with pain, anxiety, distress, and other negative aspects of life. It is an unfolding, expanding, developmental process; it is active rather than merely reactive; it is movement in a positive direction, in many positive directions. Such movement does not occur without challenges; the process of becoming human normally includes pain and the threat of destruction. But if I bend all of my energies to protecting and defending myself, I thwart my own growth and prevent myself from functioning fully. In closing off to the world, I cannot fully be myself.

To become what I am means, among other things, to move in the direction of greater openness and authenticity: to drop false facades and masks, and let my behavior transparently express my inner state. Consider, for example, a boy who is dating a girl for the first time, and is worried about how he should behave. He is eager to make a certain impression; he is acutely aware of social expectations that he fears he may not meet; he is anxious not to appear foolish, awkward, naive. As a result he may behave in ways that are not genuinely expressive of the person he actually is. He may "put on a front." When, on the other hand, the boy takes courage to become himself, he drops his facade. His behavior becomes less calculated, more spontaneous; he worries less about

113

how others will see him, and lets his behavior flow naturally from within. Instead of wearing a mask, he becomes himself.

Masks often serve not only to deceive others but also to deceive myself. If what I am does not coincide with what I want to be, or what I believe I ought to be, I may deny aspects of myself in order to maintain a false self-image. Perhaps I am angry but do not accept my anger, or fearful but do not accept my fear. Perhaps I have painful memories that I suppress and avoid. Perhaps I disapprove of some of my actions, and so I ignore them and form a false picture of my behavior. As Carl Rogers writes, "In our daily lives there are a thousand and one reasons for not letting ourselves experience our attitudes fully, reasons from our past and from the present, reasons that reside within the social situation. It seems too dangerous, too potentially damaging, to experience them fully."[1] When I regularly force my behavior and attitudes into inauthentic patterns, I come to identify myself with those patterns. What I believe myself to be diverges from what I am. I become alienated from myself, fragmented into disparate parts. I lose touch with myself; I do not know who I am.

Here, to become what I am means to recover and accept those parts of me that I have denied, to take ownership of that which I have disowned. It means to move from fragmentation toward wholeness and health, from the conflict of an internal civil war toward the harmony of a dynamic integration. For example: a man who has felt constrained to present a tough and aggressive image may come to accept and express that part of himself that is gentle and sensitive; or a woman who has disguised her intelligence for fear of seeming "unfeminine" may at last affirm and value that dimension of herself. As I come to accept more of myself, I am more able to live within myself. Instead of escaping in thought to other times and places, I learn to be present here and now, immediately aware of this passing moment, and centered in myself.

Masks to hide from others and masks to hide from myself are both expressions of a defensive, reactive strategy toward life. As I move away from masks toward authenticity and wholeness, I move away from defensiveness toward openness and vulnerability, away from rigidity toward flexibility. Instead of forcing experiences into my own preconceived forms of thought, I learn to adapt fluidly to whatever is present in experience. For example, I am less likely to judge other people by initial appearances, and more likely to see them and hear them accurately. When I encounter difficulties, hurts, anxieties, I learn to accept and deal with such challenges rather than retreating fearfully from them.

If I govern my life primarily by defensive strategies, I thwart my own long-term growth, and invite stagnation. When, on the other hand, I take the risk of greater openness and wholeness, I release creative energies and free myself for the unfolding of my potential. Being myself today helps me to become myself tomorrow.

The unfolding of the self over time follows an internal, organic logic, in which what is implicit becomes progressively more explicit, and what is potential becomes progressively more actual. Except when perverted by adverse conditions of growth, the self that emerges from this process is essentially healthy and good, according to humanistic thinkers. Because humans are naturally social creatures, they can achieve full development as individuals only under conditions of harmonious interaction with one another; there is no inherent conflict between social responsibility and self-actualization. The process of becoming human, encompassing both individual and social goods, is itself the heart of the good life. In the words of Robert Louis Stevenson, "To be what we are, and to become what we are capable of becoming, is the only end of life."[2]

The Selections

In this chapter, the first statement of becoming human as a view of the good life is by the contemporary humanistic psychologist, Carl Rogers (1902-   ). Rogers' account is drawn from many years as a practicing psychotherapist, helping troubled individuals to move toward greater wholeness and health. As a therapist, Rogers does not suggest solutions to his clients' problems, but rather seeks to create an environment of "unconditional positive regard," in which they feel safe and free to be themselves. In this climate of unconditional acceptance, Rogers finds that individuals use their psychological freedom to grow in a variety of ways toward greater health and fuller functioning. Rogers discerns certain common themes or features of such growth, and he bases his view of the good life on these observations.

The second description of the good life in this chapter is that of another highly influential humanistic psychologist, Abraham Maslow (1908-1970). Whereas Rogers bases his views on observations of troubled and disturbed persons as they grow toward greater psychological well-being, Maslow regards his subjects as already paradigms of psychological health; he describes them as "people who have developed to the full stature of which they are capable." Maslow believes that in the past, psychological theory has been unduly preoccupied with emotional illness and pathology; what is needed, he argues, is more attention to a psychology of health and self-actualization.

Maslow's model of a healthy personality rests importantly upon his theory of motivation, in which he specifies a variety of human needs and relates them to one another. In his original formulations of this theory, Maslow identifies five stages or levels of human need:

1)   **Physiological needs:**   hunger, thirst, pain avoidance, sexual release, and so on.

2) **Safety needs:** need for security, stability, protection, limits; need for freedom from fear, anxiety, chaos, and so on.

3) **Belongingness and love needs:** need for love, affection, affiliation, and so on.

4) **Esteem needs:** need for self-esteem, self-confidence, self-worth, strength, adequacy, and so on; need for esteem or respect from others, for prestige, status, recognition, and so on.

5) **Self-actualization needs:** the need to develop one's own nature, to actualize one's individual potential; the need for self-fulfillment.[3]

In Maslow's account these needs are arranged in a hierarchical fashion: under conditions of deprivation, the lower needs tend to predominate over the higher, whereas when lower needs become satisfied, higher needs become more salient. Thus a starving man is dominated by the desire for food, and can think of little else; happiness is, for him, simply something to eat. When he is adequately fed, however, he begins to be more aware of his needs for safety, love, and so on. Maslow does not hold that lower needs must be completely filled before higher needs are felt; rather, as lower needs are partially met, higher needs begin to emerge.[4] Optimal human development or self-actualization requires, however, that lower needs be relatively well satisfied so that higher needs can be addressed. Maslow found that younger, developing persons provided almost no suitable subjects for his study, perhaps because they are likely to be relatively preoccupied with meeting basic needs. In general, self-actualization develops gradually over a lengthy period of time, and emerges clearly only later in life.

NOTES

1. Carl Rogers, On Becoming a Person: A Therapist's View of Psychotherapy (Boston: Houghton Mifflin Co., 1961), p. 111.

2. Familiar Studies of Men and Books (New York: Charles Scribner's Sons, 1907), p. 167.

3. See A. H. Maslow, Motivation and Personality, Second Edition (New York: Harper and Row, 1954, 1970), pp. 35-38. In his later writings, Maslow focussed upon a yet higher level of needs or values, transcendence-needs, or "B-values." See especially A. H. Maslow, "Self-Actualization and Beyond," in Bugental, J. F. T. (ed.) Challenges of Humanistic Psychology (New York: McGraw-Hill, 1967), pp. 278-286, and Religion, Values and Peak Experiences (New York: Viking, 1970). A clear, brief review of the emergence of the concept of transcendence in Maslow's theory is given in Thomas Roberts, "Beyond Self-Actualization," in Revision, Winter, 1978, pp. 42-46.

4. "[I] f prepotent need A is satisfied only 10 percent, then need B may not be visable at all. However, as this need A becomes satisfied 25 percent, need B may emerge 5 percent, as need A becomes satisfied 75 percent, need B may emerge 50 percent, and so on." A. H. Maslow, Motivation and Personality, Second Edition, p. 54.

A THERAPIST'S VIEW OF THE GOOD LIFE:
THE FULLY FUNCTIONING PERSON*

by Carl R. Rogers

My views regarding the meaning of the good life are largely based upon my experience in working with people in the very close and intimate relationship which is called psychotherapy. These views thus have an empirical or experiential foundation, as contrasted perhaps with a scholarly or philosophical foundation. I have learned what the good life seems to be by observing and participating in the struggle of disturbed and troubled people to achieve that life.

I should make it clear from the outset that this experience I have gained comes from the vantage point of a particular orientation to psychotherapy which has developed over the years. Quite possibly all psychotherapy is basically similar, but since I am less sure of that than I once was, I wish to make it clear that my therapeutic experience has been along the lines that seem to me most effective, the type of therapy termed "client-centered."

Let me attempt to give a very brief description of what this therapy would be like if it were in every respect optimal, since I feel I have learned most about the good life from therapeutic experiences in which a great deal of movement occurred. If the therapy were optimal, intensive as well as extensive, then it would mean that the therapist has been able to enter into an intensely personal and subjective relationship with the client--relating not as a scientist to an object of study, not as a physician expecting to diagnose and cure, but as a person to a person. It would mean that the therapist feels this client to be a person of unconditional self-worth: of value no matter what his condition, his behavior, or his feelings. It would mean that the therapist is genuine, hiding behind no defensive facade, but meeting the client with the feelings which organically he is experiencing. It would mean that the therapist is able to let himself go in understanding this client; that no inner barriers keep him from sensing what it feels like to be the client at each moment of the relationship; and that he can convey something of his empathic understanding to the client. It means that the therapist has been comfortable in entering this relationship fully, without knowing cognitively where it will lead, satisfied with providing a climate which will permit the client the utmost freedom to become himself.

For the client, this optimal therapy would mean an exploration of increasingly strange and unknown and dangerous feelings in himself, the exploration proving possible only because he is gradually realizing that he is accepted unconditionally. Thus he becomes acquainted with elements

*Chapter 9 of Carl R. Rogers: <u>On Becoming A Person</u>. Copyright (c) 1961 by Houghton Mifflin Company. Used by permission.

of his experience which have in the past been denied to awareness as too threatening, too damaging to the structure of the self. He finds himself experiencing these feelings fully, completely, in the relationship, so that for the moment he is his fear, or his anger, or his tenderness, or his strength. And as he lives these widely varied feelings, in all their degrees of intensity, he discovers that he has experienced himself, that he is all these feelings. He finds his behavior changing in constructive fashion in accordance with his newly experienced self. He approaches the realization that he no longer needs to fear what experience may hold, but can welcome it freely as a part of his changing and developing self.

This is a thumbnail sketch of what client-centered therapy comes close to, when it is at its optimum. I give it here simply as a brief picture of the context in which I have formed my views of the good life.

A Negative Observation

As I have tried to live understandingly in the experiences of my clients, I have gradually come to one negative conclusion about the good life. It seems to me that the good life is not fixed state. It is not, in my estimation, a state of virtue, or contentment, or nirvana, or happiness. It is not a condition in which the individual is adjusted, or fulfilled, or actualized. To use psychological terms, it is not a state of drive-reduction, or tension-reduction, or homeostasis.

I believe that all of these terms have been used in ways which imply that if one or several of these states is achieved, then the goal of life has been achieved. Certainly, for many people happiness, or adjustment, are seen as states of being which are synonymous with the good life. And social scientists have frequently spoken of the reduction of tension, or the achievement of homeostasis or equilibrium as if these states constituted the goal of the process of living.

So it is with a certain amount of surprise and concern that I realize that my experience supports none of these definitions. If I focus on the experience of those individuals who seem to have evidenced the greatest degree of movement during the therapeutic relationships, and who, in the years following this relationship, appear to have made and to be making real progress toward the good life, then it seems to me that they are not adequately described at all by any of these terms which refer to fixed states of being. I believe they would consider themselves insulted if they were described as "adjusted," and they would regard it as false if they were described as "happy" or "contented," or even "actualized." As I have known them I would regard it as most inaccurate to say that all their drive tensions have been reduced, or that they are in a state of homeostasis. So I am forced to ask myself whether there is any way in which I can generalize about their situation, any definition which I can give of the good life which would seem to fit the facts as I have observed

118

them. I find this not at all easy, and what follows is stated very tentatively.

A Positive Observation

If I attempt to capture in a few words what seems to me to be true of these people, I believe it will come out something like this:

The good life is a <u>process</u>, not a state of being.

It is a direction, not a destination.

The direction which constitutes the good life is that which is selected by the total organism, when there is psychological freedom to move in <u>any</u> direction.

This organismically selected direction seems to have certain discernible general qualities which appear to be the same in a wide variety of unique individuals.

So I can integrate these statements into a definition which can at least serve as a basis for consideration and discussion. The good life, from the point of view of my experience, is the process of movement in a direction which the human organism selects when it is inwardly free to move in any direction, and the general qualities of this selected direction appear to have a certain universality.

The Characteristics of the Process

Let me now try to specify what appear to be the characteristic qualities of this process of movement, as they crop up in person after person in therapy.

An Increasing Openness to Experience

In the first place, the process seems to involve an increasing openness to experience. This phrase has come to have more and more meaning for me. It is the polar opposite of defensiveness. Defensiveness I have described in the past as being the organism's response to experiences which are perceived or anticipated as threatening, as incongruent with the individual's existing picture of himself, or of himself in relationship to the world. These threatening experiences are temporarily rendered harmless by being distorted in awareness, or being denied to awareness. I quite literally cannot see, with accuracy, those experiences, feelings, reactions in myself which are significantly at variance with the picture of myself which I already possess. A large part of the process of therapy is the continuing discovery by the client that he is experiencing feelings and attitudes which heretofore he has not been

119

able to be aware of, which he has not been able to "own" as being a part of himself.

If a person could be fully open to his experience, however, every stimulus--whether originating within the organism or in the environment--would be freely relayed through the nervous system without being distorted by any defensive mechanism. There would be no need of the mechanism of "subception" whereby the organism is forewarned of any experience threatening to the self. On the contrary, whether the stimulus was the impact of a configuration of form, color, or sound in the environment on the sensory nerves, or a memory trace from the past, or a visceral sensation of fear or pleasure or disgust, the person would be "living" it, would have it completely available to awareness.

Thus, one aspect of this process which I am naming "the good life" appears to be a movement away from the pole of defensiveness toward the pole of openness to experience. The individual is becoming more able to listen to himself, to experience what is going on within himself. He is more open to his feelings of fear and discouragement and pain. He is also more open to his feelings of courage, and tenderness, and awe. He is free to live his feelings subjectively, as they exist in him, and also free to be aware of these feelings. He is more able fully to live the experiences of his organism rather than shutting them out of awareness.

Increasingly Existential Living

the real questions that matter

A second characteristic of the process which for me is the good life, is that it involves an increasing tendency to live fully in each moment. This is a thought which can easily be misunderstood, and which is perhaps somewhat vague in my own thinking. Let me try to explain what I mean.

I believe it would be evident that for the person who was fully open to his new experience, completely without defensiveness, each moment would be new. The complex configuration of inner and outer stimuli which exists in this moment has never existed before in just this fashion. Consequently such a person would realize that "What I will be in the next moment, and what I will do, grows out of that moment, and cannot be predicted in advance either by me or by others." Not infrequently we find clients expressing exactly this sort of feeling.

One way of expressing the fluidity which is present in such existential living is to say that the self and personality emerge _from_ experience, rather than experience being translated or twisted to fit preconceived self-structure. It means that one becomes a participant in and an observer of the ongoing process of organismic experience, rather than being in control of it.

120

Such living in the moment means an absence of rigidity, of tight organization, of the imposition of structure on experience. It means instead a maximum of adaptability, a discovery of structure in experience, a flowing, changing organization of self and personality.

It is this tendency toward existential living which appears to me very evident in people who are involved in the process of the good life. One might almost say that it is the most essential quality of it. It involves discovering the structure of experience in the process of living the experience. Most of us, on the other hand, bring a preformed structure and evaluation to our experience to fit our preconceptions, annoyed at the fluid qualities which make it so unruly in fitting our carefully constructed pigeonholes. To open one's spirit to what is going on now, and to discover in that present process whatever structure it appears to have--this to me is one of the qualities of the good life, the mature life, as I see clients approach it.

An Increasing Trust in His Organism

Still another characteristic of the person who is living the process of the good life appears to be an increasing trust in his organism as a means of arriving at the most satisfying behavior in each existential situation. Again let me try to explain what I mean.

In choosing what course of action to take in any situation, many people rely upon guiding principles, upon a code of action laid down by some group or institution, upon the judgment of others (from wife and friends to Emily Post), or upon the way they have behaved in some similar past situation. Yet as I observe the clients whose experiences in living have taught me so much, I find that increasingly such individuals are able to trust their total organismic reaction to a new situation because they discover to an ever-increasing degree that if they are open to their experience, doing what "feels right" proves to be a competent and trustworthy guide to behavior which is truly satisfying.

As I try to understand the reason for this, I find myself following this line of thought. The person who is fully open to his experience would have access to all of the available data in the situation, on which to base his behavior; the social demands, his own complex and possibly conflicting needs, his memories of similar situations, his perception of the uniqueness of this situation, etc., etc. The data would be very complex indeed. But he could permit his total organism, his consciousness participating, to consider each stimulus, need, and demand, its relative intensity and importance, and out of this complex weighing and balancing, discover that course of action which would come closest to satisfying all his needs in the situation. An analogy which might come close to a description would be to compare this person to a giant electronic computing machine. Since he is open to his experience, all of the data from his sense impressions, from his memory, from previous learning, from his visceral and internal states, is fed into the machine. The machine takes all of these multitudinous pulls and forces which are fed in as data, and quickly computes the course of action which would be the most economical vector of need satisfaction in this existential situation. This is the behavior of our hypothetical person.

The defects which in most of us make this process untrustworthy are the inclusion of information which does <u>not</u> belong to this present situation, or the exclusion of information which <u>does</u>. It is when memories and previous learnings are fed into the computations as if they were <u>this</u> reality, and not memories and learnings, that erroneous behavioral answers arise. Or when certain threatening experiences are inhibited from awareness, and hence are withheld from the computation or fed into it in distorted form, this too produces error. But our hypothetical person would find his organism thoroughly trustworthy, because all of the available data would be used, and it would be present in accurate rather than distorted form. Hence his behavior would come as close as possible to satisfying all his needs--for enhancement, for affiliation with others, and the like.

In this weighing, balancing, and computation, his organism would not by any means be infallible. It would always give the best possible answer for the available data, but sometimes data would be missing. Because of the element of openness to experience, however, any errors, any following of behavior which was not satisfying, would be quickly corrected. The computations, as it were, would always be in process of being corrected, because they would be continually checked in behavior.

Perhaps you will not like my analogy of an electronic computing machine. Let me return to the clients I know. As they become more open to all of their experiences, they find it increasingly possible to trust their reactions. If they "feel like" expressing anger they do so and find that this comes out satisfactorily, because they are equally alive to all of their other desires for affection, affiliation, and relationship. They are surprised at their own intuitive skill in finding behavioral solutions to complex and troubling human relationships. It is only afterward that they realize how surprisingly trustworthy their inner reactions have been in bringing about satisfactory behavior.

The Process of Functioning More Fully

I should like to draw together these three threads describing the process of the good life into a more coherent picture. It appears that the person who is psychologically free moves in the direction of becoming a more fully functioning person. He is more able to live fully in and with each and all of his feelings and reactions. He makes increasing use of all his organic equipment to sense, as accurately as possible, the existential situation within and without. He makes use of all of the information his nervous system can thus supply, using it in awareness, but recognizing that his total organism may be, and often is, wiser than his awareness. He is more able to permit his total organism to function freely in all its complexity in selecting, from the multitude of possibilities, that behavior which in this moment of time will be most generally and genuinely satisfying. He is able to put more trust in his organism in this functioning, not because it is infallible, but because he can be fully open to the consequences of each of his actions and correct them if they prove to be less than satisfying.

He is more able to experience all of his feelings, and is less afraid of any of his feelings; he is his own sifter of evidence, and is more open to evidence from all sources; he is completely engaged in the process of being and becoming himself, and thus discovers that he is soundly and realistically social; he lives more completely in this moment, but learns that this is the soundest living for all time. He is becoming a more fully functioning organism, and because of the awareness of himself which flows freely in and through his experience, he is becoming a more fully functioning person.

Some Implications

Any view of what constitutes the good life carries with it many implications, and the view I have presented is no exception. I hope that these implications may be food for thought. There are two or three of these about which I would like to comment.

A New Perspective on Freedom vs Determinism

The first of these implications may not immediately be evident. It has to do with the age-old issue of "free will." Let me endeavor to spell out the way in which this issue now appears to me in a new light.

For some time I have been perplexed over the living paradox which exists in psychotherapy between freedom and determinism. In the therapeutic relationship some of the most compelling subjective experiences are those in which the client feels within himself the power of naked choice. He is free--to become himself or to hide behind a facade; to move forward or to retrogress; to behave in ways which are destructive of self and others, or in ways which are enhancing; quite literally free to live or die, in both the physiological and psychological meaning of those terms. Yet as we enter this field of psychotherapy with objective research methods, we are, like any other scientist, committed to a complete determinism. From this point of view every thought, feeling, and action of the client is determined by what preceded it. There can be no such thing as freedom. The dilemma I am trying to describe is not different than that found in other fields--it is simply brought to

123

sharper focus, and appears more insoluble.

This dilemma can be seen in a fresh perspective, however, when we consider it in terms of the definition I have given of the fully functioning person. We could say that in the optimum of therapy the person rightfully experiences the most complete and absolute freedom. He wills or chooses to follow the course of action which is the most economical vector in relationship to all the internal and external stimuli, because it is that behavior which will be most deeply satisfying. But this is the same course of action which from another vantage point may be said to be determined by all the factors in the existential situation. Let us contrast this with the picture of the person who is defensively organized. He wills or chooses to follow a given course of action, but finds that he cannot behave in the fashion that he chooses. He is determined by the factors in the existential situation, but these factors include his defensiveness, his denial or distortion of some of the relevant data. Hence it is certain that his behavior will be less than fully satisfying. His behavior is determined, but he is not free to make an effective choice. The fully functioning person, on the other hand, not only experiences, but utilizes, the most absolute freedom when he spontaneously, freely, and voluntarily chooses and wills that which is also absolutely determined.

I am not so naive as to suppose that this fully resolves the issue between subjective and objective, between freedom and necessity. Nevertheless it has meaning for me that the more the person is living the good life, the more he will experience a freedom of choice, and the more his choices will be effectively implemented in his behavior.

Creativity As An Element Of The Good Life

I believe it will be clear that a person who is involved in the directional process which I have termed "the good life" is a creative person. With his sensitive openness to his world, his trust of his own ability to form new relationships with his environment, he would be the type of person from whom creative products and creative living emerge. He would not necessarily be "adjusted" to his culture, and he would almost certainly not be a conformist. But at any time and in any culture he would live constructively, in as much harmony with his culture as a balanced satisfaction of needs demanded. In some cultural situations he might in some ways be very unhappy, but he would continue to move toward becoming himself, and to behave in such a way as to provide the maximum satisfaction of his deepest needs.

Such a person would, I believe, be recognized by the student of evolution as the type most likely to adapt and survive under changing environmental conditions. He would be able creatively to make sound adjustments to new as well as old conditions. He would be a fit vanguard of human evolution.

Basic Trustworthiness of Human Nature

It will be evident that another implication of the view I have been presenting is that the basic nature of the human being, when functioning freely, is constructive and trustworthy. For me this is an inescapable conclusion from a quarter-century of experience in psychotherapy. When we are able to free the individual from defensiveness, so that he is open to the wide range of his own needs, as well as the wide range of environmental and social demands, his reactions may be trusted to be positive, forward-moving, constructive. We do not need to ask who will socialize him, for one of his own deepest needs is for affiliation and communication with others. As he becomes more fully himself, he will become more realistically socialized. We do not need to ask who will control his aggressive impulses; for as he becomes more open to all of his impulses, his need to be liked by others and his tendency to give affection will be as strong as his impulses to strike out or to seize for himself. He will be aggressive in situations in which aggression is realistically appropriate, but there will be no runaway need for aggression. His total behavior, in these and other areas, as he moves toward being open to all his experience, will be more balanced and realistic, behavior which is appropriate to the survival and enhancement of a highly social animal.

I have little sympathy with the rather prevalent concept that man is basically irrational, and that his impulses, if not controlled, will lead to destruction of others and self. Man's behavior is exquisitely rational, moving with subtle and ordered complexity toward the goals his organism is endeavoring to achieve. The tragedy for most of us is that our defenses keep us from being aware of this rationality, so that consciously we are moving in one direction, while organismically we are moving in another. But in our person who is living the process of the good life, there would be a decreasing number of such barriers, and he would be increasingly a participant in the rationality of his organism. The only control of impulses which would exist, or which would prove necessary, is the natural and internal balancing of one need against another, and the discovery of behaviors which follow the vector most closely approximating the satisfaction of all needs. The experience of extreme satisfaction of one need (for aggression, or sex, etc.) in such a way as to do violence to the satisfaction of other needs (for companionship, tender relationship, etc.)-- an experience very common in the defensively organized person--would be greatly decreased. He would participate in the vastly complex self-regulatory activities of his organism--the psychological as well as physiological thermostatic controls--in such a fashion as to live in increasing harmony with himself and with others.

The Greater Richness of Life

One last implication I should like to mention is that this process of living in the good life involves a wider range, a greater richness, than the constricted living in which most of us find ourselves. To be a part of this process means that one is involved in the frequently frightening and frequently satisfying experience of a more sensitive living, with greater range, greater variety, greater richness. It seems to me that clients who have moved significantly in therapy live more intimately with their feelings of pain, but also more vividly with their feelings of ecstasy; that anger is more clearly felt, but so also is love; that fear is an experience they know more deeply, but so is courage. And the reason they can thus live fully in a wider range is that they have this underlying confidence in themselves as trustworthy instruments for encountering life.

I believe it will have become evident why, for me, adjectives such as happy, contented, blissful, enjoyable, do not seem quite appropriate to any general description of this process I have called the good life, even though the person in this process would experience each one of these feelings at appropriate times. But the adjectives which seem more generally fitting are adjectives such as enriching, exciting, rewarding, challenging, meaningful. This process of the good life is not, I am convinced, a life for the faint-hearted. It involves the stretching and growing of becoming more and more of one's potentialities. It involves the courage to be. It means launching oneself fully into the stream of life. Yet the deeply exciting thing about human beings is that when the individual is inwardly free, he chooses as the good life this process of becoming.

SELF-ACTUALIZING PEOPLE

by Abraham H. Maslow

The Beginnings of Self-Actualizing Studies*

My investigations on self-actualization were not planned to be research and did not start out as research. They started out as the effort of a young intelletual to try to understand two of his teachers whom he loved, adored, and admired and who were very, very wonderful people. It was a kind of high-IQ devotion. I could not be content simply to adore, but sought to understand why these two people were so different from the run-of-the-mill people in the world. These two people were Ruth Benedict and Max Wertheimer. They were my teachers after I came with a Ph.D. from the West to New York City, and they were most remarkable human beings. My training in psychology equipped me not at all for understanding them. It was as if they were not quite people but something more than people. My own investigation began as a prescientific or nonscientific activity. I made descriptions and notes on Max Wertheimer, and I made notes on Ruth Benedict. When I tried to understand them, think about them, and write about them in my journal and my notes, I realized in one wonderful moment that their two patterns could be generalized. I was talking about a kind of person, not about two noncomparable individuals. There was wonderful excitement in that. I tried to see whether this pattern could be found elsewhere, and I did find it elsewhere, in one person after another.

By ordinary standards of laboratory research, that is of rigorous and controlled research, this simply was not research at all. My generalizations grew out of _my_ selection of certain kinds of people. Obviously, other judges are needed. So far, one man has selected perhaps two dozen people whom he liked or admired very much and thought were wonderful people and then tried to figure them out and found that he was able to describe a syndrome--the kind of pattern that seemed to fit all of them. These were people only from Western cultures, people selected with all kinds of built-in biases. Unreliable as it is, that was the only operational definition of self-actualizing people as I described them in my first publication on the subject. . . .

The people I selected for my investigation were older people, people who had lived must of their lives out and were visibly successful. We do not yet know about the applicability of the findings to young people. We do not know what self-actualization means in other cultures, although studies of self-actualization in China and in India are now in process. We do not know what the findings of these new studies will be, but of one

*From Abraham H. Maslow, "Self-Actualization and Beyond" in Challenges of Humanistic Psychology, ed. by James F. T. Bugental. Copyright (c) 1967, McGraw-Hill. Used with the permission of McGraw-Hill Book Company.

thing I have no doubt: When you select out for careful study very fine and healthy people, strong people, creative people, saintly people, sagacious people--in fact, exactly the kind of people that I picked out--then you get a different view of mankind. You are asking how tall can people grow, what can a human being become? These are the Olympic gold-medal winners--the best we have. The fact that somebody can run 100 yards in less than ten seconds means that potentially any baby that is born into the world is, in theory, capable of doing so too. In that sense, any baby that is born into the world can in principle reach the heights that actually exist and can be described. . . .

A Study of Psychological Health*

Subjects and Methods

The subjects were selected from among personal acquaintances and friends, and from among public and historical figures. In addition, in a first research with young people, three thousand college students were screened, but yielded only one immediately usable subject and a dozen or two possible future subjects ("growing well").

I had to conclude that self-actualization of the sort I had found in my older subjects perhaps was not possible in our society for young, developing people. . .

The first clinical definition, on the basis of which subjects were finally chosen or rejected, had a positive as well as a merely negative side. The negative criterion was an absence of neurosis, psychopathic personality, psychosis, or strong tendencies in these directions. Possibly psychosomatic illness called forth closer scrutiny and screening. Wherever possible, Rorschach tests were given, but turned out to be far more useful in revealing concealed psychopathology than in selecting healthy people. The positive criterion for selection was positive evidence of self-actualization (SA), as yet a difficult syndrome to describe accurately. For the purposes of this discussion, it may be loosely described as the full use and exploitation of talents, capacities, potentialities, etc. Such people seem to be fulfilling themselves and to be doing the best that they are capable of doing, reminding us of Nietzsche's exhortation, "Become what thou art!" They are people who have developed or are developing to the full stature of which they are capable. These potentialities may be either idiosyncratic or species-wide.

This criterion implies also gratification, past or present, of the basic needs for safety, belongingness, love, respect, and self-respect, and of the cognitive needs for knowledge and for understanding, or in a few cases,

*Abridgement of "Self-Actualizing People" from Motivation and Personality, 2nd Edition by Abraham H. Maslow. Copyright (c) 1970 by Abraham H. Maslow. Reprinted by permission of Harper and Row, Publishers, Inc.

conquest of these needs. This is to say that all subjects felt safe and unanxious, accepted, loved and loving, respect-worthy and respected, and that they had worked out their philosophical, religious, or axiological bearings. It is still an open question as to whether this basic gratification is a sufficient or only a prerequisite condition of self-actualization. . . .

Early in this study, it was found that folk usage was so unrealistically demanding that no living human being could possibly fit the definition. We had to stop excluding a possible subject on the basis of single foibles, mistakes, or foolishness; or to put it in another way, we could not use perfection as a basis for selection, since no subject was perfect. . . .

Gathering and Presentation of the Data

Data here consist not so much in the usual gathering of specific and discrete facts as in the slow development of a global or holistic impression of the sort that we form of our friends and acquaintances. It was rarely possible to set up a situation, to ask pointed questions, or to do any testing with my older subjects (although this was possible and was done with younger subjects). Contacts were fortuitous and of the ordinary social sort. Friends and relatives were questioned where this was possible.

Because of this and also because of the small number of subjects as well as the incompleteness of the data for many subjects, any quantitative presentation is impossible: only composite impressions can be offered for whatever they may be worth.

The holistic analysis of these total impressions yields, as the most important and useful whole characteristics of self-actualizing people for further clinical and experimental study, the following:

More Efficient Perception of Reality and More Comfortable Relations With It

The first form in which this capacity was noticed was as an unusual ability to detect the spurious, the fake, and the dishonest in personality, and in general to judge people correctly and efficiently. In an informal experiment with a group of college students, a clear tendency was discerned for the more secure (the more healthy) to judge their professors more accurately than did the less secure students. . . .

As the study progressed, it slowly became apparent that this efficiency extended to many other areas of life--indeed all areas that were observed. In art and music, in things of the intellect, in scientific matters, in politics and public affairs, they seemed as a group to be able to see concealed or confused realities more swiftly and more correctly than others. Thus an informal survey indicated that their predictions of the future from whatever facts were in hand at the time seemed to be more often correct, because less based upon wish, desire, anxiety, fear, or upon generalized, character-determined optimism or pessimism. . . . It was found that self-actualizing people distinguished far more easily than most the fresh, concrete, and idiographic from the generic, abstract, and rubricized. The consequence is that they live more in the real world of nature than in the man-made mass of concepts, abstractions, expectations, beliefs, and stereotypes that most people confuse with the world. They are therefore far more apt to perceive what is there rather than their own wishes, hopes, fears, anxieties, their own theories and beliefs, or those of their cultural group. "The innocent eye," Herbert Read has very effectively called it.

The relationship with the unknown seems to be of exceptional promise as another bridge between academic and clinical psychology. Our healthy subjects are generally unthreatened and unfrightened by the unknown, being therein quite different from average men. They accept it, are comfortable with it, and, often are even _more_ attracted by it than by the known. They not only tolerate the ambiguous and unstructured; they like it. Quite characteristic is Einstein's statement, "The most beautiful thing we can experience is the mysterious. It is the source of all art and science." . . . .

Acceptance (Self, Others, Nature)

A good many personal qualities that can be perceived on the surface and that seem at first to be various and unconnected may be understood as manifestations or derivatives of a more fundamental single attitude, namely, of a relative lack of overriding guilt, of crippling shame, and of extreme or severe anxiety. This is in direct contrast with the neurotic person who in every instance may be described as crippled by guilt and/or shame and/or anxiety. Even the normal member of our culture feels unnecessarily guilty or ashamed about too many things and has anxiety in too many unnecessary situations. Our healthy individuals find it possible to accept themselves and their own nature without chagrin or complaint or for that matter, even without thinking about the matter very much.

They can accept their own human nature in the stoic style, with all its shortcomings, with all its discrepancies from the ideal image without feeling real concern. It would convey the wrong impression to say that they are self-satisfied. What we must say rather is that they can take the frailties and sins, weaknesses, and evils of human nature in the same unquestioning spirit with which one accepts the characteristics of nature. One does not complain about water because it is wet, or about rocks because they are hard, or about trees because they are green. As the child looks out upon the world with wide, uncritical, undemanding, innocent eyes, simply noting and observing what is the case, without either arguing the matter or demanding that it be otherwise, so does the self-actualizing person tend to look upon human nature in himself and in others. This is of course not the same as resignation in the eastern sense, but resignation too can be observed in our subjects, especially in the face of illness and death.

Be it observed that this amounts to saying in another form what we have already described; namely, that the self-actualized person sees reality more clearly: our subjects see human nature as it is and not as they would prefer it to be. Their eyes see what is before them without being strained through spectacles of various sorts to distort or shape or color the reality.

The first and most obvious level of acceptance is at the socalled animal level. Those self-actualizing people tend to be good animals, hearty in their appetites and enjoying themselves without regret or shame or apology. They seem to have a uniformly good appetite for food; they seem to sleep well; they seem to enjoy their sexual lives without unnecessary inhibition and so on for all the relatively physiological impulses. They are able to accept themselves not only on these low levels, but at all levels as well; e.g., love, safety, belongingness, honor, self-respect. All of these are accepted without question as worth while, simply because these people are inclined to accept the work of nature rather than to argue with her for not having constructed things to a different pattern. This shows itself in a relative lack of the disgusts and aversions seen in average people and especially in neurotics, e.g., food annoyances, disgust with body products, body odors, and body functions.

Closely related to self-acceptance and to acceptance of others is (1) their lack of defensiveness, protective coloration, or pose, and (2) their distaste for such artificialities in others. Cant, guile, hypocrisy, front, face, playing a game, trying to impress in conventional ways: these are all absent in themselves to an unusual degree. Since they can live comfortably even with their own shortcomings, these finally come to be perceived, especially in later life, as not shortcomings at all, but simply as neutral personal characteristics. . . .

What healthy people do feel guilty about (or ashamed, anxious, sad, or regretful) are (1) improvable shortcomings, e.g., laziness, thoughtlessness, loss of temper, hurting others; (2) stubborn remnants of psychological ill health, e.g., prejudice, jealousy, envy; (3) habits, which, though relatively independent of character structure, may yet be very strong, or (4) shortcomings of the species or of the culture or of the group with which they have identified. The general formula seems to be that healthy people will feel bad about discrepancies between what is and what might very well be or ought to be.

Spontaneity; Simplicity; Naturalness

Self-actualizing people can all be described as relatively spontaneous in behavior and far more spontaneous than that in their inner life, thoughts, impulses, etc. Their behavior is marked by simplicity and naturalness, and by lack of artificiality or straining for effect. This does not necessarily mean consistently unconventional behavior. If we were to take an actual count of the number of times that the self-actualizing person behaved in an unconventional manner the tally would not be high. His unconventionality is not superficial but essential or internal. It is his impulses, thought, consciousness that are so unusually unconventional, spontaneous, and natural. Apparently recognizing that the world of people in which he lives could not understand or accept this, and since he has no wish to hurt them or to fight with them over every triviality, he will go through the ceremonies and rituals of convention with a good-humored shrug and with the best possible grace. Thus I have seen a man accept an honor he laughed at and even despised in private, rather than make an issue of it and hurt the people who thought they were pleasing him.

That this conventionality is a cloak that rests very lightly upon his shoulders and is easily cast aside can be seen from the fact that the self-actualizing person infrequently allows convention to hamper him or inhibit him from doing anything that he considers very important or basic. It is at such moments that his essential lack of conventionality appears. . . .

This same inner attitude can also be seen in those moments when the person becomes keenly absorbed in something that is close to one of his main interests. He can then be seen quite casually to drop off all sorts of rules of behavior to which at other times he conforms; it is as if he has to make a conscious effort to be conventional; as if he were conventional voluntarily and by design.

Finally, this external habit of behavior can be voluntarily dropped when in the company of people who do not demand or expect routine behavior. That this relative control of behavior is felt as something of a burden is seen by our subjects' preference for such company as allows them to be more free, natural, and spontaneous, and that relieves them of what they find sometimes to be effortful conduct.

One consequence or correlate of this characteristic is that these people have codes of ethics that are relatively autonomous and individual rather than conventional. The unthinking observer might sometimes believe them to be unethical, since they can break down not only conventions but laws when the situation seems to demand it. But the very opposite is the case. They are the most ethical of people even though their ethics are not necessarily the same as those of the people around them. . . .

(A) most profound difference between self-actualizing people and others (was discovered;) namely, that the motivational life of self-actualizing people is not only quantitatively different but also qualitatively different from that of ordinary people. It seems probable that we must construct a profoundly different psychology of motivation for self-actualizing people, e.g., meta-motivation or growth motivation, rather than deficiency motivation. Perhaps it will be useful to make a distinction between living and preparing to live. Perhaps the ordinary concept of motivation should apply only to nonself-actualizers. Our subjects no longer strive in the ordinary sense, but rather develop. They attempt to grow to perfection and to develop more and more fully in their own style. The motivation of ordinary men is a striving for the basic need gratifications that they lack. But self-actualizing people in fact lack none of these gratifications; and yet they have impulses. They work, they try, and they are ambitious, even though in an unusual sense. For them motivation is just character growth, character expression, maturation, and development; in a word self-actualization. Could these self-actualizing people be more human, more revealing of the original nature of the species, closer to the species type in the taxonomical sense? Ought a biological species to be judged by its crippled, warped, only partially developed specimens, or by examples that have been overdomesticated, caged, and trained?

Problem Centering

Our subjects are in general strongly focused on problems outside themselves. In current terminology they are problem centered rather than ego centered. They generally are not problems for themselves and are not generally much concerned about themselves; e.g., as contrasted with the ordinary introspectiveness that one finds in insecure people. These individuals customarily have some mission in life, some task to fulfill, some problem outside themselves which enlists much of their energies.

This is not necessarily a task that they would prefer or choose for themselves; it may be a task that they feel is their responsibility, duty, or obligation. This is why we use the phrase "a task that they must do" rather than the phrase "a task that they want to do." In general these tasks are nonpersonal or unselfish, concerned rather with the good of mankind in general, or of a nation in general, or of a few individuals in the subject's family.

With a few exceptions we can say that our subjects are ordinarily concerned with basic issues and eternal questions of the type that we have learned to call philosophical or ethical. Such people live customarily in the widest possible frame of reference. They seem never to get so close to the trees that they fail to see the forest. They work within a framework of values that are broad and not petty, universal and not local, and in terms of a century rather than the moment. In a word, these people are all in one sense or another philosophers, however homely.

Of course, such an attitude carries with it dozens of implications for every area of daily living. For instance, one of the main presenting symptoms orginally worked with (bigness, lack of smallness, triviality, or pettiness) can be subsumed under this more general heading. This impression of being above small things, of having a larger horizon, a wider breadth of vision, of living in the widest frame of reference, sub specie aeternitatis, is of the utmost social and interpersonal importance; it seems to impart a certain serenity and lack of worry over immediate concerns that make life easier not only for themselves but for all who are associated with them.

The Quality of Detachment; The Need for Privacy

For all my subjects it is true that they can be solitary without harm to themselves and without discomfort. Furthermore, it is true for almost all that they positively like solitude and privacy to a definitely greater degree than the average person.

It is often possible for them to remain above the battle, to remain unruffled, undisturbed by that which produces turmoil in others. They find it easy to be aloof, reserved, and also calm and serene; thus it becomes possible for them to take personal misfortunes without reacting violently as the ordinary person does. They seem to be able to retain their dignity even in undignified surroundings and situations. Perhaps this comes in part from their tendency to stick by their own interpretation of a situation rather than to rely upon what other people feel or think about the matter. This reserve may shade over into austerity and remoteness.

This quality of detachment may have some connection with certain other qualities as well. For one thing it is possible to call my subjects more objective (in all senses of that word) than average people. We have seen that they are more problem centered than ego centered. This is true even when the problem concerns themselves, their own wishes, motives, hopes, or aspirations. Consequently, they have the ability to concentrate to a degree not usual for ordinary men. Intense concentration produces as a by-product such phenomena as absent-mindedness, the ability to forget and to be oblivious of outer surroundings. Examples are the ability to sleep soundly, to have undisturbed appetite, to be able to smile and laugh through a period of problems, worry, and responsibility.

In social relations with most people, detachment creates certain troubles and problems. It is easily interpreted by "normal" people as coldness, snobbishness, lack of affection, unfriendliness, or even hostility. . . .

Autonomy; Independence of Culture and Environment; Will; Active Agents

One of the characteristics of self-actualizing people, which to a certain extent crosscuts much of what we have already described, is their relative independence of the physical and social environment. Since they are propelled by growth motivation rather than by deficiency motivation, self-actualizing people are not dependent for their main satisfactions on the real world, or other people or culture or means to ends or, in general, on extrinsic satisfactions. Rather they are dependent for their own development and continued growth on their own potentialities and latent resources. Just as the tree needs sunshine and water and food, so do most people need love, safety, and the other basic need gratifications that can come only from without. But once these external satisfiers are obtained, once these inner deficiencies are satiated by outside satisfiers, the true problem of individual human development begins, e.g., self-actualization.

This independence of environment means a relative stability in the face of hard knocks, blows, deprivations, frustrations, and the like. These people can maintain a relative serenity in the midst of circumstances that would drive other people to suicide; they have also been described as "self-contained."

Deficiency-motivated people must have other people available, since most of their main need gratifications (love, safety, respect, prestige, belongingness) can come only from other human beings. But growth-motivated people may actually be hampered by others. The determinants of satisfaction and of the good life are for them now inner-individual and not social. They have become strong enough to be independent of the good opinion of other people, or even of their affection. The honors, the status, the rewards, the popularity, the prestige, and the love they can bestow must have become less important than self-development and inner growth. We must remember that the best technique we know, even though not the only one, for getting to this point of relative independence from love and respect, is to have been given plenty of this very same love and respect in the past.

Continued Freshness of Appreciation

Self-actualizing people have the wonderful capacity to appreciate again and again, freshly and naively, the basic goods of life, with awe, pleasure, wonder, and even ecstasy, however stale these experiences may have become to others--what C. Wilson has called "newness". Thus for such a person, any sunset may be as beautiful as the first one, any flower may be of breath-taking loveliness, even after he has seen a million flowers. The thousandth baby he sees is just as miraculous a product as the first one he saw. He remains as convinced of his luck in marriage thirty years after his marriage and is as surprised by his wife's beauty when she is sixty as he was forty years before. For such people, even the casual workaday, moment-to-moment business of living can be thrilling, exciting, and ecstatic. These intense feelings do not come all the time; they come occasionally rather than usually, but at the most unexpected moments. The person may cross the river on the ferry ten times and at the eleventh crossing have a strong recurrence of the same feelings, reaction of beauty, and excitement as when he rode the ferry for the first time.

There are some differences in choice of beautiful objects. Some subjects go primarily to nature. For others it is primarily children, and for a few subjects it has been primarily great music; but it may certainly be said that they derive ecstasy, inspiration, and strength from the basic experiences of life. No one of them, for instance, will get this same sort of reaction from going to a night club or getting a lot of money or having a good time at a party.

Perhaps one special experience may be added. For several of my subjects the sexual pleasures and particularly the orgasm provided, not passing pleasure alone, but some kind of basic strengthening and revivifying that some people derive from music or nature. I shall say more about this in the section on the mystic experience.

It is probable that this acute richness of subjective experience is an aspect of closeness of relationship to the concrete and fresh, per se reality discussed above. Perhaps what we call staleness in experience is a consequence of rubricizing or ticketing off a rich perception into one or another category or rubric as it proves to be no longer advantageous, or useful, or threatening or otherwise ego involved. . . .

The Mystic Experience; The Peak Experience

Those subjective expressions that have been called the mystic experience and described so well by William James are a fairly common experience for our subjects though not for all. The strong emotions described in the previous section sometimes get strong enough, chaotic, and widespread enough to be called mystic experiences. My interest and attention in this subject was first enlisted by several of my subjects who described their sexual orgasms in vaguely familiar terms which later I remembered had been used by various writers to describe what they called the mystic experience. There were the same feelings of limitless horizons opening up to the vision, the feeling of being simultaneously more powerful and also more helpless than one ever was before, the feeling of great ecstasy and wonder and awe, the loss of placing in time and space with, finally, the conviction that something extremely important and valuable had happened, so that the subject is to some extent transformed and strengthened even in his daily life by such experiences.

It is quite important to dissociate this experience from any theological or supernatural reference, even though for thousands of years they have been linked. Because this experience is a natural experience, well within the jurisdiction of science, I call it the peak experience.

We may also learn from our subjects that such experiences can occur in a lesser degree of intensity. The theological literature has generally assumed an absolute, qualitative difference between the mystic experience and all others. As soon as it is divorced from supernatural reference and studied as a natural phenomenon, it becomes possible to place the mystic experience on a quantitative continuum from intense to mild. We discover then that the mild mystic experience occurs in many, perhaps even most individuals, and that in the favored individual it occurs often, perhaps even daily. . . .

Gemeinschaftsgefühl

This word, invented by Alfred Adler, is the only one available that describes well the flavor of the feelings for mankind expressed by self-actualizing subjects. They have for human beings in general a deep feeling of identification, sympathy, and affection in spite of the occasional anger, impatience, or disgust described below. Because of this they have a genuine desire to help the human race. It is as if they were all members of a single family. One's feelings toward his brothers would be on the whole affectionate, even if these brothers were foolish, weak, or even if they were sometimes nasty. They would still be more easily forgiven than strangers. . . .

Interpersonal Relations

Self-actualizing people have deeper and more profound interpersonal relations than any other adults (although not necessarily deeper than those of children). They are capable of more fusion, greater love, more perfect identification, more obliteration of the ego boundaries than other people would consider possible. There are, however, certain special characteristics of these relationships. In the first place, it is my observation that the other members of these relationships are likely to be healthier and closer to self-actualization than the average, often much closer. There is high selectiveness here, considering the small proportion of such people in the general population.

One consequence of this phenomenon and of certain others as well is that self-actualizing people have these especially deep ties with rather few individuals. Their circle of friends is rather small. The ones that they love profoundly are few in number. Partly this is for the reason that being very close to someone in this self-actualizing style seems to require a good deal of time. Devotion is not a matter of a moment. One subject expressed it like this: "I haven't got time for many friends. Nobody has, that is, if they are to be real friends.". . . .

All the subjects for whom I have data show in common another characteristic that is appropriate to mention here, namely, that they attract at least some admirers, friends or even disciples or worshippers. The relation between the individual and his train of admirers is apt to be rather one-sided. The admirers are apt to demand more than our individual is willing to give. And furthermore, these devotions can be rather embarrassing, distressing, and even distasteful to the self-actualizing person, since they often go beyond ordinary bounds. The usual picture is of our subject being kind and pleasant when forced into these relationships, but ordinarily trying to avoid them as gracefully as possible.

The Democratic Character Structure

All my subjects without exception may be said to be democratic people in the deepest possible sense. . . . They can be and are friendly with anyone of suitable character regardless of class, education, political belief, race, or color. As a matter of fact it often seems as if they are not even aware of these differences, which are for the average person so obvious and so important.

They have not only this most obvious quality but their democratic feeling goes deeper as well. For instance they find it possible to learn from anybody who has something to teach them--no matter what other characteristics he may have. In such a learning relationship they do not try to maintain any outward dignity or to maintain status or age prestige or the like. It should even be said that my subjects share a quality that could be called humility of a certain type. They are all quite well aware of how little they know in comparison with what <u>could</u> be known and what <u>is</u> known by others. Because of this it is possible for them without pose to be honestly respectful and even humble before people who can teach them something that they do not know or who have a skill they do not possess. They give this honest respect to a carpenter who is a good carpenter; or for that matter to anybody who is a master of his own tools or his own craft.

The careful distinction must be made between this democratic feeling and a lack of discrimination in taste, of an undiscriminating equalizing of any one human being with any other. These individuals, themselves elite, select for their friends elite, but this is an elite of character, capacity, and talent, rather than of birth, race, blood, name, family, age, youth, fame, or power.

Most profound, but also most vague is the hard-to-get-at-tendency to give a certain quantum of respect to <u>any</u> human being just because he is a human individual; our subjects seem not to wish to go beyond a certain minimum point, even with scoundrels, of demeaning, of derogating, of robbing of dignity. And yet this goes along with their strong sense of right and wrong, of good and evil. They are <u>more</u> likely rather than less likely to counterattack against evil men and evil behavior. They are far less ambivalent, confused or weak-willed about their own anger than average men are.

Discrimination Between Good and Evil

I have found none of my subjects to be chronically unsure about the difference between right and wrong in his actual living. Whether or not they could verbalize the matter, they rarely showed in their day-to-day living the chaos, the confusion, the inconsistency, or the conflict that are so common in the average person's ethical dealings. This may be phrased also in the following terms: these individuals are strongly ethical, they have definite moral standards, they do right and do not do wrong. Needless to say, their notions of right and wrong and of good and evil are often not the conventional ones. . . .

Philosophical, Unhostile Sense of Humor

One very early finding that was quite easy to make, because it was common to all my subjects, was that their sense of humor is not of the ordinary type. They do not consider funny what the average man considers to be funny. Thus they do not laugh at hostile humor (making people laugh by hurting someone) or superiority humor (laughing at someone else's inferiority) or authority-rebellion humor (the unfunny, Oedipal, or smutty joke). Characteristically what they consider humor is more closely allied to philosophy than to anything else. It may also be called the humor of the real because it consists in large part in poking fun at human beings in general when they are foolish, or forget their place in the universe, or try to be big when they are actually small. This can take the form of poking fun at themselves, but this is not done in any masochistic or clownlike way. Lincoln's humor can serve as a suitable example. . . .

Creativeness

This is a universal characteristic of all the people studied or observed. There is no exception. Each one shows in one way or another a special kind of creativeness or originality or inventiveness that has certain peculiar characteristics. . . . The creativeness of the self-actualized man seems . . . to be kin to the naive and universal creativeness of unspoiled children. It seems to be more a fundamental characteristic of common human nature--a potentiality given to all human beings at birth. Most human beings lose this as they become enculturated, but some few individuals seem either to retain this fresh and naive, direct way of looking at life, or if they have lost it, as most people do, they later in life recover it. Santayana called this the "second naivete," a very good name for it.

139

This creativeness appears in some of our subjects not in the usual forms of writing books, composing music, or producing artistic objects, but rather may be much more humble. It is as if this special type of creativeness, being an expression of healthy personality, is projected out upon the world or touches whatever activity the person is engaged in. In this sense there can be creative shoemakers or carpenters or clerks. Whatever one does can be done with a certain attitude, a certain spirit that arises out of the nature of the character of the person performing the act. One can even <u>see</u> creatively as the child does.

This quality is differentiated out here for the sake of discussion, as if it were something separate from the characteristics that precede it and follow it, but this is not actually the case. Perhaps when we speak of creativeness here we are simply describing from another point of view, namely, from the point of view of consequences, what we have described above as a greater freshness, penetration, and efficiency of perception. These people seem to see the true and the real more easily. It is because of this that they seem to other more limited men creative.

Furthermore, as we have seen, these individuals are less inhibited, less constricted, less bound, in a word, less enculturated. In more positive terms, they are more spontaneous, more natural, more human. This too would have as one of its consequences what would seem to other people to be creativeness. If we assume, as we may from our study of children, that all people were once spontaneous, and perhaps in their deepest roots still are, but that these people have in addition to their deep spontaneity a superficial but powerful set of inhibitions, then this spontaneity must be checked so as not to appear very often. If there were no choking-off forces, we might expect that every human being would show this special type of creativeness. . . .

The Imperfections of Self-Actualizing People

. . . Our subjects show many of the lesser human failings. They too are equipped with silly, wasteful, or thoughtless habits. They can be boring, stubborn, irritating. They are by no means free from a rather superficial vanity, pride, partiality to their own productions, family, friends, and children. Temper outbursts are not rare.

Our subjects are occasionally capable of an extraordinary and unexpected ruthlessness. It must be remembered that they are very strong people. This makes it possible for them to display a surgical coldness when this is called for, beyond the power of the average man. The man who found that a long-trusted acquaintance was dishonest cut himself off from this friendship sharply and abruptly and without any observable pangs whatsoever. Another woman who was married to someone she did not love, when she decided on divorce, did it with a decisiveness that looked almost like ruthlessness. Some of them recover

140

so quickly from the death of people close to them as to seem heartless. . . .

We may mention one more example that arises primarily from the absorption of our subjects in an impersonal world. In their concentration, in their fascinated interest, in their intense concentration on some phenomenon or question, they may become absent-minded or humorless and forget their ordinary social politeness. In such circumstances, they are apt to show themselves more clearly as essentially not interested in chatting, gay conversation, party-going, or the like, they may use language or behavior that may be very distressing, shocking, insulting, or hurtful to others. Other undesirable (at least from the point of view of others) consequences of detachment have been listed above.

Even their kindness can lead them into mistakes, e.g., marrying out of pity, getting too closely involved with neurotics, bores, unhappy people, and then being sorry for it, allowing scoundrels to impose on them for a while, giving more than they should so that occasionally they encourage parasites and psychopaths, etc.

Finally, it has already been pointed out that these people are not free of guilt, anxiety, sadness, self-castigation, internal strife, and conflict. The fact that these arise out of nonneurotic sources is of little consequence to most people today (even to most psychologists) who are therefore apt to think them unhealthy for this reason.

What this has taught me I think all of us had better learn. There are no perfect human beings! Persons can be found who are good, very good indeed, in fact, great. There do in fact exist creators, seers, sages, saints, shakers, and movers. This can certainly give us hope for the future of the species even if they are uncommon and do not come by the dozen. And yet these very same people can at times be boring, irritating, petulant, selfish, angry, or depressed. To avoid disillusionment with human nature, we must first give up our illusions about it.

CRITIQUE

Focussing especially upon the topic of morality, the British philosopher Hastings Rashdall (1858-1924) subjects self-realization theories to critical analysis. Rashdall distinguishes several interpretations of the doctrine that "Self-realization is the end of life," and refutes each in turn. In a trivial sense, I need not "realize" myself because I already exist as a person. But if I understand self-realization theories to call for the development of potentials that I have not yet realized, then which of my potentials shall I develop? For in everything I do, however trivial or wrong, I am in some respect "realizing my capacities." Most critically: I have the potential to be either a morally admirable or a morally criminal person. The doctrine of self-realization is not helpful here, says Rashdall, for it does not distinguish between good and bad forms of self-realization.

If the ideal of self-realization means realizing all of my capacities, then it sets an impossible task. For realization of some potentials rules out others; "There can be no self-realization without self-sacrifice." We must choose some paths of development over others; and the doctrine of self-realization provides no help in such choices. Finally, if the doctrine of self-realization is interpreted to require that we develop our "highest capacities by the sacrifice of the lower," it is so general as to be of little or no value.

Maslow's study of self-actualizing persons receives a methodological criticism from the prominant contemporary psychologist, Brewster Smith (1919-   ). Smith states that Maslow's selection of subjects for his study is not based upon clearly objective citeria, but rather reflects Maslow's own value biases. "In the inherent nature of the case, the dice are loaded toward Maslow's own values. I like them, but that is beside the point." Thus the self-actualizing syndrome as described by Maslow cannot form the basis for a scientific treatment of values. Smith also criticizes Maslow's notion that certain potentialities for self-actualization are "uniquely predetermined" in humans. Human potentials are indeterminate; "the young person has an extremely broad range of multiple potentialities." Echoing Rashdall's criticism, Smith suggests that "Vice and evil are as much in the range of human potentiality. . .as virtue."

SELF-REALIZATION IDEALS ARE UNHELPFUL*

by Hastings Rashdall

I shall here . . . confine myself to the purely ethical aspect of this fascinating formula--'Self-realization is the end of life.'

In order to subject the doctrine to any profitable criticism, it seems necessary to attempt the by no means easy task of distinguishing the various possible senses in which this watchword seems to be used by its devotees. The formula would probably have proved less attractive, had these various senses been distinguished by those to whom it presents itself as a 'short and easy way' out of all ethical perplexities.

(1) Firstly, then, we may suppose that the upholder of self-realization means exactly what he says. If he does, it seems easy to show that what he is committing himself to is mere self-contradictory nonsense. To realize means to make real. You cannot make real what is real already, and the self must certainly be regarded as real before we are invited to set about realizing it. . . .

(2) But of course it will be said that what is actually meant by self-realization is the realization of some potentiality or capacity of the self which is at present unrealized. In this sense no doubt it is true enough that Morality must consist in some kind of self-realization. But to say so is to say something 'generally admitted indeed but obscure' . . . as Aristotle would have put it. In this sense the formula gives us just no information at all. For whatever you do or abstain from doing, if you only sit still or go to sleep, you must still be realizing some one of your capacities: since nobody can by any possibility do anything which he was not first capable of doing. Morality is self-realization beyond a doubt, but then so is immorality. The precious formula leaves out the whole differentia of Morality; and it is a differentia presumably which we are in search of when we ask, 'What is Morality?' and are solemnly told, 'It is doing or being something which you are capable of doing or being.'

(3) It may be maintained that Morality is the realization of all the capacities of human nature. But this is impossible, since one capacity can only be realized by the non-realization or sacrifice of some other capacity. There can be no self-realization without self-sacrifice. The good man and the bad alike realize one element or capacity of their nature, and sacrifice another. The whole question is which capacity is to be realized and which is to be sacrified. And as to this our formula gives us just no information.

*From The Theory of Good and Evil, Second Edition, Vol. II (London: Oxford University Press, 1907, 1924).

(4)   Or more vaguely self-realization may be interpreted to mean an equal, all-round development of one's whole nature--physical, intellectual, emotional. To such a view I should object that, interpreted strictly and literally, it is just as impracticable as the last.   It is impossible for the most gifted person to become a first-rate Musician without much less completely realizing any capacity he has of becoming a first-rate Painter. It is impossible to become really learned in one subject without remaining ignorant of many others: impossible to develop one's athletic capacities to the full without starving and stunting the intellect, impossible (as a simple matter of Physiology) to carry to its highest point the cultivation of one's intellectual faculties without some sacrifice of physical efficiency. There is a similar collision between the demands of intellectual cultivation and those of practical work. . . . Up to a certain point it is no doubt desirable that a man should endeavour to develop different sides of his nature: but that point is soon reached. Beyond that point there must come the inevitable sacrifice--of body to mind or of mind to body, of learning or speculative insight to practical efficiency or of practical efficiency to learning or insight. . .

And there is a more formidable objection to come. If the ideal of self-realization is to be logically carried out, it must involve the cultivation of a man's capacity for what vulgar prejudice calls Immorality as well as of his capacity for Morality. It is quite arbitrary to exclude certain kinds of activity as 'bad,' because what we are in search of was some definition of the good in conduct, and we were told that it was the development of all his capacities. . . .

(5)   One possible interpretation of our formula remains.   Self-realization may mean the realization of a man's highest capacities by the sacrifice of the lower. No doubt, in a sense every school of Moral Philosophy which allows of the distinction between a 'higher' and a 'lower' at all would admit that Morality does mean the sacrifice of the lower to the higher--though it might be objected that this ideal, taken literally, is too ascetic: the lower capacities of human nautre have a certain value: they ought to be realized to a certain extent--to be subordinated, not 'sacrificed,' except in so far as their realization is inconsistent with that of the higher. But then there is nothing of all this in the word 'self-realization.'   And even with the gloss that 'self-realization' means realization of the 'true' or 'higher' self, it tell us just nothing at all about the question what this true self-realization is. In fact the formula which is presented to us as the key to the ethical problem of the end of life, turns out on examination to mean merely 'The end of life is the end of life.'

FLAWS IN MASLOW'S STUDY*

by Brewster Smith

The crucial flaw, one that I noted in 1959. . . has to do with the boot-straps operation by which (Maslow) selected his "sample" of self-actualizing people. In effect, Maslow eliminated people with gross pathology--the Dostoyevskis and Van Goghs--and selected people for whom, after close scrutiny, he had the highest admiration as human specimens. His empirical definition of psychological health or self-actualization thus rests, at root, on his own implicit values that underlie this global judgment. The array of characteristics that he reports must then be regarded not as an empirical description of the fully human (the value-laden facts that he claims to have established), but rather as an explication of his implicit conception of the fully human, of his orienting frame of human values. This is still interesting because of our respect for Maslow's discriminations of human quality, but it is not the factual foundation for humanistic values that he claims it to be.

The trouble is apparent when we look at the names of his seven cases of "fairly sure" or "highly probable" public and historical figures: Abe Lincoln in his last years, Thomas Jefferson, Albert Einstein, Eleanor Roosevelt, Jane Addams, William James, and Spinoza. Why not also George Washington in his later years, Casanova in his earlier years, Napoleon, Thomas Edison, or Lenin? All of these could equally be said to be making, in the phrasing of Maslow's criterion statement of self-actualization, "the full use . . . of talents, capacities, potentialities, . . . , to be fulfilling themselves and to be doing the best they were capable of doing, reminding us of Nietzsche's exhortation, 'Become what thou art!'" In the inherent nature of the case, the dice are loaded toward Maslow's own values. I like them, but that is beside the point.

The Problem of Potentialities

The methodological point shades into a theoretical one. How, indeed, are we to understand the "human potentialities" that get actualized? The term is most at home in an Aristotelian, finalistic conception, in which development is conceived as the realization of potentialities that are in some sense uniquely predetermined. As I subsequently suggest, that is not so bad a fit to the biological facts when we are dealing with the adaptive products of long-term evolution (even though most biologists do not regard it as a viable theoretical formulation). Maslow stretches the biological analogy to cover the case of human psychology, as in the following:

*From Brewster Smith, "On Self-Actualization: A Transambivalent Examination of a Focal Theme in Maslow's Psychology," in Journal of Humanistic Psychology," Vol. 13, No. 2 (Spring 1973), pp. 24f. Copyright (c) 1973 by the Association for Humanistic Psychology. Reprinted by permission of Sage Publications, Inc. and Brewster Smith.

> Man demonstrates in his own nature a pressure toward fuller and fuller Being, more and more perfect actualization of his humanness in exactly the same naturalistic, scientific sense (sic) that an acorn may be said to be "pressing toward" being an oak tree, or that a tiger can be observed to "push toward" being tigerish, or a horse toward being equine. . . . the environment does not give him potentialities or capacities; he has them in inchoate or embryonic form, just as he has embryonic arms and legs.

This will hardly do. except for some universals of the human species like language and symbolization, constructiveness, interdependence, and maybe reactive aggression that have an entrenched evolutionary status and probably fit the acorn–oak tree model as well as the plant itself does (which is to ignore the complex interactive processes of epigenesis), the young person has an extremely broad range of multiple potentialities. The course of life, including the choices of the emerging self, excludes some of them, sets limits on others, and elaborates upon still others. Vice and evil are as much in the range of human potentiality, I would argue, as virtue; specialization as much as "well-rounded" development. Our biology cannot be made to carry our ethics as Maslow would have it.

I see that I am resorting here to sheer assertions to counter Maslow's. But the burden of proof is upon him. The kinds of people that he excludes from his self-actualizing sample, its bias toward Maslovian values undermine his case of the distinctive humanness of the particular human potentialities that his sample exemplifies. These are among the attractive possibilities of human existence; its interest, its tragedy, and I think its glory lie in the fact that they are not "built in" but exist as possibilities among a range of very different ones, any of which can be regarded as an actualization of potentiality, though trivially so, when it occurs.

Generally, I think the doctrine of potentiality is more misleading than helpful.

STUDY QUESTIONS FOR CHAPTER IV

Questions for Review:

1. Why do we adopt masks or facades, according to the point of view of this chapter? What does it mean to drop them?

2. What assumptions about human nature are made by the authors in this chapter?

3. What sorts of people form the basis of Rogers' views on the good life?

4. Restate Maslow's hierarchy of needs.

5. What does Rogers mean by "client-centered" therapy?

6. When clients feel that they are unconditionally accepted, how do they usually use that freedom, according to Rogers?

7. What sorts of definitions of the good life are <u>not</u> correct, in Rogers' view?

8. Summarize in your own words the following concepts from Rogers: "openness to experience"; "existential living"; "trust in one's organism."

9. What is the "new perspective on freedom vs. determinism" offered by Rogers?

10. How did Maslow form the sample for his study of self-actualizing persons?

11. Review the main characteristics of self-actualizing people, and formulate each in your own words.

12. What sorts of behaviors promote self-actualization, according to Maslow?

13. Review Rashdall's various formulations of the self-realization ethic, and his refutation of each.

14. What are Brewster Smith's chief objections to Maslow's study? Why does he think the doctrine of potentiality is misleading?

Questions for Reflection:

1. What masks or facades do I use to hide myself from my world? What sort of person am I, underneath my masks?

2. Under what conditions do I feel most myself? Under what conditions do I feel least myself?

3. What feelings in me do I fight off or deny?

4. Do I trust myself? To what degree do I believe that I must suppress myself, out of fear of what I may do if I am spontaneous?

5. To what degree are my needs (as outlined by Maslow) satisfied at the present time?

6. To what degree do I "live existentially"?

7. To what degree do I see in my own life the qualities described by Maslow? Which of those qualities do I feel the greatest need for?

Questions for Discussion:

1. Do you think that the underlying, deepest inclinations of human beings are positive or trustworthy?

2. Is the "fully functioning person" in fact desirable as an ideal?

3. Is the "self-actualizing person" in fact desirable as an ideal?

4. Do the criticisms of Rashdall successfully refute the views of Rogers and Maslow?

5. Do you agree with Smith's critique of Maslow? If Smith's objections are granted, are Maslow's results seriously undermined?

6. Are ideals of becoming human as depicted in this chapter fundamentally opposed to ideals of detachment, as presented in the previous chapter?

SUGGESTIONS FOR FURTHER READING

Abe Arkov, ed., Psychology and Personal Growth, Second edition (Allyn and Bacon, 1980)

Richard P. Dennis and Edwin P. Moldof, eds., Becoming Human, Vols. One and Two (Great Books Foundation, 1977)

Nicholas S. DiCaprio, The Good Life: Models for a Healthy Personality (Prentice-Hall, Spectrum, 1976) Summaries of various psychological theories of a healthy personality.

John Hospers, Human Conduct: Problems in Ethics, Chapter 5 (Harcourt Brace Jovanovich, 1961, 1972) Good discussion of self-realization theories.

Paul Kurtz, ed., The Humanist Alternative: Some Definitions of Humanism (Prometheus, 1973)

Christopher Lasch, The Culture of Narcissism (W. W. Norton, 1979)

David L. Norton, Personal Destinies: A Philosophy of Ethical Individualism (Princeton, 1976) A contemporary philosophical theory of self-realization.

Fredrick S. Perls, M.D., Ph.D., Gestalt Therapy Verbatim (Real People Press and Bantam Books, 1969, 1971).

Carl Rogers, On Becoming a Person (Houghton Mifflin, 1961)

Edwin Schur, The Awareness Trap: Self-Absorption Instead of Social Change (Quadrangle, 1976).

Chapter Five:

Nature

Chapter V: NATURE

Introduction

Come forth into the light of things / Let nature be your teacher," urges the poet Wordsworth.[1]   As humans we are, first and foremost, natural beings of the natural world--one form of life among innumerable others. The world of earth, air, sky and water is our home. Yet we turn away from that home and its rhythms, walling ourselves off in warrens of plastic and concrete, steel and glass--paving the earth, fouling the air and water, submitting ourselves to stresses that violate our own biology. Thereby we become strangers to our natural home and to our organism; we alienate ourselves from our own being. Divorced from our roots, our lives become pathological. The rebreathed air of our hot-house society becomes lifeless and oppressive.   By convention and artifice, by technology and self-indulgence, we transform our disposition toward good health into a proclivity for the artifical and unhealthy. Such conditions render the good life impossible. Living well requires that we loosen the strangle-hold of excessive social constraints, and reawaken to our deeper nature.

The good life is indeed a process of self-actualizing, of growing toward the fullest functioning of one's organism. But such growth is blocked or distorted when we become too preoccupied with human culture, and see the rest of the world as merely raw material for the factory of "civilization."   Becoming ourselves requires that we look beyond that which is peculiarly human, to our affinity with the non-human world.   Aristotle declared that human beings are essentially rational animals.   An anthropocentric egotism prompts us to emphasize our differences from other forms of life as evidence of our superiority, and

151

glorify our rationality at the expense of our animality. Such an attitude encourages us to exploit the rest of nature, and blinds us to our own organic needs: for healthy nutrition, for adequate rest and exercise, for warmth and nurturance, and so on. In contrast, as we identify with nature we become more aware of our natural needs. Our most complete good lies, not in setting ourselves apart, but in coming to understand our unity with the rest of the natural world.

What does it mean to cultivate our affinity with nature? In an extended sense, the word "nature" designates all that exists in space and time and is subject to scientific law. In this sense, the products of human culture--a radio, a bomb, a symphony--are as "natural" as trees or planets. All conform to the "laws of nature" and all may appropriately be the object of scientific inquiry. More specifically, however, the word "nature" is reserved for that which has not been produced or altered by self-conscious human contrivance. Thus a wilderness area represents nature to us, whereas a city street does not; and we see a timber wolf as more "natural" than a poodle.

A related ambiguity is found in the advice to live "naturally" or "in harmony with nature." In the extended sense of the word explained above, we live "naturally" no matter how we conduct our lives. Shooting heroin and sleeping are both events in space and time, subject to natural laws, and thus are equally a part of nature in the extended sense. Yet in the more specific sense, shooting heroin is clearly less natural than sleeping: one who uses heroin not only intervenes deliberately in the course of things, but does so in a way that violates his or her own life-supporting processes, thereby endangering health and well-being.

This example brings to light some underlying assumptions of naturalism as a view of the good life: as human beings, we are not infinitely pliant pieces of clay, to be molded without harm by any desires that we or others may have; nor are we empty vessels, to be filled with whatever content is dictated by our particular culture and upbringing. Rather, from our beginning we are complex organisms, endowed with inherent potentialities for development and growth; when properly nurtured, we manifest inborn imperatives and flourish according to our own developmental logic. In short, we have a nature: an internal configuration of traits and propensities, needs and possibilities, that can be cultivated and expressed in various ways, or thwarted and perverted in others, but that cannot be wholly denied except by destroying ourselves.

Living naturally means, therefore, that we respect our entire human organism, and behave in ways that nurture and cultivate it rather than undermine it and damage it. Instead of reverting to a non-human way of life, living naturally means that we experience our human uniqueness as grounded in a deeper commonality with all being.

Nature and Society

Nor does adopting a naturalistic view of the good life mean that we must separate ourselves from society. We are, as Aristotle and many others have observed, social animals, naturally inclined to live with other humans rather than alone. And among known species, our behavior is less dominated by instinct, and more easily modified by learning and intelligence. Civilization and culture are natural expressions of our humanness, and a naturalistic approach to the good life includes their benefits: security and order, community and mutual support, the enrichment of the mind, opportunity for play and leisure, and many others. But the demands of one's particular culture and setting rarely coincide fully with the natural needs of one's organism. The fit between the social order and our individuality is often uncomfortable and sometimes harmful. Perhaps we are filled with rage at a time when the social setting happens to call for quiescence; perhaps social norms stereotype our gender, forcing us to be "masculine" or "feminine" in ways that suppress the full range of our natural propensities; perhaps we simply want privacy when we must be immersed in crowds, or want companionship when no one is there. Further, the entanglements of society may render our lives so complex and confusing that we lose awareness of who we are. When civilization and culture become agents not for the enhancement of life, but for the confusion of consciousness and the humiliation of the body, when they blind us to all but themselves, their effect upon us is pernicious. At such times, writes Thoreau, "we need the tonic of wildness": we need to remove ourselves for a time from the confusion of the human world, to immerse ourselves in a larger reality that lifts us out of our narrow preoccupations, simplifies our lives, and restores to us a healthier perspective and peace of mind. Such a retreat need not be "escapist" in any negative sense, but rather a way of redressing an imbalance, of recovering our well being by yielding to the healing power of natural beauty.

Natural Beauty and Spirituality

In turning to natural beauty, we discover our own depths: the experience of beauty opens the soul. In the stirrings of our being, we sense a resonance with that which lies around us. Alone in the forest, playing in the ocean, or simply gazing at a bed of flowers--as we awaken to our roots, we feel our separateness melt away, and we slip into a growing sense of our harmony with all things. In open receptivity we become one with the world. Thereby we take on new life: we are renewed and refreshed, and we feel vitality coursing through our veins. Nature has restored us to ourselves again.

Such experiences are often felt as spiritual: through overcoming the limits of one's conventional self, one is lifted to a communion and renewal that breathe light and joy into every cell, reminding us of possibilities we

153

had forgotten. Wordsworth writes

> And I have felt
> A presence that disturbs me with the joy
> Of elevated thoughts; a sense sublime
> Of something far more deeply interfused,
> Whose dwelling is the light of setting suns
> And the round ocean and the living air,
> And the blue sky, and in the mind of man;
> A motion and a spirit, that impels
> All thinking things, all objects of all thought,
> All rolls through all things.[2]

But though naturalists may recognize a spiritual quality in the experience of nature, they are typically less willing to grant a supernatural spirituality that transcends nature: a god beyond this world. The natural world can be seen, heard, felt; its qualities can be experienced directly and known through one's body. Such is not true of the supernatural. To project a supernatural realm and being is to demote the real in favor of an imagined ideal; it is to betray an unwillingness to accept one's humanness, one's mortality and physical nature. Those who have not learned a full appreciation of this life may feel a need for another; and those who insist upon perfection will create for themselves a perfect fantasy. According to naturalism, such impulses are understandable but mistaken. For those who are alive to their own natural being, this world is enough.

Morality and the Good Life

According to a naturalistic view of the good life, morality is not the revelation of a supernatural will, delivered from above, but an outgrowth of human intelligence and need. Like other social animals, we function best within an environment with some degree of mutual trust and cooperation. In order to achieve and maintain such an environment, we must have some agreement regarding how we shall live together: which forms of behavior will be prohibited and which required. Differing moral codes are the responses of various cultures to this common need. Morality is thus an effort to provide the conditions for the good life. Living well is a kind of happiness: not simply happiness as a pleasant state of mind, apart from one's activities, but that happiness which lies in the free-flowing exercise of one's natural functions, capacities and talents--happiness as a flourishing of the entire person.

A naturalistic view of the good life thus affirms that we achieve our highest good through the fullest exercise of our human capacities, and that such flourishing requires both an honoring of our own organic nature, and an appreciation of our affinity with the natural world around us. It invites us to let go of our human conceit and to experience the non-human world with respect and reverence. While affirming the importance of civilization and culture, naturalism cautions against excessive preoccupation with purely human concerns, and urges us to simplify our lives through an appreciation of the larger non-human setting of such concerns: to recover ourselves through immersion in natural beauty, and to return to a deeper awareness of the harmony of all things. The quality of such an experience may be appreciated for itself, and need not be taken as grounds for turning away from nature toward an imagined supernatural realm. Morality needs no supernatural foundation; it may be understood as the human effort to provide the conditions for the fullest possible flourishing of the human organism.

The Selections

The first selection in this chapter is from the Chinese poet Tao Chien (372-427 A.D.). Tao Chien notes a paradox: although he lives among other humans, he is far away from them, in lovely solitude--for "A heart that is distant creates a wilderness round it." In a few deft strokes, he evokes that experience of nature which touches the deepest parts of us.

Whereas Tao Chien lives "in a zone of human habitation," Henry David Thoreau (1817-1862) built his house in the woods apart from other humans. But like Tao Chien, Thoreau uses his experience of nature as a stimulus for wide-ranging musings and reflections, enabling him to live in a world of his own choosing. "Both time and place were changed, and I dwelt nearer to those parts of the universe and to those eras in history which had most attracted me." An astringent social critic, Thoreau used the isolation of Walden Pond to gain perspective upon the political stupidities and social foibles of his day: slavery, militarism, an exaggerated notion of one's material needs, and so on. Physically, Thoreau lived a mile from his nearest neighbor; in thought, however, he was much farther away, in "a withdrawn, but forever new and unprofaned, part of the universe."

Thoreau achieved his ends in large part by simplifying his life and limiting his needs. His experiment illustrates how much a determined and resourceful person may do, at little expense, to bring the conditions of life into conformity with desire. "If you have built castles in the air, your work need not be lost; that is where they should be. Now put the foundations under them."

In the character of Zorba, from Nikos Kazanzakis' novel, Zorba the Greek, we encounter a sharply contrasting form of naturalism. Whereas Tao Chien and Thoreau use their experience of nature to withdraw from society and find liberation in solitude, Zorba is engrossed in both the world of people--their loves and hates, their noble aspirations and their foolish preoccupations--and the non-human world of nature as well. Tao

Chien and Thoreau seek a reflective detachment; Zorba is thoroughly immersed in all of his experience, and powerfully attached to many things in it. He responds with amazement and wonder to a woman, a tree, a glass of wine. In some respects Zorba seems atavistic, a throwback to a more primitive type. "Man is a brute," he declares. Yet he is also a philosopher, in his passionate desire to understand himself and his world. Zorba articulates no "theory" of the good life; but his response to the world serves as a vivid, commanding model, exemplifying a compelling point of view.

NOTES

1. From "The Tables Turned," in The Complete Poetical Works of William Wordsworth, with an Introduction by John Morley (London: Macmillan and Co., LTD., 1888, 1930), p. 85.

2. From "Lines Composed a Few Miles Above Tintern Abbey," Ibid, p. 94.

UNTITLED*

by Tao Chien

I built my hut in a zone of human habitation,
Yet near me there sounds no noise of horse or coach,
Would you know how that is possible?
A heart that is distant creates a wilderness round it.
I pluck chrysanthemums under the eastern hedge,
Then gaze long at the distant summer hills.
The mountain air is fresh at the dusk of day;
The flying birds two by two return.
In these things there lies a deep meaning;
Yet when we would express it, words suddenly fail us.

*From TRANSLATIONS FROM THE CHINESE, translated by Arthur Waley. Copyright 1919 and renewed 1947 by Arthur Waley. Reprinted by permission of Alfred A. Knopf, Inc.

WALDEN*

by Henry David Thoreau

When I wrote the following pages, or rather the bulk of them, I lived alone, in the woods, a mile from any neighbor, in a house which I had built myself, on the shore of Walden Pond, in Concord, Massachusetts, and earned my living by the labor of my hands only. I lived there two years and two months. At present I am a sojourner in civilized life again. . .

When first I took up my abode in the woods, that is, began to spend my nights as well as days there, which, by accident, was on Independence Day, or the Fourth of July, 1845, my house was not finished for winter, but was merely a defence against the rain, without plastering or chimney, the walls being of rough, weather-stained boards, with wide chinks, which made it cool at night. The upright white hewn studs and freshly planed door and window casings gave it a clean and airy look, especially in the morning, when its timbers were saturated with dew, so that I fancied that by noon some sweet gum would exude from them. . . . I found myself suddenly neighbor to the birds; not by having imprisoned one, but having caged myself near them. I was not only nearer to some of those which commonly frequent the garden and the orchard, but to those wilder and more thrilling songsters of the forest which never, or rarely, serenade a villager,--the wood thrush, the veery, the scarlet tanager, the field sparrow, the whip-poor-will, and many others.

I was seated by the shore of a small pond, about a mile and a half south of the village of Concord and somewhat higher than it, in the midst of an extensive wood between that town and Lincoln, and about two miles south of that our only field known to fame, Concord Battle Ground; but I was so low in the woods that the opposite shore, half a mile off, like the rest, covered with wood, was my most distant horizon. For the first week, whenever I looked out on the pond it impressed me like a tarn high up on the side of a mountain, its bottom far above the surface of other lakes, and, as the sun arose, I saw it throwing off its nightly clothing of mist, and here and there, by degrees, its soft ripples or its smooth reflecting surface was revealed, while the mists, like ghosts, were stealthily withdrawing in every direction into the woods, as at the breaking up of some nocturnal conventicle. The very dew seemed to hang upon the trees later into the day than usual, as on the sides of mountains.

This small lake was of most value as a neighbor in the intervals of a gentle rain-storm in August, when, both air and water being perfectly still, but the sky overcast, mid-afternoon had all the serenity of evening, and the wood thrush sang around, and was heard from shore to shore. A lake like this is never smoother than at such a time; and the clear portion of the air above it being shallow and darkened by clouds, the water, full of

*Excerpts from H. D. Thoreau, <u>Walden</u> (London: Walter Scott, 1886). Breaks are indicated by elipses.

158

light and reflections, becomes a lower heaven itself so much the more important. . . .

Though the view from my door was still more contracted, I did not feel crowded or confined in the least. There was pasture enough for my imagination. The low shrub oak plateau to which the opposite shore arose stretched away toward the prairies of the West and the steppes of Tartary, affording ample room for all the roving families of men. "There are none happy in the world but beings who enjoy freely a vast horizon,"-- said Damodara, when his herds required new and larger pastures.

Both place and time were changed, and I dwelt nearer to those parts of the universe and to those eras in history which had most attracted me. Where I lived was as far off as many a region viewed nightly by astronomers. We are wont to imagine rare and delectable places in some remote and more celestial corner of the system, behind the constellation of Cassiopeia's Chair, far from noise and disturbance. I discovered that my house actually had its site in such a withdrawn, but forever new and unprofaned, part of the universe. . . .

Every morning was a cheerful invitation to make my life of equal simplicity, and I may say innocence, with Nature herself. I have been as sincere a worshipper of Aurora as the Greeks. I got up early and bathed in the pond; that was a religious exercise, and one of the best things which I did. They say that characters were engraven on the bathing tub of King Tching-thang to this effect: "Renew thyself completely each day; do it again, and again, and forever again." I can understand that. Morning brings back the heroic ages. I was as much affected by the faint hum of a mosquito making its invisible and unimaginable tour through my apartment at earliest dawn, when I was sitting with door and windows open, as I could be by any trumpet that ever sang of fame. It was Homer's requiem; itself an Iliad and Odyssey in the air, singing its own wrath and wanderings. There was something cosmical about it; a standing advertisement, till forbidden, of the everlasting vigor and fertility of the world. The morning, which is the most memorable season of the day, is the awakening hour. Then there is least somnolence in us; and for an hour, at least, some part of us awakes which slumbers all the rest of the day and night. Little is to be expected of that day, if it can be called a day, to which we are not awakened by our Genius, but by the mechanical nudgings of some servitor, are not awakened by our own newly acquired force and aspirations from within, accompanied by the undulations of celestial music, instead of factory bells, and a fragrance filling the air--to a higher life than we fell asleep from; and thus the darkness bear its fruit, and prove itself to be good, no less than the light. That man who does not believe that each day contains an earlier, more sacred, and auroral hour than he has yet profaned, has despaired of life, and is pursuing a descending and darkening way. After a partial cessation of his sensuous life, the soul of man, or its organs rather, are reinvigorated each day, and his Genius tries again what noble life it can make. All memorable events, I should say, transpire in morning time and in a morning atmosphere. The Vedas say, "All intelligences awake with the morning." Poetry and art, and the fairest and most memorable of the actions of men, date from such an hour. All poets and heroes, like Memnon, are the children of Aurora, and emit their music at sunrise. To him whose elastic and vigorous thought keeps pace with the sun, the day is a perpetual morning. It matters not what the clocks say or the attitudes and labors of men. Morning is when I am awake and there is a dawn in me. Moral reform is the effort to throw off sleep. Why is it that men give so poor an account of their day if they have not been slumbering? They are not such poor calculators. If they had not been overcome with drowsiness, they would have performed something. The millions are awake enough for physical labor; but only one in a million is awake enough for effective intellectual exertion, only one in a hundred millions to a poetic or divine life. To be awake is to be alive. I have never yet met a man who was quite awake. How could I have looked him in the face?

We must learn to reawaken and keep ourselves awake, not by mechanical aids, but by an infinite expectation of the dawn, which does not forsake us in our soundest sleep. I know of no more encouraging fact than the unquestionable ability of man to elevate his life by a conscious endeavor. It is something to be able to paint a particular picture, or to carve a statue, and so to make a few objects beautiful; but it is far more glorious to carve and paint the very atmosphere and medium through which we look, which morally we can do. To affect the quality of the day, that is the highest of arts. Every man is tasked to make his life, even in its details, worthy of the contemplation of his most elevated and critical hour. If we refused, or rather used up, such paltry information as we get, the oracles would distinctly inform us how this might be done.

I went to the woods because I wished to live deliberately, to front only the essential facts of life, and see if I could not learn what it had to teach, and not, when I came to die, discover that I had not lived. I did not wish to live what was not life, living is so dear; nor did I wish to practise resignation, unless it was quite necessary. I wanted to live deep and suck out all the marrow of life, to live so sturdily and Spartan-like as to put to rout all that was not life, to cut a broad swath and shave close, to drive life into a corner, and reduce it to its lowest terms, and, if it proved to be mean, why then to get the whole and genuine meanness of it, and publish its meanness to the world; or if it were sublime, to know it by experience, and be able to give a true account of it in my next excursion. For most men, it appears to me, are in strange uncertainty about it, whether it is of the devil or of God, and have <u>somewhat hastily</u> concluded that it is the chief end of man here to "glorify God and enjoy him forever."

Still we live meanly, like ants; though the fable tells us that we were long ago changed into men; like pygmies we fight with cranes; it is error upon error, and clout upon clout, and our best virtue has for its occasion a superfluous and evitable wretchedness. Our life is frittered away by detail. An honest man has hardly need to count more than his ten fingers, or in extreme cases he may add his ten toes, and lump the rest. Simplicity, simplicity, simplicity! I say, let your affairs be as two or three, and not a hundred or a thousand; instead of a million count half a dozen, and keep your accounts on your thumb-nail. In the midst of this chopping sea of civilized life, such are the clouds and storms and quicksands and thousand-and-one items to be allowed for, that a man has to live, if he would not founder and go to the bottom and not make his port at all, by dead reckoning, and he must be a great calculator indeed who succeeds. Simplify, simplify. Instead of three meals a day, if it be necessary eat but one; instead of a hundred dishes, five; and reduce other things in proportion. . . .

I did not read books the first summer; I hoed beans. Nay, I often did better than this. There were times when I could not afford to sacrifice the bloom of the present moment to any work, whether of the head or hands. I love a broad margin to my life. Sometimes, in a summer morning, having taken my accustomed bath, I sat in my sunny doorway from sunrise till noon, rapt in a revery, amidst the pines and hickories and sumachs, in undisturbed solitude and stillness, while the birds sang around or flitted noiseless through the house, until by the sun falling in at my west window, or the noise of some traveller's wagon on the distant highway, I was reminded of the lapse of time. I grew in those seasons like corn in the night, and they were far better than any work of the hands would have been. They were not time subtracted from my life, but so much over and above my usual allowance. I realized what the Orientals mean by contemplation and the forsaking of works. For the most part, I minded not how the hours went. The day advanced as if to light some work of mine; it was morning, and lo, now it is evening, and nothing memorable is accomplished. Instead of singing like the birds, I silently smiled at my incessant good fortune. As the sparrow had its trill, sitting on the hickory before my door, so had I my chuckle or suppressed warble which he might hear out of my nest. My days were not days of the week, bearing the stamp of any heathen deity, nor were they minced into hours and fretted by the ticking of a clock. . . .

I kept neither dog, cat, cow, pig, nor hens, so that you would have said there was a deficiency of domestic sounds; neither the churn, nor the spinning-wheel, nor even the singing of the kettle, nor the hissing of the urn, nor children crying, to comfort one. An old-fashioned man would have lost his senses or died of ennui before this. Not even rats in the wall, for they were starved out, or rather were never baited in,--only squirrels on the roof and under the floor, a whip-poor-will on the ridge-pole, a blue jay screaming beneath the window, a hare or woodchuck under the house, a screech owl or a cat owl behind it, a flock of wild geese or a laughing loon on the pond, and a fox to bark in the night. Not even a lark or an oriole, those mild plantation birds, ever visited my clearing. No cockerels to crow nor hens to cackle in the yard. No yard! but unfenced nature reaching up to your very sills. A young forest growing up under your windows, and wild sumachs and blackberry vines breaking through into your cellar; sturdy pitch pines rubbing and creaking against the shingles for want of room, their roots reaching quite under the house. Instead of a scuttle or a blind blown off in the gale,--a pine tree snapped off or torn up by the roots behind your house for fuel. Instead of no path to the front-yard gate in the Great Snow,--no gate--no front-yard,--and no path to the civilized world. . . .

This is a delicious evening, when the whole body is one sense, and imbibes delight through every pore. I go and come with a strange liberty in Nature, a part of herself. As I walk along the stony shore of the pond in my shirt-sleeves, though it is cool as well as cloudy and windy, and I see nothing special to attract me, all the elements are unusually congenial to me. The bullfrogs trump to usher in the night, and the note of the whip-poor-will is borne on the rippling wind from over the water. Sympathy with the fluttering alder and poplar leaves almost takes away my breath; yet, like the lake, my serenity is rippled but not ruffled. . . .

There can be no very black melancholy to him who lives in the midst of nature and has his senses still. There was never yet such a storm but it was AEolian music to a healthy and innocent ear. Nothing can rightly compel a simple and brave man to a vulgar sadness. While I enjoy the friendship of the seasons I trust that nothing can make life a burden to me. The gentle rain which waters my beans and keeps me in the house to-day is not drear and melancholy, but good for me too. Though it prevents my hoeing them, it is of far more worth than my hoeing. If it should continue so long as to cause the seeds to rot in the ground and destroy the potatoes in the low lands, it would still be good for the grass on the uplands, and, being good for the grass, it would be good for me. Sometimes, when I compare myself with other men, it seems as if I were more favored by the gods than they, beyond any deserts that I am conscious of; as if I had a warrant and surety at their hands which my fellows have not, and were especially guided and guarded. I do not flatter myself, but if it be possible they flatter me. I have never felt lonesome, or in the least oppressed by a sense of solitude, but once, and that was a few weeks after I came to the woods, when, for an hour, I doubted if the near neighborhood of man was not essential to a serene and healthy life. To be alone was something unpleasant. But I was at the same time conscious of a slight insanity in my mood, and seemed to foresee my recovery. In the midst of a gentle rain while these thoughts prevailed, I was suddenly sensible of such sweet and beneficent society in Nature, in the very pattering of the drops, and in every sound and sight around my house, an infinite and unaccountable friendliness all at once like an atmosphere sustaining me, as made the fancied advantages of human neighborhood insignificant, and I have never thought of them since.

Every little pine needle expanded and swelled with sympathy and befriended me. I was so distinctly made aware of the presence of something kindred to me, even in scenes which we are accustomed to call wild and dreary, and also that the nearest of blood to me and humanest was not a person nor a villager, that I thought no place could ever be strange to me again.--. .

I set out one afternoon to go a-fishing to Fair Haven, through the woods, to eke out my scanty fare of vegetables. . . When at length I had made one cast over the pickerel-weed, standing up to my middle in water, I found myself suddenly in the shadow of a cloud, and the thunder began to rumble with such emphasis that I could do no more than listen to it. The gods must be proud, thought I, with such forked flashes to rout a poor unarmed fisherman. So I made haste for shelter to the nearest hut, which stood half a mile from any road, but so much the nearer to the pond, and had long been uninhabited:--. . . therein, as I found, dwelt now John Field, an Irishman, and his wife, and several children, from the broad-faced boy who assisted his father at his work, and now came running to his side from the bog to escape the rain, to the wrinkled, sibyl-like, cone-headed infant that sat upon its father's knee as in the palaces of nobles, and looked out from its home in the midst of wet and hunger inquisitively upon the stranger, with the privilege of infancy, not knowing but it was the last of a noble line, and the hope and cynosure of the world, instead of John Field's poor starveling brat. There we sat together under that part of the roof which leaked the least, while it showered and thundered without. I had sat there many times of old before the ship was built that floated this family to America. An honest, hard-working, but shiftless man plainly was John Field; and his wife, she too was brave to cook so many successive dinners in the recesses of that lofty stove; with round greasy face and bare breast, still thinking to improve her condition one day; with the never absent mop in one hand, and yet no effects of it visible anywhere. The chickens, which had also taken shelter here from the rain, stalked about the room like members of the family, too humanized, methought, to roast well. They stood and looked in my eye or pecked at my shoe significantly. Meanwhile my host told me his story, how hard he worked "bogging" for a neighboring farmer, turning up a meadow with a spade or bog hoe at the rate of ten dollars an acre and the use of the land with manure for one year, and his little broad-faced son worked cheerfully at his father's side the while, not knowing how poor a bargain the latter had made. I tried to help him with my experience, telling him that he was one of my nearest neighbors, and that I too, who came a-fishing here, and looked like a loafer, was getting my living like himself; that I lived in a tight, light, and clean house, which hardly cost more than the annual rent of such a ruin as his commonly amounts to; and how, if he chose, he might in a month or two built himself a palace of his own; that I did not use tea, nor coffee, nor butter, nor milk, nor fresh meat, and so did not have to work to get them; again, as I did not work hard, I did not have to eat hard, and it cost me but a trifle for my food; but as he began with tea, and

163

coffee, and butter, and milk, and beef, he had to work hard to pay for them, and when he had worked hard he had to eat hard again to repair the waste of his system,--and so it was as broad as it was long, indeed it was broader than it was long, for he was discontented and wasted his life into the bargain; and yet he had rated it as a gain in coming to America, that here you could get tea, and coffee, and meat every day. But the only true America is that country where you are at liberty to pursue such a mode of life as may enable you to do without these, and where the state does not endeavor to compel you to sustain the slavery and war and other superfluous expenses which directly or indirectly result from the use of such things. For I purposely talked to him as if he were a philosopher, or desired to be one. I should be glad if all the meadows on the earth were left in a wild state, if that were the consequence of men's beginning to redeem themselves. A man will not need to study history to find out what is best for his own culture. . . I told him, that as he worked so hard at bogging, he required thick boots and stout clothing, which yet were soon soiled and worn out, but I wore light shoes and thin clothing, which cost not half so much, though he might think that I was dressed like a gentleman (which, however, was not the case), and in an hour or two, without labor, but as a recreation, I could, if I wished, catch as many fish as I should want for two days, or earn enough money to support me a week. If he and his family would live simply, they might all go a-huckleberrying in the summer for their amusement. John heaved a sigh at this, and his wife stared with arms a-kimbo, and both appeared to be wondering if they had capital enough to begin such a course with, or arithmetic enough to carry it through. It was sailing by dead reckoning to them, and they saw not clearly how to make their port so; therefore I suppose they still take life bravely, after their fashion, face to face, giving it tooth and nail, not having skill to split its massive columns with any fine entering wedge, and rout it in detail;--thinking to deal with it roughly, as one should handle a thistle. But they fight at an overwhelming disadvantage,--living, John Field, alas! without arithmetic and failing so.

"Do you ever fish?" I asked. "Oh yes, I catch a mess now and then when I am lying by; good perch I catch." "What's your bait?" "I catch shiners with fishworms, and bait the perch with them." "You'd better go now, John," said his wife, with glistening and hopeful face; but John demurred.

The shower was now over, and a rainbow above the eastern woods promised a fair evening; so I took my departure. When I had got without I asked for a drink, hoping to get a sight of the well bottom, to complete my survey of the premises; but there, alas! are shallows and quicksands, and rope broken withal, and bucket irrecoverable. Meanwhile the right culinary vessel was selected, water was seemingly distilled, and after consultation and long delay passed out to the thirsty one,--not yet suffered to cool, not yet to settle. Such gruel sustains life here, I thought; so, shutting my eyes, and excluding the motes by a skillfully directed undercurrent, I drank to genuine hospitality the heartiest draught I could. I am not squeamish in such cases when manners are concerned.

As I was leaving the Irishman's roof after the rain, bending my steps again to the pond, my haste to catch pickerel, wading in retired meadows, in sloughs and bogholes, in forlorn and savage places, appeared for an instant trivial to me who had been sent to school and college; but as I ran down the hill toward the reddening west, with the rainbow over my shoulder, and some faint tinkling sounds borne to my ear through the cleansed air, from I know not what quarter, my Good Genius seemed to say,--Go fish and hunt far and wide day by day,--farther and wider,--and rest thee by many brooks and hearth-sides without misgiving. Remember thy Creator in the days of thy youth. Rise free from care before the dawn, and seek adventures. Let the noon find thee by other lakes, and the night overtake thee everywhere at home. There are no larger fields than these, no worthier games than may here be played. Grow wild according to thy nature, like these sedges and brakes, which will never become English hay. Let the thunder rumble; what if it threaten ruin to farmers' crops? that is not its errand to thee. Take shelter under the cloud, while they flee to carts and sheds. Let not to get a living be thy trade, but thy sport. Enjoy the land, but own it not. Through want of enterprise and faith men are where they are, buying and selling, and spending their lives like serfs. . .

Men come tamely home at night only from the next field or street, where their household echoes haunt, and their life pines because it breathes its own breath over again; their shadows, morning and evening, reach farther than their daily steps. We should come home from far, from adventures, and perils, and discoveries every day, with new experience and character.

Before I had reached the pond some fresh impulse had brought out John Field, with altered mind, letting go "bogging" ere this sunset. But he, poor man, disturbed only a couple of fins while I was catching a fair string, and he said it was his luck; but when we changed seats in the boat luck changed seats too. Poor John Field!--I trust he does not read this, unless he will improve by it,--thinking to live by some derivative old-country mode in this primitive new country,-- to catch perch with shiners. It is good bait sometimes, I allow. With his horizon all his own, yet he a poor man, born to be poor, with his. . .boggy ways, not to rise in this world, he nor his posterity, till their wading webbed bog-trotting feet get talaria to their heels. . . .

The north wind had already begun to cool the pond, though it took many weeks of steady blowing to accomplish it, it is so deep. When I began to have a fire at evening, before I plastered my house, the chimney carried smoke particularly well, because of the numerous chinks between the boards. Yet I passed some cheerful evenings in that cool and airy

165

apartment, surrounded by the rough brown boards full of knots, and rafters with the bark on high overhead. My house never pleased my eye so much after it was plastered, though I was obliged to confess that it was more comfortable. Should not every apartment in which man dwells be lofty enough to create some obscurity overhead, where flickering shadows may play at evening about the rafters? These forms are more agreeable to the fancy and imagination than fresco paintings or other the most expensive furniture. I now first began to inhabit my house, I may say, when I began to use it for warmth as well as shelter. I had got a couple of old fire-dogs to keep the wood from the hearth, and it did me good to see the soot form on the back of the chimney which I had built, and I poked the fire with more right and more satisfaction than usual. My dwelling was small, and I could hardly entertain an echo in it; but it seemed larger for being a single apartment and remote from neighbors. All the attractions of a house were concentrated in one room; it was kitchen, chamber, parlor, and keeping-room; and whatever satisfaction parent or child, master or servant, derive from living in a house, I enjoyed it all. . . .

After a still winter night I awoke with the impression that some question had been put to me, which I had been endeavoring in vain to answer in my sleep, as what--how--when--where? But there was dawning Nature, in whom all creatures live, looking in at my broad windows with serene and satisfied face, and no question on her lips. I awoke to an answered question, to Nature and daylight. The snow lying deep on the earth dotted with young pines, and the very slope of the hill on which my house is placed, seemed to say, "Forward!" Nature puts no question and answers none which we mortals ask. She has long ago taken her resolution. "O Prince, our eyes contemplate with admiration and transmit to the soul the wonderful and varied spectacle of this universe. The night veils without doubt a part of this glorious creation; but day comes to reveal to us this great work, which extends from earth even into the plains of the ether."

Then to my morning work. First I take an axe and pail and go in search of water, if that be not a dream. After a cold and snowy night it needed a divining-rod to find it. Every winter the liquid and trembling surface of the pond, which was so sensitive to every breath, and reflected every light and shadow, becomes solid to the depth of a foot or a foot and a half, so that it will support the heaviest teams, and perchance the snow covers it to an equal depth, and it is not to be distinguished from any level field. Like the marmots in the surrounding hills, it closes its eyelids and becomes dormant for three months or more. Standing on the snow-covered plain, as if in a pasture amid the hills, I cut my way first through a foot of snow, and then a foot of ice, and open a window under my feet, where, kneeling to drink, I look down into the quiet parlor of the fishes, pervaded by a softened light as through a window of ground glass, with its bright sanded floor the same as in summer; there a perennial waveless serenity reigns as in the amber twilight sky, corresponding to the cool and even temperament of the inhabitants. Heaven is under our feet as well as over our heads. . . .

At the approach of spring the red squirrels got under my house, two at a time, directly under my feet as I sat reading or writing, and kept up the queerest chuckling and chirruping and vocal pirouetting and gurgling sounds that ever were heard; and when I stamped they only chirruped the louder, as if past all fear and respect in their mad pranks, defying humanity to stop them. No, you don't--chickaree--chickaree. They were wholly deaf to my arguments, or failed to perceive their force, and fell into a strain of invective that was irresistible.

The first sparrow of spring! The year beginning with younger hope than ever! The faint silvery warblings heard over the partially bare and moist fields from the bluebird, the song sparrow, and the red-wing, as if the last flakes of winter tinkled as they fell! What at such a time are histories, chronologies, traditions, and all written revelations? The brooks sing carols and glees to the spring. The marsh hawk, sailing low over the meadow, is already seeking the first slimy life that awakes. The sinking sound of melting snow is heard in all dells, and the ice dissolves apace in the ponds. The grass flames up on the hillsides like a spring fire,--"et primitus oritur herba imbribus primoribus evocata,"--as if the earth sent forth an inward heat to greet the returning sun; not yellow but green is the color of its flame;--the symbol of perpetual youth, the grass-blade, like a long green ribbon, streams from the sod into the summer, checked indeed by the frost, but anon pushing on again, lifting its spear of last year's hay with the fresh life below. It grows as steadily as the rill oozes out of the ground. It is almost identical with that, for in the growing days of June, when the rills are dry, the grass-blades are their channels, and from year to year the herds drink at this perennial green stream, and the mower draws from it betimes their winter supply. So our human life but dies down to its root, and still puts forth its green blade to eternity.

Walden is melting apace. There is a canal two rods wide along the northerly and westerly sides, and wider still at the east end. A great field of ice has cracked off from the main body. I hear a song sparrow singing from the bushes on the shore,--olit, olit, olit,--chip, chip, chip, che char,--che wiss, wiss, wiss. He too is helping to crack it. How handsome the great sweeping curves in the edge of the ice, answering somewhat to those of the shore, but more regular! It is unusually hard, owing to the recent severe but transient cold, and all watered or waved like a palace floor. But the wind slides eastward over its opaque surface in vain, till it reaches the living surface beyond. It is glorious to behold this ribbon of water sparkling in the sun, the bare face of the pond full of glee and youth, as if it spoke the joy of the fishes within it, and of the sands on its shore,--a silvery sheen as from the scales of a leuciscus, as it were all one active fish. Such is the contrast between winter and spring. Walden was dead and is alive again. But this spring it broke up more steadily, as I have said.

The change from storm and winter to serene and mild weather, from dark and sluggish hours to bright and elastic ones, is a memorable crisis which all things proclaim. It is seemingly instantaneous at last. Suddenly an influx of light filled my house, though the evening was at hand, and the clouds of winter still overhung it, and the eaves were dripping with sleety rain. I looked out the window, and lo! where yesterday was cold gray ice there lay the transparent pond already calm and full of hope as in a summer evening, reflecting a summer evening sky in its bosom, though none was visible overhead, as if it had intelligence with some remote horizon. I heard a robin in the distance, the first I had heard for many a thousand years, methought, whose note I shall not forget for many a thousand more,--the same sweet and powerful song as of yore. O the evening robin, at the end of a New England summer day! If I could ever find the twig he sits upon! I mean he; I mean the twig. . . The pitch pines and shrub oaks about my house, which had so long drooped, suddenly resumed their several characters, looked brighter, greener, and more erect and alive, as if effectually cleansed and restored by the rain. I knew that it would not rain any more. You may tell by looking at any twig of the forest, ay, at your very wood-pile, whether its winter is past or not. As it grew darker, I was startled by the honking of geese flying low over the woods, like weary travellers getting in late from Southern lakes, and indulging at last in unrestrained complaint and mutual consolation. Standing at my door, I could hear the rush of their wings; when, driving toward my house, they suddenly spied my light, and with hushed clamor wheeled and settled in the pond. So I came in, and shut the door, and passed my first spring night in the woods. . .

Our village life would stagnate if it were not for the unexplored forests and meadows which surround it. We need the tonic of wildness,--to wade sometimes in marshes where the bittern and the meadow-hen lurk, and hear the booming of the snipe; to smell the whispering sedge where only some wilder and more solitary fowl builds her nest, and the mink crawls with its belly close to the ground. At the same time that we are earnest to explore and learn all things, we require that all things be mysterious and unexplorable, that land and sea be infinitely wild, unsurveyed and unfathomed by us because unfathomable. We can never have enough of nature. We must be refreshed by the sight of inexhaustible vigor, vast and titanic features, the sea-coast with its wrecks, the wilderness with its living and its decaying trees, the thunder-cloud, and the rain which lasts three weeks, and produces freshets. We need to witness our own limits transgressed, and some life pasturing freely where we never wander. . . .

I left the woods for as good a reason as I went there. Perhaps it seemed to me that I had several more lives to live, and could not spare any more time for that one. It is remarkable how easily and insensibly we fall into a particular route, and make a beaten track for ourselves. I had not lived there a week before my feet wore a path from my door to the pondside; and though it is five or six years since I trod it, it is still quite distinct. It is true, I fear, that others may have fallen into it, and so helped to keep it open. The surface of the earth is soft and impressible by the feet of men; and so with the paths which the mind travels. How worn and dusty, then, must be the highways of the world, how deep the ruts of tradition and conformity! I did not wish to take a cabin passage, but rather to go before the mast and on the deck of the work, for there I could best see the moonlight amid the mountains. I do not wish to go below now.

I learned this, at least, by my experiment: that if one advances confidently in the direction of his dreams, and endeavors to live the life which he has imagined, he will meet with a success unexpected in common hours. He will put some things behind, will pass an invisible boundary; new, universal, and more liberal laws will begin to establish themselves around and within him; or the old laws be expanded, and interpreted in his favor in a more liberal sense, and he will live with the license of a higher order of beings. In proportion as he simplifies his life, the laws of the universe will appear less complex, and solitude will not be solitude, nor poverty poverty, nor weakness weakness. If you have built castles in the air, your work need not be lost; that is where they should be. Now put the foundations under them. . .

I do not say that John or Jonathan will realize all this; but such is the character of that morrow which mere lapse of time can never make to dawn. The light which puts out our eyes is darkness to us. Only that day dawns to which we are awake. There is more day to dawn. The sun is but a morning star.

ZORBA THE GREEK*

by Nikos Kazantzakis

"Talk, Zorba, talk!"

When he speaks, the whole of Macedonia is immediately spread before my gaze, laid out in the little space between Zorba and myself, with its mountains, its forests, its torrents, its <u>comitadjis</u>, its hard-working women and great, heavily-built men. And also Mount Athos with its twenty-one monasteries, its arsenals and its broad-bottomed idlers. Zorba would shake his head as he finished his tales of monks and say, roaring with laughter: "God preserve you, boss, from the stern of mules and the stem of monks!"

Every evening Zorba takes me through Greece, Bulgaria and Constantinople. I shut my eyes and I see. He has been all over the racked and chaotic Balkans and observed everything with his little falcon-like eyes, which he constantly opens wide in amazement. Things we are accustomed to, and which we pass by indifferently, suddenly rise up in front of Zorba like fearful enigmas. Seeing a woman pass by, he stops in consternation.

"What is that mystery?" he asks. "What is a woman, and why does she turn our heads? Just tell me, I ask you, what's the meaning of that?"

He interrogates himself with the same amazement when he sees a man, a tree in blossom, a glass of cold water. Zorba sees everything every day as if for the first time.

We were sitting yesterday in front of the hut. When he had drunk a glass of wine, he turned to me in alarm:

"Now whatever is this red water, boss, just tell me! An old stock grows branches, and at first there's nothing but a sour bunch of beads hanging down. Time passes, the sun ripens them, they become as sweet as honey, and then they're called grapes. We trample on them; we extract the juice and put it into casks; it ferments on its own, we open it on the feast day of St. John the Drinker, it's become wine! It's a miracle! You drink the red juice and, lo and behold, your soul grows big, too big for the old carcass, it challenges God to a fight. Now tell me, boss, how does it happen?

I did not answer. I felt, as I listened to Zorba, that the world was recovering its pristine freshness. All the dulled daily things regained the brightness they had in the beginning, when we came out of the hands of God. Water, women, the stars, bread, returned to their mysterious, primitive origin and the divine whirlwind burst once more upon the air. . .

On one of these Sundays, as we were returning from the copious feast, I decided to speak and tell Zorba of my plans. He listened, gaping and forcing himself to be patient. But from time to time he shook his great head with anger. My very first words had sobered him, the fumes left his brain. When I had finished, he nervously plucked two or three hairs from his moustache.

"I hope you don't mind my saying so, boss, but I don't think your brain is quite formed yet. How old are you?"

"Thirty-five."

"Then it never will be."

Thereupon he burst out laughing. I was stung to the quick.

"You don't believe in man, do you?" I retorted.

"Now, don't get angry, boss. No, I don't believe in anything. If I believed in man, I'd believe in God, and I'd believe in the devil, too. And that's a whole business. Things get all muddled then, boss, and cause me a lot of complications."

He became silent, took off his beret, scratched his head frantically and tugged again at his moustache, as if he meant to tear it off. He wanted to say something, but he restrained himself. He looked at me out of the corner of his eye; looked at me again and decided to speak.

"Man is a brute," he said, striking the pebbles with his stick. "A great brute. Your lordship doesn't realize this. It seems everything's been too easy for you, but you ask me! A brute, I tell you! If you're cruel to him, he respects and fears you. If you're kind to him, he plucks your eyes out.

"Keep your distance, boss! Don't make men too bold, don't go telling them we're all equal, we've got the same rights, or they'll go straight and trample on your rights; they'll steal your bread and leave you to die of hunger. Keep your distance, boss, by all the good things I wish you!"

"But don't you believe in anything?" I exclaimed in exasperation.

"No, I don't believe in anything. How many times must I tell you that? I don't believe in anything or anyone; only in Zorba. Not because Zorba is better than the others; not at all, not a little bit! He's a brute

171

like the rest! But I believe in Zorba because he's the only being I have in my power, the only one I know. All the rest are ghosts. I see with these eyes, I hear with these ears, I digest with these guts. All the rest are ghosts, I tell you. When I die, everything'll die. The whole Zorbatic world will go to the bottom!"

"What egoism!" I said sarcastically.

"I can't help it, boss! That's how it is. I eat beans, I talk beans; I am Zorba, I talk like Zorba.

I said nothing. Zorba's words stung me like whiplashes. I admired him for being so strong, for despising men to that extent, and at the same time wanting to live and work with them. I should either have become an ascetic or else have adorned men with false feathers so that I could put up with them.

Zorba looked round at me. By the light of the stars I could see he was grinning from ear to ear.

"Have I offended you, boss?" he said, stopping abruptly. We had arrived at the hut. Zorba looked at me tenderly and uneasily.

I did not reply. I felt my mind was in agreement with Zorba, but my heart resisted, wanted to leap out and escape from the brute, to go its own road.

"I'm not sleepy this evening, Zorba," I said. "You go to bed."

The stars were shining, the sea was sighing and licking the shells, a glow-worm lit under its belly its little erotic lantern. Night's hair was streaming with dew.

I lay face downward, plunged in silence, thinking of nothing. I was now one with night and the sea; my mind was like a glow-worm that had lit its little lantern and settled on the damp, dark earth, and was waiting.

The stars were travelling round, the hours were passing--and, when I arose, I had, without knowing how, engraved on my mind the double task I had to accomplish on this shore:

Escape from Buddha, rid myself by words of all my metaphysical cares and free my mind from vain anxiety;

Make direct and firm contact with men, starting from this very moment.

I said to myself: "Perhaps it is not yet too late.". .

When I had finished reading Zorba's letter I was for a while in two minds--no, three. I did not know whether to be angry, or laugh, or just admire this primitive man who simply cracked life's shell--logic, morality, honesty--and went straight to its very substance. All the little virtues which are so useful are lacking in him. All he has is an uncomfortable, dangerous virtue which is hard to satisfy and which urges him continually and irresistibly towards the utmost limits, towards the abyss.

When he writes, this ignorant workman breaks his pens in his impetuosity. Like the first men to cast off their monkey skins, or like the great philosophers, he is dominated by the basic problems of mankind. He lives them as if they were immediate and urgent necessities. Like the child, he sees everything for the first time. He is forever astonished and wonders why and wherefore. Everything seems miraculous to him, and each morning when he opens his eyes he sees trees, sea, stones and birds, and is amazed.

"What is this miracle?" he cries. "What are these mysteries called: trees, seas, stones, birds?"

One day, I remember, when we were making our way to the village, we met a little old man astride a mule. Zorba opened his eyes wide as he looked at the beast. And his look was so intense that the peasant cried out in terror:

"For God's sake, brother, don't give him the evil eye!" And he crossed himself.

I turned to Zorba.

"What did you do to the old chap to make him cry out like that?" I asked him.

"Me? What d'you think I did? I was looking at his mule, that's all! Didn't it strike you, boss?"

"What?"

"Well . . . that there are such things as mules in this world!"

Another day, I was reading, stretched out on the shore, and Zorba came and sat down opposite me, placed his santuri on his knees and began to play. I raised my eyes to look at him. Gradually his expression changed and a wild joy took possession of him. He shook his long, creased neck and began to sing.

Macedonian songs, Klepht songs, savage cries; the human throat became as it was in prehistoric times, when the cry was a great synthesis which bore within it all we call today by the names of poetry, music and thought. "Akh! Akh!" The cry came from the depth of Zorba's being and the whole thin crust of what we call civilization cracked and let out the immortal beast, the hairy god, the terrifying gorilla.

Lignite, profits and losses, Dame Hortense and plans for the future, all vanished. That cry carried everything before it; we had no need of anything else. Immobile, on that solitary coast of Crete, we both held in our breasts all the bitterness and sweetness of life. Bitterness and sweetness no longer existed. The sun went down, night came, the Great Bear danced round the immovable axis of the sky, the moon rose and gazed in horror at two tiny beasts who were singing on the sands and fearing no one. . .

Zorba looked at the sky with open mouth in a sort of ecstasy, as though he were seeing it for the first time.

"What can be happening up there?" he murmured.

A moment later he decided to speak.

"Can you tell me, boss," he said, and his voice sounded deep and earnest in the warm night, "what all these things mean? Who made them all? And why? And, above all"--here Zorba's voice trembled with anger and fear--"why do people die?"

"I don't know, Zorba," I replied, ashamed, as if I had been asked the simplest thing, the most essential thing, and was unable to explain it.

"You don't know!" said Zorba in round-eyed astonishment, just like his expression the night I had confessed I could not dance.

He was silent a moment and then suddenly broke out.

"Well, all those damned books you read--what good are they? Why do you read them? If they don't tell you that, what do they tell you?"

"They tell me about the perplexity of mankind, who can give no answer to the question you've just put me, Zorba."

"Oh, damn their perplexity!" he cried, tapping his foot on the ground in exasperation.

The parrot started up at these noises.

"Canavaro! Canavaro!" he called, as if for help.

174

"Shut up! You, too!" shouted Zorba, banging on the cage with his fist.

He turned back to me.

"I want you to tell me where we come from and where we are going to. During all those years you've been burning yourself up consuming their black books of magic, you must have chewed over about fifty tons of paper! What did you get out of them?"

There was so much anguish in his voice that my heart was wrung with distress. Ah! how I would have liked to be able to answer him!

I felt deep within me that the highest point a man can attain is not Knowledge, or Virtue, or Goodness, or Victory, but something even greater, more heroic and more despairing: Sacred Awe!

"Can't you answer?" asked Zorba anxiously.

I tried to make my companion understand what I meant by Sacred Awe.

"We are little grubs, Zorba, minute grubs on the small leaf of a tremendous tree. This small leaf is the earth. The other leaves are the stars that you see moving at night. We make our way on this little leaf examining it anxiously and carefully. We smell it; it smells good or bad to us. We taste it and find it eatable. We beat on it and it cries out like a living thing.

"Some men--the more intrepid ones--reach the ege of the leaf. From there we stretch out, gazing into chaos. We tremble. We guess what a frightening abyss lies beneath us. In the distance we can hear the noise of the other leaves of the tremendous tree, we feel the sap rising from the roots to our leaf and our hearts swell. Bent thus over the awe-inspiring abyss, with all our bodies and all our souls, we tremble with terror. From that moment begins . . ."

I stopped. I wanted to say "from that moment begins poetry," but Zorba would not have understood. I stopped.

"What begins?" asked Zorba's anxious voice. "Why did you stop?"

". . . begins the great danger, Zorba. Some grow dizzy and delirious, others are afraid; they try to find an answer to strengthen their hearts, and they say: 'God!' Others again, from the edge of the leaf, look over the precipice calmly and bravely and say: 'I like it.'"

175

Zorba reflected for a long time. He was straining to understand.

"You know," he said at last, "I think of death every second. I look at it and I'm not frightened. But never, never, do I say I like it. No, I don't like it at all! I don't agree!"

He was silent, but soon broke out again.

"No, I'm not the sort to hold out my neck to Charon like a sheep and say: 'Cut my throat, Mr. Charon, please: I want to go straight to Paradise!'"

I listened to Zorba in perplexity. Who was the sage who tried to teach his disciples to do voluntarily what the law ordered should be done? To say "yes" to necessity and change the inevitable into something done of their own free will? That is perhaps the only human way to deliverance. It is a pitiable way, but there is no other.

But what of revolt? The proud, quixotic reaction of mankind to conquer Necessity and make external laws conform to the internal laws of the soul, to deny all that is and create a new world according to the laws of one's own heart, which are contrary to the inhuman laws of nature--to create a new world which is purer, better and more moral than the one that exists?

Zorba looked at me, saw that I had no more to say to him, took up the cage carefully so that he should not wake the parrot, placed it by his head and stretched out on the pebbles.

"Good night, boss!" he said. "That's enough."

A strong south wind was blowing from Africa. It was making the vegetables and fruits and Cretan breasts all swell and grow. I felt it on my forehead, lips and neck; and like a fruit my brain cracked and swelled.

I could not and would not sleep. I thought of nothing. I just felt something, someone growing to maturity inside me in the warm night. I lived lucidly through a most surprising experience: I saw myself change. A thing that usually happens only in the most obscure depths of our bowels was this time occurring in the open, before my eyes. Crouched by the sea, I watched this miracle take place.

The stars grew dim, the sky grew light and against this luminous background appeared, as if delicately traced in ink, the mountains, trees and gulls.

Dawn was breaking.

CRITIQUE

John Stuart Mill (1806-1873) challenges Wordsworth's advice to "Let nature be your teacher." If we understand "nature" in the extended sense--as "the entire system of things, with the aggregate of all their properties"--then we can do nothing else but follow nature; for all of our behavior, whether good or bad, accords with natural laws. But if we understand by "nature" that which takes place "apart from human intervention," then the advice to follow nature is, according to Mill, "irrational and immoral." For nearly everything that is of value in human life requires that we somehow alter the course of nature to suit our needs. The cultivation of food, the creation of clothing, the construction of shelter, all involve a conscious human intervention in the course of things. And analogues of behaviors that we abhor--such as torture, exploitation, arbitary injustice--are found throughout the world of non-human nature. Conceptions of human good should not be patterned on the natural order.

Erich Fromm (1900-1980) suggests another reason why the good life for humans cannot be adequately defined in naturalistic terms. The evolution of homo sapiens has produced in us a new order of being, characterized by a level of consciousness that goes far beyond anything found in the natural world. "Self-awareness, reason and imagination disrupt the 'harmony' which characterizes animal existence." Like Adam and Eve, we cannot return to the natural innocence of Eden, but must accept our uniqueness, and look forward rather than backward. The yearning to return to nature is like the desire to return to the womb; it is, after all, a kind of escapism, an effort to forget one's unique humanness, its burdens, responsibilities and freedoms. We are more than merely natural beings, and must seek our destiny not in a return to nature, but elsewhere.

NATURE CANNOT TEACH US HOW TO LIVE*

by John Stuart Mill

We must recognize at least two principal meanings in the word Nature. In one sense, it means all the powers existing in either the outer or the inner world and everything which takes place by means of those powers. In another sense, it means, not everything which happens, but only what takes place without the agency, or without the voluntary and intentional agency, of man. This distinction is far from exhausting the ambiguities of the word; but it is the key to most of those on which important consequences depend.

Such, then, being the two principal senses of the word Nature; in which of these is it taken, or is it taken in either, when the word and its derivatives are used to convey ideas of commendation, approval, and even moral obligation?. . .

When it is asserted, or implied, that Nature, or the laws of Nature, should be conformed to, is the Nature which is meant, Nature in the first sense of the term, meaning all which is--the powers and properties of all things? But in this signification, there is no need of a recommendation to act according to nature, since it is what nobody can possibly help doing, and equally whether he acts well or ill. There is no mode of acting which is not conformable to Nature in this sense of the term, and all modes of acting are so in exactly the same degree. Every action is the exertion of some natural power, and its effects of all sorts are so many phenomena of nature, produced by the powers and properties of some of the objects of nature, in exact obedience to some law or laws of nature. When I voluntarily use my organs to take in food, the act, and its consequences, take place according to laws of nature: if instead of food I swallow poison, the case is exactly the same. To bid people conform to the laws of nature when they have no power but what the laws of nature give them--when it is a physical impossibility for them to do the smallest thing otherwise than through some law of nature, is an absurdity. The thing they need to be told is, what particular law of nature they should make use of in a particular case. When, for example, a person is crossing a river by a narrow bridge to which there is no parapet, he will do well to regulate his proceedings by the laws of equilibrium in moving bodies, instead of conforming only to the law of gravitation, and falling into the river. . .

Let us then consider whether we can attach any meaning to the supposed practical maxim of following Nature, in this second sense of the word, in which Nature stands for that which takes place without human intervention. In Nature as thus understood, is the spontaneous course of things when left to themselves, the rule to be followed in endeavouring to

*From John Stuart Mill, <u>Three Essays on Religion</u> (New York: Henry Holt & Co., 1884).

adapt things to our use? But it is evident at once that the maxim, taken in this sense, is not merely, as it is in the other sense, superfluous and unmeaning, but palpably absurd and self-contradictory. For while human action cannot help conforming to Nature in the one meaning of the term, the very aim and object of action is to alter and improve Nature in the other meaning. If the natural course of things were perfectly right and satisfactory, to act at all would be a gratuitous meddling, which as it could not make things better, must make them worse. Or if action at all could be justified, it would only be when in direct obedience to instincts, since these might perhaps be accounted part of the spontaneous order of Nature; but to do anything with forethought and purpose, would be a violation of that perfect order. If the artificial is not better than the natural, to what end are all the arts of life? To dig, to plough, to build, to wear clothes, are direct infringements of the injunction to follow nature.

Accordingly it would be said by every one, even of those most under the influence of the feelings which prompt the injunction, that to apply it to such cases as those just spoken of, would be to push it too far. Everybody professes to approve and admire many great triumphs of Art over Nature: the junction by bridges of shores which Nature had made separate, the draining of Nature's marshes, the excavation of her wells, the dragging to light of what she has buried at immense depths in the earth; the turning away of her thunderbolts by lightning rods, of her inundations by embankments, of her ocean by breakwaters. But to commend these and similar feats, is to acknowledge that the ways of Nature are to be conquered, not obeyed: that her powers are often towards man in the position of enemies, from whom he must wrest, by force and ingenuity, what little he can for his own use, and deserves to be applauded when that little is rather more than might be expected from his physical weakness in comparison to those gigantic powers. All praise of Civilization, or Art, or Contrivance, is so much dispraise of Nature; an admission of imperfection, which it is man's business, and merit, to be always endeavouring to correct or mitigate. . .

In sober truth, nearly all the things which men are hanged or imprisoned for doing to one another, are nature's every day performances. Killing, the most criminal act recognized by human laws, Nature does once to every being that lives; and in a large proportion of cases, after protracted tortures such as only the greatest monsters whom we read of ever purposely inflicted on their living fellow-creatures. If, by an arbitrary reservation, we refuse to account anything murder but what abridges a certain term supposed to be allotted to human life, nature also does this to all but a small percentage of lives, and does it in all the modes, violent or insidious, in which the worst human beings take the lives of one another. Nature impales men, breaks them as if on the wheel, casts them to be devoured by wild beasts, burns them to death, crushes them with stones like the first christian martyr, starves them with hunger, freezes them with cold, poisons them by the quick or slow venom of her exhalations, and has hundreds of other hideous deaths in reserve, such as the ingenious cruelty of a Nabis or a Domitian never surpassed. All this, Nature does with the most supercilious disregard both of mercy and of justice, emptying her shafts upon the best and noblest indifferently with the meanest and worst; upon those who are engaged in the highest and worthiest enterprises, and often as the direct consequence of the noblest acts; and it might almost be imagined as a punishment for them. She mows down those on whose existence hangs the well-being of a whole people, perhaps the prospects of the human race for generations to come, with as little compunction as those whose death is a relief to themselves, or a blessing to those under their noxious influence. Such are Nature's dealings with life. Even when she does not intend to kill, she inflicts the same tortures in apparent wantonness. In the clumsy provision which she has made for that perpetual renewal of animal life, rendered necessary by the prompt termination she puts to it in every individual instance, no human being ever comes into the world but another human being is literally stretched on the rack for hours or days, not unfrequently issuing in death. Next to taking life (equal to it according to a high authority) is taking the means by which we live; and Nature does this too on the largest scale and with the most callous indifference. A single hurricane destroys the hopes of a season; a flight of locusts, or an inundation, desolates a district; a trifling chemical change in an edible root, starves a million of people. The waves of the sea, like banditti seize and appropriate the wealth of the rich and the little all of the poor with the same accompaniments of stripping, wounding, and killing as their human antitypes. Everything in short, which the worst men commit either against life or property is perpetrated on a larger scale by natural agents. . .

But, it is said, all these things are for wise and good ends. On this I must first remark that whether they are so or not, is altogether beside the point. Supposing it true that contrary to appearances these horrors when perpetrated by Nature, promote good ends, still as no one believes that good ends would be promoted by our following the example, the course of Nature cannot be a proper model for us to imitate. Either it is right that we should kill because nature kills; torture because nature tortures; ruin and devastate because nature does the like; or we ought not to consider at all what nature does, but what it is good to do. If there is such a thing as a reductio ad absurdum, this surely amounts to one. If it is a sufficient reason for doing one thing, that nature does it, why not another thing? If not all things, why anything? The physical government of the world being full of the things which when done by men are deemed the greatest enormities, it cannot be religious or moral in us to guide our actions by the analogy of the course of nature. . . .

It will be useful to sum up in a few words the leading conclusions of this Essay.

The word Nature has two principal meanings: it either denotes the entire system of things, with the aggregate of all their properties, or it denotes things as they would be, apart from human intervention.

In the first of these senses, the doctrine that man ought to follow nature is unmeaning; since man has no power to do anything else than follow nature; all his actions are done through, and in obedience to, some one or many of nature's physical or mental laws.

In the other sense of the term, the doctrine that man ought to follow nature, or in other words, ought to make the spontaneous course of things the model of his voluntary actions, is equally irrational and immoral.

Irrational, because all human action whatever, consists in altering, and all useful action in improving, the spontaneous course of nature:

Immoral, because the course of natural phenomena being replete with everything which when committed by human beings is most worthy of abhorrence, any one who endeavoured in his actions to imitate the natural course of things would be universally seen and acknowledged to be the wickedest of men.

The scheme of Nature regarded in its whole extent, cannot have had, for its sole or even principal object, the good of human or other sentient beings. What good it brings to them, is mostly the result of their own exertions. Whatsoever, in nature, gives indication of beneficent design, proves this beneficence to be armed only with limited power; and the duty of man is to co-operate with the beneficent powers, not by imitating but by perpetually striving to amend the course of nature--and bringing that part of it over which we can exercise control, more nearly into conformity with a high standard of justice and goodness.

HUMAN LIFE TRANSCENDS NATURE*

by Erich Fromm

Man, in respect to his body and his physiological functions, belongs to the animal kingdom. The functioning of the animal is determined by instincts, by specific action patterns which are in turn determined by inherited neurological structures. The higher an animal is in the scale of development, the more flexibility of action pattern and the less completeness of structural adjustment do we find at birth. In the higher primates we even find considerable intelligence; that is, use of thought for the accomplishment of desired goals, thus enabling the animal to go far beyond the instinctively prescribed action pattern. But great as the development within the animal kingdom is, certain basic elements of existence remain the same.

The animal "is lived" through biological laws of nature; it is part of nature and never transcends it. It has no conscience of a moral nature, and no awareness of itself and of its existence; it has no reason, if by reason we mean the ability to penetrate the surface grasped by the senses and to understand the essence behind that surface; therefore the animal has no concept of the truth, even though it may have an idea of what is useful.

Animal existence is one of harmony between the animal and nature; not, of course, in the sense that the natural conditions do not often threaten the animal and force it to a bitter fight for survival, but in the sense that the animal is equipped by nature to cope with the very conditions it is to meet, just as the seed of a plant is equipped by nature to make use of the conditions of soil, climate, etcetera, to which it has become adapted in the evolutionary process.

At a certain point of animal evolution, there occurred a unique break, comparable to the first emergence of matter, to the first emergence of life, and to the first emergence of animal existence. This new event happens when in the evolutionary process, action ceases to be essentially determined by instinct; when the adaptation of nature loses its coercive character; when action is no longer fixed by hereditarily given mechanisms. When the animal transcends nature, when it transcends the purely passive role of the creature, when it becomes, biologically speaking, the most helpless animal, <u>man is born</u>. At this point, the animal has emancipated itself from nature by erect posture, the brain has grown far beyond what it was in the highest animal. This birth of man may have lasted for hundreds of thousands of years, but what matters is that a new species arose, transcending nature, that <u>life became aware of itself</u>.

*From THE SANE SOCIETY by Erich Fromm. Copyright (c) 1955 by Erich Fromm. Reprinted by permission of Holt, Rinehart and Winston, Publishers.

Self-awareness, reason and imagination disrupt the "harmony" which characterizes animal existence. Their emergence has made man into an anomaly, into the freak of the universe. He is part of nature, subject to her physical laws and unable to change them, yet he transcends the rest of nature. He is set apart while being a part; he is homeless, yet chained to the home he shares with all creatures. Cast into this world at an accidental place and time, he is forced out of it, again accidentally. Being aware of himself, he realizes his powerlessness and the limitations of his existence. He visualizes his own end: death. Never is he free from the dichotomy of his existence: he cannot rid himself of his mind, even if he should want to; he cannot rid himself of his body as long as he is alive-- and his body makes him want to be alive.

Reason, man's blessing, is also his curse; it forces him to cope everlastingly with the task of solving an insoluble dichotomy. Human existence is different in this respect from that of all other organisms; it is in a state of constant and unavoidable disequilibrium. Man's life cannot "be lived" by repeating the pattern of his species; he must live. Man is the only animal that can be bored, that can feel evicted from paradise. Man is the only animal who finds his own existence a problem which he has to solve and from which he cannot escape. He cannot go back to the prehuman state of harmony with nature; he must proceed to develop his reason until he becomes the master of nature, and of himself.

But man's birth ontogenetically as well as phylogenetically is essentially a negative event. He lacks the instinctive adaptation to nature, he lacks physical strength, he is the most helpless of all animals at birth, and in need of protection for a much longer period of time than any of them. While he has lost the unity with nature, he has not been given the means to lead a new existence outside of nature. His reason is most rudimentary, he has no knowledge of nature's processes, nor tools to replace the lost instincts; he lives divided into small groups, with no knowledge of himself or of others; indeed, the biblical Paradise myth expresses the situation with perfect clarity. Man, who lives in the Garden of Eden, in complete harmony with nature but without awareness of himself, begins his history by the first act of freedom, disobedience to a command. Concomitantly, he becomes aware of himself, of his separateness, of his helplessness; he is expelled from Paradise, and two angels with fiery swords prevent his return.

Man's evolution is based on the fact that he has lost his original home, nature--and that he can never return to it, can never become an animal again. There is only one way he can take: to emerge fully from his natural home, to find a new home--one which he creates, by making the world a human one and by becoming truly human himself.

STUDY QUESTIONS FOR CHAPTER V

Questions for Review:

1. What are the extended and the specific senses of the word "nature"?

2. According to the editor, what does it mean to say that humans have "a nature"?

3. In what ways may our involvement in society interfere with living well, according to the editor?

4. What is the role of the experience of natural beauty in naturalistic views of the good life, as described by the editor?

5. What attitude do naturalists typically take toward the hypothesis of supernatural and transcendant realms of being?

6. What is the naturalist's account of morality, according to the editor?

7. What is the naturalist's account of happiness, according to the editor?

8. How does Tao Chien achieve wilderness in the midst of people?

9. Describe the immediate environment of Thoreau's house.

10. What are Thoreau's claims about life in the morning?

11. "I went to the woods because I wished to live deliberately. . ." Restate in your own words the basic ideas expressed by Thoreau in this paragraph.

12. Summarize Thoreau's advice concerning simplicity.

13. Describe how Thoreau overcomes his doubts that perhaps it is unhealthy to live alone.

14. What, in Thoreau's opinion, was wrong with the way John Field lived his life? What is the core of Thoreau's advice to John Field?

15. What is it that we need from wild nature, according to Thoreau?

16. Why did Thoreau leave the woods?

17. In the selection from Kazanzakis, what are the chief lessons that the narrator learns from Zorba?

18. What does Zorba believe in?

19. What is Zorba's attitude toward death?

20. Summarize the contrast between acceptance and revolt as attitudes toward life and death, as described by the narrator in Kazanzakis's story.

21. What are the "two principal meanings in the word Nature" as stated by John Stuart Mill? Are they the same as the "extended" and the "specific" senses outlined by the editor?

22. Summarize Mill's critique of the doctrine that we should "follow nature."

23. Why is it necessary for human morality to diverge from nature, according to Mill?

24. What grounds are given by Fromm for his claim that human life transcends nature? What is new about human beings, as compared with their evolutionary forbearers?

25. What are the "two conflicting tendencies" in human nature, according to Fromm?

26. One central theme of naturalism is an affirmation of the physical, biological dimensions of human life, and an emphasis upon common features of human and non-human life. To what degree is this theme found in Tao Chien, Thoreau and Zorba?

Questions for Reflection:

1. When I am in a natural environment that is relatively unchanged by humans, how do I usually react? What is the difference between those times that I am uplifted, and those times that I am indifferent or bothered by nature?

2. Do I have needs that are met by being immersed in natural settings? Do I meet those needs often enough to satisfy me? If not, why not? What might I do to gain greater satisfaction of this kind?

3. How might I simplify my life, in the spirit of Thoreau?

4. What are some of the "castles in the air" that I have built in fantasy? Which one or two of them stir me most deeply? How might I "put the foundations under them" and "advance confidently in the direction of my dreams"?

5. How do I feel about the kind of person that Zorba is? Would I like to be more like him? If so, what might I do to bring about such a change in myself?

Questions for Discussion:

1. Is the suggestion to "let nature be your teacher" good advice? What might nature teach us?

2. Are Tao Chien and Thoreau "escapists" in some negative sense? Is their withdrawal unhealthy?

3. Are those dimensions of human life that are shared with the non-human world commonly emphasized too much or too little (or neither) in the way people live their lives?

4. Is Zorba simplistic? Is he naive?

5. What are the chief benefits of living life as Zorba does? What are the chief drawbacks?

6. Do you agree with Mill's criticism of the advice to follow nature?

7. Is it true that human life transcends nature, as Fromm asserts?

8. If one denies any transcendent or supernatural realm, is this world enough for a good life?

SUGGESTIONS FOR FURTHER READING

John Burroughs, ed., Songs of Nature (McClure, Phillips, 1901)

Walter H. Capps, ed., Seeing With A Native Eye: Essays on Native American Religion (Harper & Row, 1976)

R. G. Collingwood, The Idea of Nature (Oxford, Galaxy, 1960)

John Hospers, Human Conduct: Problems of Ethics, Chapter 6 (Harcourt Brace Jovanovich, 1961, 1972) Excellent discussion of naturalism.

Y. H. Krikorian, ed., Naturalism and the Human Spirit (Columbia University Press, 1944)

J. W. Krutch, The Best Nature Writing of Joseph Wood Krutch (Morrow, 1969)

John Muir, The Wilderness World of John Muir, ed. by Edwin Way Teale (Houghton Mifflin, 1954)

John Ruskin, The Genius of John Ruskin, ed. by John Rosenberg (G. Braziller, 1963)

Ways of Wisdom

Chapter Six:

God

Chapter VI: GOD

Introduction

Know that the Lord is God!
It is he that made us, and we are his.
(Psalm 100)

Where, then, does human good lie? Captivating images float in our minds, of lives that are whole, and strong, and free. Eagerly we invest our energies in various projects and strivings, seeking satisfaction and fulfillment. If only we can remake our world to fit our impulses, then surely the hunger within us will be eased, and we will live in harmony and happiness.

For the theist, however, no human-centered endeavors can satisfy the deepest longings of our hearts; and no human-based projects can finally overcome the egocentricity of our private selves. Bold constructions of human effort reach upward like new towers of Babel, then topple and disintegrate into a cacaphony of confused, contentious voices. Our good lies in another way, a way that does not begin with the merely human. Our futility is transformed into power, love and joy only when at last we acknowledge that we belong, not to ourselves but to another; when we yield up our willful human pride and humble ourselves before an awesome power and unfathomable wisdom; when we lay our minds and hearts open to the cleansing light, the fearful and wonderful workings of the spirit of God.

189

No account of the good life can provide lasting and trustworthy guidance, unless it shows us a deeper understanding of our relationship to God, according to traditional Western monotheism. And no well-meaning projects--personal, social, or political--will liberate us, unless they lead us to a more complete obedience to God's will. Human freedom, human joy and fulfillment are found only by rising above the purely human, to a way of life that is sanctified by submission to the ultimate source of our being.

The Poverty of Naturalism

As humans we are indeed natural creatures of the physical world, subject to scientific law, possessing animal-like instincts and needs. And living rightly requires that we attend to our bodies, caring for them and respecting them rather than abusing them. But in the eyes of the theist, we are more than animals; we have needs and potentialities that cannot be satisfied through mere identification with the natural world. If appreciation of nature enriches our lives, it is not through sinking back into the physical, but through a process of heightening and uplifting by which we become aware of spiritual possibilities that go beyond what can be seen with our eyes. Joy in natural beauty is ultimately joy in the beauty of the supernatural; "The heavens are telling the glory of God; and the firmament proclaims his handiwork." To praise a spiritual quality in nature while refusing to acknowledge its true source is like exclaiming at the beautiful color of the sunset while ignoring the sun itself.

Thus without grounding in that which transcends this world, our lives are ultimately hollow and pointless, lacking in true meaning. We may find ways to enjoy ourselves; we may become wealthy and live comfortably; we may gain the admiration and respect of others; we may be regarded by most people as successful in everything we do. But without God, our lives will be like empty pantomimes, gestures without feeling. In itself, this world in not enough.

Ethical Monotheism

The dominant view of the good life in Western thought has been, for many centuries, some version of ethical monotheism, the belief in one supremely good God. As first developed in Judaism and then elaborated in differing ways by its chief offspring, Christianity and Islam, ethical monotheism declares that God, the creater and sustainer of the universe, is benevolent and just, sovereign over us and all else that exists--infinitely transcending us in power, knowledge and goodness, yet more intimately infused into our lives than the breath that we draw into our lungs, or the blood that circulates in our veins. When we penetrate deeply into ourselves, we find that our own nature is grounded in the divine: God is not only above, but also within. The God of all is also a specific force in history, entering dramatically into human affairs at definite points in time: speaking with a chosen few, forming covenants with the many, inspiring sages and prophets, punishing the evil and guiding the righteous. Such events are not merely colorful incidents that embroider an abstract faith; rather they are critical moments of God's revelation in human history, forming the foundation of traditional Western theism.

The universe that God has created is orderly and good, originally a fit place for human habitation. Within the universe, humans occupy a unique position, brought into being as God's culminating act of creation: we are made in God's own image, and are intended by God to have dominion over the rest of the created world, "over the fish of the sea, and over the birds of the air, and over the cattle, and over all the earth, and over every creeping thing that creeps upon the earth." Human nature is two-fold: intermingled with our physical being is the capacity for intelligent choice, and the potential for an exalted spirituality, endowing us with an inherent dignity and worth. Our very likeness to God presents us with powerful temptation, however: like Adam and Eve, we may choose to deny our dependency upon God and, turning away from God's will and love for us, strike out on our own, seeking to work our private wills upon the world, trying to become like gods to ourselves. In doing so, we mask our perverse and willful pride with an illusion of self-sufficiency, eventually bringing down upon ourselves confusion and conflict, toil and ruin. Living rightly requires that we release our wayward arrogance and submit our lives to the stern and loving discipline of God, as expressed in God's will. Such submission requires faith, the willingness to trust ourselves to a wisdom more profound and a vision more discerning than that provided by our own faulty understanding. Through lives guided by divine law and bathed in divine love, we may discover genuine fulfillment and happiness, the good life that God intends for us.

The Good Life

Living rightly and living well, the two complementary dimensions of the good life, are here hardly distinguishable. For in doing the will of God, which is the essence of right choice, we come to experience a beauty and joy, a wholeness and satisfaction, that transform our lives. As expressed in the 19th Psalm:

The law of the Lord is perfect, reviving the soul;
The testimony of the Lord is sure, making wise the simple;
The precepts of the Lord are right, rejoicing the heart;
The commandment of the Lord is pure, enlightening the eyes;
The fear of the Lord is clean, enduring for ever;
The ordinances of the Lord are true, and righteous altogether.
More to be desired are they than gold, even much fine gold;
Sweeter also than honey, and drippings of honeycomb.

As evidenced here, doing God's will is not a mere technique or means to gain a pleasant life for oneself, as if one were trading good behavior for a reward. Such motivation is still self-centered and manipulative, an attempt to use God for one's own personal gain. The bounty of God's goodness is available to us only to the degree that we let go of our private egoism and give ourselves whole-heartedly to the service of God's will, in dedication and devotion. In the greatest commandment of all, Moses declared: "Hear, O Israel: The Lord our God is one Lord; and you shall love the Lord your God with all your heart, and with all your soul, and with all your might. And these words which I command you this day shall be upon your heart . . . . " Though God's commandment is exacting and all-encompassing, it is not placed at a distance from us, as something to attain by a lengthy journey; as Moses also said, "the word is very near to you; it is in your mouth and in your heart, so that you can do it."

Commitment to do God's will is no guarantee of a continuously pleasant life. We are still likely to feel doubt and conflict, fear and anguish, at various times in our lives. But in the midst of such experiences, genuine commitment opens the way to a deeper source of reassurance and strength. Reverence and awe, delight and praise, arise spontaneously in those who yield fully to God's majesty and love. Perhaps we experience such power through the veneration of God's sacred words and in the observance of holy ritual. Perhaps we feel a complete peace and serenity in the faith that all--everything--is sustained by loving arms. Perhaps we experience the divine as an actual and living presence, infusing every cell of our body with transfiguring light and love. As we give ourselves over increasingly to God, we find that our lives acquire a growing rightness, order and inherent beauty. In an exalted form, displayed in the lives of many men and women throughout history, life itself is transformed into an experience of holiness (in Hebrew, Kedushah). The present moment is fraught with the sacred; God's immense power and love evoke a human response of awe, mystery, fear and joy; one is immersed in radiance, so that the very ground beneath one's feet is felt to be holy. Life is sanctified in humility before God.

The Selections

The selections in this chapter representing a theistic view of the good life are taken from scripture recognized as sacred by all three major Western religious traditions--Judaism, Christianity and Islam--and shared in common among them. Selections from Genesis, Exodus and Deuteronomy, three of the first five books of the Bible, recount major events in the story of God's direct involvement in human affairs, from the creation itself through the delivery of the Ten Commandments to Moses. Whether viewed as literal truth or as symbolic myth and allegory, these passages establish the fundamental framework of generic Western monotheism. In the selections from the Psalms, we find expression of the human response to God: inspired songs of praise and thanksgiving, of doubt and pain, of entreaty and dedication--lyrical records of human experience of the good life, as centered in God.

God's supreme sovereignty over all the universe is apparent in the creation story from Genesis. Unlike creation myths in numerous other traditions, where gods are often depicted as arbitrary or even malicious,God is shown here to be benevolent, just and wise. God's creation is orderly and good throughout. Disorder, fear, pain and toil are introduced through the wrong actions of the first man and woman, Adam and Eve, who disobeyed God's order to refrain from eating fruit from the tree of the knowledge of good and evil. Thus a perennial theme of Western monotheism is struck: we introduce misery into our lives when we, through the desire to become like gods to ourselves, disobey God's will for us. Banished from the Garden of Eden, each of us retains a faint memory of its innocent beauty and peace. Our life struggles are fueled by an urge to regain our original state of bliss.

The story of the Garden of Eden, like other biblical stories, has been given a remarkable variety of interpretations. According to one analysis, it is primarily a description of the discovery of sexuality; according to another, the heart of the story is the human assumption of moral responsibility. Yet another reading sees the events as the awakening of our intellectual capacities. Each interpretation may be supported by explicit passages in the text.

The story of Abraham, appearing later in the book of Genesis, depicts an archetype of the ideal faith relationship with God. By doing God's will, Abraham learns to trust God's love; life becomes good through faith and obedience. As a willing servant of God, Abraham enjoys the abundance of God's beneficence. God tests the depth of Abraham's faith by commanding him to sacrifice his son, Isaac, intervening only at the last moment when Abraham is about to carry out his charge. Human judgment shall not oppose God's will, even for seemingly the best of reasons; the ideal faith relationship requires that we be ready to sacrifice that which is most dear to us, in order to unite with God's way.

In the excerpts from Exodus, the dramatic story of the escape from Egypt, and Deuteronomy, the delivery by Moses of God's new covenant with Israel, the biblical account of the right way of life is further elaborated. God's will is expressed in a series of precepts, so that humans may better know what is expected of them. For those who obey, God pledges not death, but a bountiful life; "therefore choose life, that you and your descendants may live, loving the Lord your God, obeying his voice, and cleaving to him..."

The Psalms convey, in poetry of surpassing beauty, heightened moments in human lives that are guided by the love of God and the effort to do God's will. In some Psalms, disconsolate voices cry out of pain and loneliness, yearning for God's reassurance and solace; others pour out glad praise of God's majesty, power and wisdom. All, from the measured dignity of the first, through the serene faith of the twenty-third, to the awestruck wonder of the 139th, testify to the human need for God and to the joy of a life that finds acceptance in God's eyes.

From

GENESIS*

In the beginning God created the heavens and the earth. The earth was without form and void, and darkness was upon the face of the deep; and the Spirit of God was moving over the face of the waters:

And God said, "Let there be light"; and there was light. And God saw that the light was good; and God separated the light from the darkness. God called the light Day, and the darkness he called Night. And there was evening and there was morning, one day.

And God said, "Let there be a firmament in the midst of the waters, and let it separate the waters from the waters." And God made the firmament and separated the waters which were under the firmament from the waters which were above the firmament. And it was so. And God called the firmament Heaven. And there was evening and there was morning, a second day.

And God said, "Let the waters under the heavens be gathered together into one place, and let the dry land appear." And it was so. God called the dry land Earth, and the waters that were gathered together he called Seas. And God saw that it was good. And God said, "Let the earth put forth vegetation, plants yielding seed, and fruit trees bearing fruit in which is their seed, each according to its kind, upon the earth." And it was so. The earth brought forth vegetation, plants yielding seed according to their own kinds, and trees bearing fruit in which is their seed, each according to its kind. And God saw that it was good. And there was evening and there was morning, a third day.

And God said, "Let there be lights in the firmament of the heavens to separate the day from the night; and let them be for signs and for seasons and for days and years, and let them be lights in the firmament of the heavens to give light upon the earth." And it was so. And God made the two great lights, the greater light to rule the day, and the lesser light to rule the night; he made the stars also. And God set them in the firmament of the heavens to give light upon the earth, to rule over the day and over the night, and to separate the light from the darkness. And God saw that it was good. And there was evening and there was morning, a fourth day.

And God said, "Let the waters bring forth swarms of living creatures, and let birds fly above the earth across the firmament of the

---

*Selections from Genesis, Exodus, Deuteronomy, and Psalms are taken from the Revised Standard Version of the Bible, copyrighted 1946, 1952, (c) 1971, 1973. (Toronto, Edinburgh, New York: Thomas Nelson & Sons, 1953). Selections from Genesis are 1:1-2:9, 2:15-3:24, 17:1-8, 22:1-18.

195

heavens." So God created the great sea monsters and every living creature that moves, with which the waters swarm, according to their kinds, and every winged bird according to its kind. And God saw that it was good. And God blessed them, saying, "Be fruitful and multiply and fill the waters in the seas, and let birds multiply on the earth." And there was evening and there was morning, a fifth day.

And God said, "Let the earth bring forth living creatures according to their kinds: cattle and creeping things and beasts of the earth according to their kinds." And it was so. And God made the beasts of the earth according to their kinds and the cattle according to their kinds, and everything that creeps upon the ground according to its kind. And God saw that it was good.

Then God said, "Let us make man in our image, after our likeness; and let them have dominion over the fish of the sea, and over the birds of the air, and over the cattle, and over all the earth, and over every creeping thing that creeps upon the earth." So God created man in his own image, in the image of God he created him; male and female he created them. And God blessed them, and God said to them, "Be fruitful and multiply, and fill the earth and subdue it; and have dominion over the fish of the sea and over the birds of the air and over every living thing that moves upon the earth." And God said, "Behold, I have given you every plant yielding seed which is upon the face of all the earth, and every tree with seed in its fruit; you shall have them for food. And to every beast of the earth, and to every bird of the air, and to everything that creeps on the earth, everything that has the breath of life, I have given every green plant for food." And it was so. And God saw everything that he had made, and behold, it was very good. And there was evening and there was morning, a sixth day.

Thus the heavens and the earth were finished, and all the host of them. And on the seventh day God finished his work which he had done, and he rested on the seventh day from all his work which he had done. So God blessed the seventh day and hallowed it, because on it God rested from all his work which he had done in creation.

These are the generations of the heavens and the earth when they were created.

In the day that the Lord God made the earth and the heavens, when no plant of the field was yet in the earth and no herb of the field had yet sprung up--for the Lord God had not caused it to rain upon the earth, and there was no man to till the ground; but a mist went up from the earth and watered the whole face of the ground--then the Lord God formed man of dust from the ground, and breathed into his nostrils the breath of life; and man became a living being. And the Lord God planted a garden in Eden, in the east; and there he put the man whom he had formed. And out of the ground the Lord God made to grow every tree that is pleasant to the sight and good for food, the tree of life also in the midst of the garden, and the tree of the knowledge of good and evil. . . .

The Lord God took the man and put him in the garden of Eden to till it and keep it. And the Lord God commanded the man, saying "You may freely eat of every tree of the garden; but of the tree of the knowledge of good and evil you shall not eat, for in the day that you eat of it you shall die."

Then the Lord God said, "It is not good that the man should be alone; I will make him a helper fit for him." So out of the ground the Lord God formed every beast of the field and every bird of the air, and brought them to the man to see what he would call them; and whatever the man called every living creature, that was its name. The man gave names to all cattle, and to the birds of the air, and to every beast of the field; but for the man there was not found a helper fit for him. So the Lord God caused a deep sleep to fall upon the man, and while he slept took one of his ribs and closed up its place with flesh; and the rib which the Lord God had taken from the man he made into a woman and brought her to the man. Then the man said,

> "This at last is bone of my bones
>   and flesh of my flesh;
> she shall be called Woman,
>   because she was taken out of Man."

Therefore a man leaves his father and his mother and cleaves to his wife, and they become one flesh. And the man and his wife were both naked, and were not ashamed.

Now the serpent was more subtle than any other wild creature that the Lord God had made. He said to the women, "Did God say, 'You shall not eat of any tree of the garden'?" And the woman said to the serpent, "We may eat of the fruit of the trees of the garden; but God said, 'You shall not eat of the fruit of the tree which is in the midst of the garden, neither shall you touch it, lest you die.'" But the serpent said to the woman, "You will not die. For God knows that when you eat of it your eyes will be opened, and you will be like God, knowing good and evil." So when the woman saw that the tree was good for food, and that it was a delight to the eyes, and that the tree was to be desired to make one wise, she took of its fruit and ate; and she also gave some to her husband, and he ate. Then the eyes of both were opened, and they knew that they were naked; and they sewed fig leaves together and made themselves aprons.

And they heard the sound of the Lord God walking in the garden in the cool of the day, and the man and his wife hid themselves from the presence of the Lord God among the trees of the garden. But the Lord

God called to the man, and said to him, "Where are you?" And he said, "I heard the sound of thee in the garden, and I was afraid, because I was naked; and I hid myself." He said, "Who told you that you were naked? Have you eaten of the tree of which I commanded you not to eat?" The man said, "The woman whom thou gavest to be with me, she gave me fruit of the tree, and I ate." Then the Lord God said to the woman, "What is this that you have done?" The woman said, "The serpent beguiled me, and I ate." The Lord God said to the serpent,

> "Because you have done this,
> > cursed are you above all cattle,
> > and above all wild animals;
> upon your belly you shall go,
> > and dust you shall eat
> > all the days of your life.
> I will put enmity between you and the woman,
> > and between your seed and her seed;
> he shall bruise your head,
> > and you shall bruise his heel."
> To the woman he said,
> "I will greatly multiply your pain in childbearing;
> > in pain you shall bring forth children,
> > yet your desire shall be for your husband,
> > and he shall rule over you.",
> And to Adam he said,
> "Because you have listened to the voice of your wife,
> > and have eaten of the tree
> of which I commanded you,
> > 'You shall not eat of it,'
> cursed is the ground because of you:
> > in toil you shall eat of it all the days of your life;
> thorns and thistles it shall bring forth to you;
> > and you shall eat the plants of the field.
> In the sweat of your face
> > you shall eat bread
> till you return to the ground,
> > for out of it you were taken;
> you are dust,
> > and to dust you shall return."

The man called his wife's name Eve, because she was the mother of all living. And the Lord God made for Adam and for his wife garments of skins, and clothed them.

Then the Lord God said, "Behold, the man has become like one of us, knowing good and evil; and now, lest he put forth his hand and take also of the tree of life, and eat, and live for ever"--therefore the Lord God sent him forth from the garden of Eden, to till the ground from which he was taken. He drove out the man; and at the east of the garden of Eden he placed the cherubim, and a flaming sword which turned every way, to guard the way to the tree of life. . . .

When Abram was ninety-nine years old the Lord appeared to Abram, and said to him, "I am God Almighty; walk before me, and be blameless. And I will make my covenant between me and you, and will multiply you exceedingly." Then Abram fell on his face; and God said to him, "Behold, my covenant is with you, and you shall be the father of a multitude of nations. No longer shall your name be Abram, but your name shall be Abraham; for I have made you the father of a multitude of nations. I will make you exceedingly fruitful; and I will make nations of you, and kings shall come forth from you. And I will establish my covenant between me and you and your descendants after you throughout their generations for an everlasting covenant, to be God to you and to your descendants after you. And I will give to you, and to your descendants after you, the land of your sojournings, all the land of Canaan, for an everlasting possession; and I will be their God.". . . .

After these things God tested Abraham, and said to him, "Abraham!" And he said, "Here am I." He said, "Take your son, your only son Isaac, whom you love, and go to the land of Mori'ah, and offer him there as a burnt offering upon one of the mountains of which I shall tell you." So Abraham rose early in the morning, saddled his ass, and took two of his young men with him, and his son Isaac; and he cut the wood for the burnt offering, and arose and went to the place of which God had told him. On the third day Abraham lifted up his eyes and saw the place afar off. Then Abraham said to his young men, "Stay here with the ass; I and the lad will go yonder and worship, and come again to you." And Abraham took the wood of the burnt offering, and laid it on Isaac his son; and he took in his hand the fire and the knife. So they went both of them together. And Isaac said to his father Abraham, "My father!" And he said, "Here am I, my son." He said, "Behold, the fire and the wood; but where is the lamb for a burnt offering?" Abraham said, "God will provide himself the lamb for a burnt offering, my son." So they went both of them together.

When they came to the place of which God had told him, Abraham built an altar there, and laid the wood in order, and bound Isaac his son, and laid him on the altar, upon the wood. Then Abraham put forth his hand, and took the knife to slay his son. But the angel of the Lord called to him from heaven, and said, "Abraham, Abraham!" And he said, "Here am I." He said, "Do not lay your hand on the lad or do anything to him; for now I know that you fear God, seeing you have not withheld your son, your only son, from me." And Abraham lifted up his eyes and looked, and behold, behind him was a ram, caught in a thicket by his horns; and Abraham went and took the ram, and offered it up as a burnt offering instead of his son. So Abraham called the name of that place The Lord will provide; as it is said to this day, "On the mount of the Lord it shall be provided."

And the angel of the Lord called to Abraham a second time from heaven, and said, "By myself I have sworn, says the Lord, because you have done this, and have not withheld your son, your only son, I will indeed bless you, and I will multiply your descendants as the stars of heaven and as the sand which is on the seashore. And your descendants shall possess the gate of their enemies, and by your descendants shall all the nations of the earth bless themselves, because you have obeyed my voice." . . .

From

EXODUS*

These are the names of the sons of Israel who came to Egypt with Jacob, each with his household: Reuben, Simeon, Levi, and Judah, Is'sachar, Zeb'ulun, and Benjamin, Dan and Naph'tali, Gad and Asher. All the offspring of Jacob were seventy persons; Joseph was already in Egypt. Then Joseph died, and all his brothers, and all that generation. But the descendants of Israel were fruitful and increased greatly; they multiplied and grew exceedingly strong; so that the land was filled with them.

Now there arose a new king over Egypt, who did not know Joseph. And he said to his people, "Behold, the people of Israel are too many and too mighty for us. Come, let us deal shrewdly with them, lest they multiply, and, if war befall us, they join our enemies and fight against us and escape from the land." Therefore they set taskmasters over them to afflict them with heavy burdens; and they built for Pharaoh store cities, Pithom and Ra-am'ses. But the more they were oppressed, the more they multiplied and the more they spread abroad. And the Egyptians were in dread of the people of Israel. So they made the people of Israel serve with rigor, and made their lives bitter with hard service, in mortar and brick, and in all kinds of work in the field; in all their work they made them serve with rigor. . . .

In the course of those many days the king of Egypt died. And the people of Israel groaned under their bondage, and cried out for help, and their cry under bondage came up to God. And God heard their groaning, and God remembered his covenant with Abraham, with Isaac, and with Jacob. And God saw the people of Israel, and God knew their condition.

Now Moses was keeping the flock of his father-in-law, Jethro, the priest of Mid'ian; and he led his flock to the west side of the wilderness, and came to Horeb, the mountain of God. And the angel of the Lord appeared to him in a flame of fire out of the midst of a bush; and he looked, and lo, the bush was burning, yet it was not consumed. And Moses said, "I will turn aside and see this great sight, why the bush is not burnt." When the Lord saw that he turned aside to see, God called to him out of the bush, "Moses, Moses!" And he said, "Here am I." Then he said, "Do not come near; put off your shoes from your feet, for the place on which you are standing is holy ground." And he said, "I am the God of your father, the God of Abraham, the God of Isaac, and the God of Jacob." And Moses hid his face, for he was afraid to look at God.

Then the Lord said, "I have seen the affliction of my people who are in Egypt, and have heard their cry because of their taskmasters; I know

*Selections from Exodus are 1:8-14, 2:23-3:17.

201

their sufferings, and I have come down to deliver them out of the hand of the Egyptians, and to bring them up out of that land to a good and broad land, a land flowing with milk and honey, to the place of the Canaanites, the Hittites, the Amorites, the Per'izzites, the Hivites, and the Jeb'usites. And now, behold, the cry of the people of Israel has come to me, and I have seen the oppression with which the Egyptians oppress them. Come, I will send you to Pharaoh that you may bring forth my people, the sons of Israel, out of Egypt." But Moses said to God, "Who am I that I should go to Pharaoh, and bring the sons of Israel out of Egypt?" He said, "But I will be with you; and this shall be the sign for you, that I have sent you: when you have brought forth the people out of Egypt, you shall serve God upon this mountain."

Then, Moses said to God, "If I come to the people of Israel and say to them, 'The God of your fathers has sent me to you,' and they ask me, 'What is his name?' what shall I say to them?" God said to Moses, "I AM WHO I AM." And he said, "Say this to the people of Israel, 'I AM has sent me to you.'" God also said to Moses, "Say this to the people of Israel, 'The Lord, the God of your fathers, the God of Abraham, the God of Isaac, and the God of Jacob, has sent me to you': this is my name for ever, and thus I am to be remembered throughout all generations. Go and gather the elders of Israel together, and say to them, 'The Lord, the God of your fathers, the God of Abraham, of Isaac, and of Jacob, has appeared to me, saying, "I have observed you and what has been done to you in Egypt; and I promise that I will bring you up out of the affliction of Egypt, to the land of Canaanites, the Hittites, the Amorites, the Per'izzites, the Hivites, and the Jeb'usites, a land flowing with milk and honey.'"

From

DEUTERONOMY*

And Moses summoned all Israel, and said to them, "Hear, O Israel, the statutes and the ordinances which I speak in your hearing this day, and you shall learn them and be careful to do them. The Lord our God made a covenant with us in Horeb. Not with our fathers did the Lord make this covenant, but with us, who are all of us here alive this day. The Lord spoke with you face to face at the mountain, out of the midst of the fire, while I stood between the Lord and you at that time, to declare to you the word of the Lord; for you were afraid because of the fire, and you did not go up into the mountain. He said:

"'I am the Lord your God, who brought you out of the land of Egypt, out of the house of bondage.

"'You shall have no other gods before me.

"'You shall not make for yourself a graven image, or any likeness of anything that is in heaven above, or that is on the earth beneath, or that is in the water under the earth; you shall not bow down to them or serve them; for I the Lord your God am a jealous God, visiting the iniquity of the fathers upon the children to the third and fourth generation of those who hate me, but showing steadfast love to thousands of those who love me and keep my commandments.

"'You shall not take the name of the Lord your God in vain: for the Lord will not hold him guiltless who takes his name in vain.

"'Observe the sabbath day, to keep it holy, as the Lord your God commanded you. Six days you shall labor, and do all your work; but the seventh day is a sabbath to the Lord your God; in it you shall not do any work, you, or your son, or your daughter, or your manservant, or your maidservant, or your ox, or your ass, or any of your cattle, or the sojourner who is within your gates, that your manservant and your maidservant may rest as well as you. You shall remember that you were a servant in the land of Egypt, and the Lord your God brought you out thence with a mighty hand and an outstretched arm; therefore the Lord your God commanded you to keep the sabbath day.

"'Honor your father and your mother, as the Lord your God commanded you; that your days may be prolonged, and that it may go well with you, in the land which the Lord your God gives you.

"'You shall not kill.

*Selections from Deuteronomy are 5:1-6:9, 30:1-20.

"'Neither shall you commit adultery.

"'Neither shall you steal.

"'Neither shall you bear false witness against your neighbor.

"'Neither shall you covet your neighbor's wife; and you shall not desire your neighbor's house, his field, or his manservant, or his maidservant, his ox, or his ass, or anything that is your neighbor's.'

"These words the Lord spoke to all your assembly at the mountain out of the midst of the fire, the cloud, and the deep gloom, with a loud voice; and he added no more. And he wrote them upon two tables of stone, and gave them to me. And when you heard the voice out of the midst of the darkness, while the mountain was burning with fire, you came near to me, all the heads of your tribes, and your elders; and you said, 'Behold, the Lord our God has shown us his glory and greatness, and we have heard his voice out of the midst of the fire; we have this day seen God speak with man and man still live. Now therefore why should we die? For this great fire will consume us; if we hear the voice of the Lord our God any more, we shall die. For who is there of all flesh, that has heard the voice of the living God speaking out of the midst of fire, as we have, and has still lived? Go near, and hear all that the Lord our God will say; and speak to us all that the Lord our God will speak to you; and we will hear and do it.'

"And the Lord heard your words, when you spoke to me; and the Lord said to me, 'I have heard the words of this people, which they have spoken to you; they have rightly said all that they have spoken. Oh that they had such a mind as this always, to fear me and to keep all my commandments, that it might go well with them and with their children for ever! Go and say to them, "Return to your tents." But you, stand here by me, and I will tell you all the commandment and the statutes and the ordinances which you shall teach them, that they may do them in the land which I give them to possess.' You shall be careful to do therefore as the Lord your God has commanded you; you shall not turn aside to the right hand or to the left. You shall walk in all the way which the Lord your God has commanded you, that you may live, and that it may go well with you, and that you may live long in the land which you shall possess.

"Now this is the commandment, the statutes and the ordinances which the Lord your God commanded me to teach you, that you may do them in the land to which you are going over, to possess it; that you may fear the Lord your God, you and your son and your son's son, by keeping all his statutes and his commandments, which I command you, all the days of your life; and that your days may be prolonged. Hear therefore, O Israel, and be careful to do them; that it may go well with you, and that you may multiply greatly, as the Lord, the God of your fathers, has promised you, in a land flowing with milk and honey.

"Hear, O Israel: The Lord our God is one Lord; and you shall love the Lord your God with all your heart, and with all your soul, and with all your might. And these words which I command you this day shall be upon your heart; and you shall teach them diligently to your children, and shall talk of them when you sit in your house, and when you walk by the way, and when you lie down, and when you rise. And you shall bind them as a sign upon your hand, and they shall be as frontlets between your eyes. And you shall write them on the doorposts of your house and on your gates. . . .

"And when all these things come upon you, the blessing and the curse, which I have set before you, and you call them to mind among all the nations where the Lord your God has driven you, and return to the Lord your God, you and your children, and obey his voice in all that I command you this day, with all your heart and with all your soul; then the Lord your God will restore your fortunes, and have compassion upon you, and he will gather you again from all the peoples where the Lord your God has scattered you. If your outcasts are in the uttermost parts of heaven, from there the Lord your God will gather you, and from there he will fetch you; and the Lord your God will bring you into the land which your fathers possessed, that you may possess it; and he will make you more prosperous and numerous than your fathers. And the Lord your God will circumcise your heart and the heart of your offspring, so that you will love the Lord your God with all your heart and with all your soul, that you may live. And the Lord your God will put all these curses upon your foes and enemies who persecuted you. And you shall again obey the voice of the Lord, and keep all his commandments which I command you this day. The Lord your God will make you abundantly prosperous in all the work of your hand, in the fruit of your body, and in the fruit of your cattle, and in the fruit of your ground; for the Lord will again take delight in prospering you, as he took delight in your fathers, if you obey the voice of the Lord your God, to keep his commandments and his statutes which are written in this book of the law, if you turn to the Lord your God with all your heart and with all your soul.

"For this commandment which I command you this day is not too hard for you, neither is it far off. It is not in heaven, that you should say, 'Who will go up for us to heaven, and bring it to us, that we may hear it and do it?' Neither is it beyond the sea, that you should say, 'Who will go over the sea for us, and bring it to us, that we may hear it and do it?' But the word is very near you; it is in your mouth and in your heart, so that you can do it.

"See, I have set before you this day life and good, death and evil. If you obey the commandments of the Lord your God which I command you this day, by loving the Lord your God, by walking in his ways, and by keeping his commandments and his statutes and his ordinances, then you shall live and multiply, and the Lord your God will bless you in the land which you are entering to take possession of it. But if your heart turns away, and you will not hear, but are drawn away to worship other gods and serve them, I declare to you this day, that you shall perish; you shall not live long in the land which you are going over the Jordan to enter and possess. I call heaven and earth to witness against you this day, that I have set before you life and death, blessing and curse; therefore choose life, that you and your descendants may live, loving the Lord your God, obeying his voice, and cleaving to him; for that means life to you and length of days, that you may dwell in the land which the Lord swore to your fathers, to Abraham, to Isaac, and to Jacob, to give them."

From

THE PSALMS*

1 Blessed is the man
    who walks not in the counsel of
       the wicked,
nor stands in the way of sinners,
    nor sits in the seat of scoffers;
but his delight is in the law of the
       Lord,
    and on his law he meditates day
       and night.
He is like a tree
    planted by streams of water,
that yields its fruit in its season,
    and its leaf does not wither,
In all that he does, he prospers.

The wicked are not so,
    but are like chaff which the wind
       drives away.
Therefore the wicked will not stand
    in the judgment,
    nor sinners in the congregation of
       the righteous;
for the Lord knows the way of the
       righteous,
    but the way of the wicked will
       perish.

8 O Lord, our Lord,
how majestic is thy name in all
       the earth!

Thou whose glory above the heavens
    is chanted
    by the mouth of babes and infants,
thou hast founded a bulwark because
    of thy foes,
    to still the enemy and the
       avenger.

When I look at thy heavens, the
    work of thy fingers,
    the moon and the stars which

thou hast established;
what is man that thou art mindful
    of him,
    and the son of man that thou
       dost care for him?

Yet thou hast made him little less
    than God, (should be angel)
    and dost crown him with glory
       and honor.
Thou hast given him dominion over
    the works of thy hands;
thou hast put all things under his
    feet,
all sheep and oxen,
    and also the beasts of the
       field,
the birds of the air, and the fish of
    the sea,
    whatever passes along the
       paths of the sea.
O Lord, our Lord,
    how majestic is thy name in
       all the earth!

19 The heavens are telling the
       glory of God;
and the firmament proclaims his
    handiwork.
Day to day pours forth speech,
    and night to night declares
       knowledge.
There is no speech, nor are there
    words;
    their voice is not heard;
yet their voice goes out through
    all the earth,
    and their words to the end of
       the world.
In them he has set a tent for the
    sun,
    which comes forth like a bride-

*The following Psalms are selected: 1, 8, 19, 23, 24, 42, 51, 84, 100, 103, 121, 139.

207

groom leaving his chamber,
and like a strong man runs its
course with joy.

Its rising is from the end of the
heavens,
and its circuit to the end of them;
and there is nothing hid from its
heat.

The law of the Lord is perfect,
reviving the soul;
the testimony of the Lord is sure,
making wise the simple;
the precepts of the Lord are right,
rejoicing the heart;
the commandment of the Lord is
pure,
enlightening the eyes;
the fear of the Lord is clean,
enduring for ever;
the ordinances of the Lord are true,
and righteous altogether.
More to be desired are they than
gold,
even much fine gold;
sweeter also than honey
and drippings of the honeycomb.

Moreover by them is thy servant
warned;
in keeping them there is great reward.
But who can discern his errors?
clear thou me from hidden faults.
Keep back thy servant also from
presumptuous sins;
let them not have dominion over
me!
Then I shall be blameless
and innocent of great transgres-
sion.

Let the words of my mouth and the
meditation of my heart
be acceptable in thy sight,
O Lord, my rock and my re-
deemer.

23 The Lord is my shepherd, I
shall not want;
he makes me lie down in green
pastures.
He leads me beside still waters;
he restores my soul.
He leads me in paths of righteousness
for his name's sake.

Even though I walk through the
valley of the shadow of death,
I fear no evil;
for thou art with me;
thy rod and thy staff,
they comfort me.

Thou preparest a table before me
in the presence of my enemies;
thou anointest my head with oil,
my cup overflows.
Surely goodness and mercy shall
follow me
all the days of my life;
and I shall dwell in the house of
the Lord
for ever.

24 The earth is the Lord's and
the fulness thereof,
the world and those who dwell
therein;
for he has founded it upon the seas,
and established it upon the
rivers.

Who shall ascend the hill of the
Lord?
And who shall stand in his holy
place?
He who has clean hands and a pure
heart,
who does not lift up his soul to
what is false,
and does not swear deceitfully.
He will receive blessing from the
Lord,
and vindication from the God of

his salvation.

Such is the generation of those who
seek him,
who seek the face of the God of
Jacob.
Lift up your heads, O gates!
and be lifted up, O ancient doors!
that the King of glory may come
in.
Who is the King of glory?
The Lord, strong and mighty,
the Lord, mighty in battle!
Lift up your heads, O gates!
and be lifted up, O ancient
doors!
that the King of glory may come
in!
Who is this King of glory?
The Lord of hosts,
he is the King of glory!

42 As a hart longs
for flowing steams,
so longs my soul
for thee, O God.
My soul thirsts for God,
for the living God.
When shall I come and behold
the face of God?
My tears have been my food
day and night,
while men say to me continually,
"Where is your God?"

These things I remember,
as I pour out my soul:
how I went with the throng,
and led them in procession to
the house of God,
with glad shouts and songs of
thanksgiving,
a multitude keeping festival.
Why are you cast down, O my soul,
and why are you disquieted within me?
Hope in God; for I shall again
praise him,

my help and my God.

My soul is cast down within me,
therefore I remember thee
from the land of Jordan and of
Hermon,
from Mount Mizar.
Deep calls to deep
at the thunder of thy cataracts;
all thy waves and thy billows
have gone over me.
By day the Lord commands his
steadfast love;
and at night his song is with me,
a prayer to the God of my life.

I say to God, my rock;
"why hast thou forgotten me?
Why go I mourning
because of the oppression of the
enemy?

As with a deadly wound in my
body,
my adversaries taunt me,
while they say to me continually,
"Where is your God?"

Why are you cast down, O my soul,
and why are you disquieted within me?
Hope in God; for I shall again
praise him,
my help and my God.

51 Have mercy on me, O God,
according to thy steadfast love;
according to thy abundant mercy
blot out my transgressions.
Wash me thoroughly from my iniquity,
and cleanse me from my sin!

For I know my transgressions,
and my sin is ever before me.
Against thee, thee only, have I
sinned,
and done that which is evil in

thy sight,
so that thou art justified in thy
sentence
and blameless in thy judgment.
Behold, I was brought forth in iniquity,
and in sin did my mother conceive me.

Behold, thou desirest truth in the
inward being,
therefore teach me wisdom in
my secret heart.
Purge me with hyssop, and I shall
be clean;
wash me, and I shall be whiter
than snow.
Fill me with joy and gladness;
let the bones which thou hast
broken rejoice.
Hide thy face from my sins,
and blot out all my iniquities.

Create in me a clean heart, O God,
and put a new and right spirit
within me.
Cast me not away from thy presence,
and take not thy holy Spirit from
me.

Restore to me the joy of thy salvation,
and uphold me with a willing
spirit.

Then I will teach transgressors thy
ways,
and sinners will return to thee.
Deliver me from bloodguiltiness,
O God,
thou God of my salvation,
and my tongue will sing aloud of
thy deliverance.

O Lord, open thou my lips,
and my mouth shall show forth
thy praise.

For thou hast no delight in sacrifice;
were I to give a burnt offering,
thou wouldst not be pleased.
The sacrifice acceptable to God is
a broken spirit;
a broken and contrite heart, O
God, thou wilt not despise.

Do good to Zion in thy good pleasure;
rebuild the walls of Jerusalem,
then wilt thou delight in right
sacrifices,
in burnt offerings and whole
burnt offerings;
then bulls will be offered on thy
altar.

84 How lovely is thy dwelling
place,
O Lord of hosts!
My soul longs, yea, faints
for the courts of the Lord;
my heart and flesh sing for joy
to the living God.

Even the sparrow finds a home,
and the swallow a nest for herself,
where she may lay her young,
at thy altars, O Lord of hosts,
my king and my God.
Blessed are those who dwell in thy
house,
ever singing thy praise!

Blessed are the men whose
strength is in thee,
in whose heart are the highways
to Zion.
As they go through the valley of
Baca
they make it a place of springs;
the early rain also covers it with
pools.
They go from strength to strength;
the God of gods will be seen in

Zion.

O Lord God of hosts, hear my
    prayer;
  give ear, O God of Jacob!

Behold our shield, O God;
  look upon the face of thine
    anointed!

For a day in thy courts is better
  than a thousand elsewhere
I would rather be a doorkeeper in
    the house of my God
  than dwell in the tents of wicked-
    ness.
For the Lord God is a sun and
    shield;
  he bestows favor and honor.
No good thing does the Lord with-
    hold
  from those who walk uprightly.
O Lord of hosts,
  blessed is the man who trusts in
    thee!

100 Make a joyful noise to the
    Lord, all the lands!
Serve the Lord with gladness!
Come into his presence with
    singing!

Know that the Lord is God!
  It is he that made us, and we are
    his;
  we are his people, and the sheep
    of his pasture.

Enter his gates with thanksgiving,
  and his courts with praise!
  Give thanks to him, bless his
    name!

For the Lord is good;
  his steadfast love endures for
    ever,
  and his faithfulness to all gene-
    rations.

103 Bless the Lord, O my soul;
  and all that is within me,
    bless his holy name!
Bless the Lord, O my soul,
  and forget not all his benefits,
who forgives all your iniquity,
  who heals all your diseases,
who redeems your life from the
    Pit, who crowns you with
    steadfast love and mercy,
who satisfies you with good as long
    as you live
  so that your youth is renewed
    like the eagle's.

The Lord works vindication
  and justice for all who are op-
    pressed.
He made known his ways to Moses,
  his acts to the people of Israel.
The Lord is merciful and gracious,
  slow to anger and abounding in
    steadfast love.
He will not always chide,
  nor will he keep his anger for
    ever.
He does not deal with us accord-
    ing to our sins,
  nor requite us according to our
    iniquities.
For as the heavens are high above
    the earth,
  so great is his steadfast love to-
    ward those who fear him;
as far as the east is from the west,
  so far does he remove our trans-
    gressions from us.
As a father pities his children,
  so the Lord pities those who fear
    him.

For he knows our frame;
  he remembers that we are dust.

As for man, his days are like grass;
  he flourishes like a flower of the
    field;
for the wind passes over it, and it

is gone,
and its place knows it no more.

But the steadfast love of the Lord
is from everlasting to everlasting
upon those who fear him,
and his righteousness to children's children,
to those who keep his covenant
and remember to do his commandments.

The Lord has established his
throne in the heavens,
and his kingdom rules over all.
Bless the Lord, O you his angels,
you mighty ones who do his
word,
hearkening to the voice of his
word!
Bless the Lord, all his hosts,
his ministers that do his will!
Bless the Lord, all his works,
in all places of his dominion.
Bless the Lord, O my soul!

121 I lift up my eyes to the
hills.
From whence does my help
come?
My help comes from the Lord,
who made heaven and earth.

He will not let your foot be moved,
he who keeps you will not
slumber.
Behold, he who keeps Israel
will neither slumber nor sleep.

The Lord is your keeper;
the Lord is your shade
on your right hand.
The sun shall not smite you by day,
nor the moon by night.

The Lord will keep you from all
evil;

he will keep your life.
The Lord will keep
your going out and your coming
in
from this time forth and for
evermore.

139 O Lord, thou hast searched
me and known me!
Thou knowest when I sit down and
when I rise up;
thou discernest my thoughts
from afar.
Thou searchest out my path and
my lying down,
and art acquainted with all my
ways.
Even before a word is on my
tongue,
lo, O Lord, thou knowest it altogether.
Thou dost beset me behind and
before,
and layest thy hand upon me.
Such knowledge is too wonderful
for me;
it is high, I cannot attain it.

Whither shall I go from thy Spirit?
Or whither shall I flee from thy
presence?
If I ascend to heaven, thou art
there!
If I make my bed in Sheol, thou
art there!
If I take the wings of the morning
and dwell in the uttermost parts
of the sea,
even there thy hand shall lead me,
and thy right hand shall hold me.
If I say, "Let only darkness cover
me,
and the light about me be night,"
even the darkness is not dark to
thee,
for night is bright as the day;
for darkness is as light with
thee.

For thou didst form my inward
    parts,
  thou didst knit me together in
  my mother's womb.
I praise thee, for thou art fearful
and wonderful.

  Wonderful are thy works!
Thou knowest me right well;
  my frame was not hidden from
  thee,
when I was being made in secret,
  intricately wrought in the depths
  of the earth.
Thy eyes beheld my unformed substance;
  in thy book were written, every
  one of them,
the days that were formed for me,
  when as yet there was none of
  them.
How precious to me are thy
  thoughts, O God!
  How vast is the sum of them!

If I would count them, they are
  more than the sand.
When I awake, I am still with
  thee.

O that thou wouldst slay the
  wicked, O God,
  and that men of blood would depart from me,
men who maliciously defy thee,
  who lift themselves up against
  thee for evil!
Do I not hate them that hate thee,
  O Lord?
  And do I not loathe them that
  rise up against thee?
I hate them with perfect hatred;
  I count them my enemies.
Search me, O God, and know my
  heart!
And see if there be any wicked
  way in me,
  and lead me in the way
everlasting!

CRITIQUE

In his The Future of an Illusion, Sigmund Freud (1856-1939) offers a psychological account of the origin of religious beliefs. Humans find themselves largely at the mercy of powerful natural forces. In order to render the natural world more comprehensible, and to achieve a feeling of control over their lives, humans seek to explain the world in anthropomorphic terms, first attributing natural events to the actions of powerful person-like spirits or gods, then eventually coalescing these beings into a single, all-powerful deity, who constitutes a kind of father-figure, a source of love and reassurance, of justice and punishment. Such explanations are, according to Freud, products of wishful thinking; they are in fact illusions, incapable of proof.

Freud imagines a hypothetical critic who argues that it is cruel to destroy the illusions of religion, because people depend upon those illusions for consolation and hope. Freud replies that while it is not feasible to change the minds of those who have received religious indoctrination since childhood, one can start afresh with others, who can be "sensibly brought up" to face the hard facts of life without relying upon illusion. Freud calls this "education to reality." For "surely infantilism is destined to be surmounted. Men cannot remain children for ever . . . "

It is often argued that if there is no God, human life can have no meaning or purpose, since human existence is then merely an accident of evolution, without any design or goal that transcends itself. In reply to this line of reasoning, the philosopher Kurt Baier (1917-   ) distinguishes two senses of the word "purpose." One, self-generated purpose, is the intention of conscious persons to bring about some goal or end; the second, externally imposed purpose, is usually attributed to things created or arranged by humans. Thus a pencil has no intentions of its own, but has a definite purpose as envisioned by those who make it and those who use it.

Without the agency of a higher being, human life has no externally imposed purpose: we are not artifacts of God, put here to serve God's goals. It does not follow, however, that our lives must be lacking in self-generated purposes, argues Baier. We may conceive plans and undertake projects that make our lives meaningful and purposeful, within their own terms. Although Baier directs his remarks to Christianity, the excerpt included here applies to theism generally: without God, human life may still have meaning.

ESCAPE FROM REALITY:

RELIGION AS WISH-FULFILLMENT AND ILLUSION*

by Sigmund Freud

...No one is under the illusion that nature has already been vanquished; and few dare hope that she will ever be entirely subjected to man. There are the elements, which seem to mock at all human control: the earth, which quakes and is torn apart and buries all human life and its works; water, which deluges and drowns everything in a turmoil; storms, which blow everything before them; there are diseases, which we have only recently recognized as attacks by other organisms; and finally there is the painful riddle of death, against which no medicine has yet been found, nor probably will be. With these forces nature rises up against us, majestic, cruel and inexorable; she brings to our mind once more our weakness and helplessness, which we thought to escape through the work of civilization. One of the few gratifying and exalting impressions which mankind can offer is when, in the face of an elemental catastrophe, it forgets the discordancies of its civilization and all its internal difficulties and animosities, and recalls the great common task of preserving itself against the superior power of nature.

For the individual, too, life is hard to bear, just as it is for mankind in general. The civilization in which he participates imposes some amount of privation on him, and other men bring him a measure of suffering, either in spite of the precepts of his civilization or because of its imperfections. To this are added the injuries which untamed nature--he calls it fate--inflicts on him. One might suppose that this condition of things would result in a permanent state of anxious expectation in him and a severe injury to his natural narcissism. . . . Man's self-regard, seriously menaced, calls for consolation; life and the universe must be robbed of their terrors; moreover his curiosity, moved, it is true, by the strongest practical interest, demands an answer. . . .

Once before, one has found oneself in a similar state of helplessness: as a small child, in relation to one's parents. One had reason to fear them, and especially one's father; and yet one was sure of his protection against the dangers one knew. Thus it was natural to assimilate the two situations. Here, too, wishing played its part, as it does in dream life. . . . In the same way, a man makes the forces of nature not simply into persons with whom he can associate as he would with his equals--that would not do justice to the overpowering impression which those forces make on him--but he gives them the character of a father. He turns them into gods. . .

*Reprinted from The Future of An Illusion by Sigmund Freud, translated and edited by James Strachey. With the permission of W. W. Norton & Company, Inc. Copyright (c) 1961 by James Strachey.

And thus a store of ideas is created, born from man's need to make his helplessness tolerable and built up from the material of memories of the helplessness of his own childhood and the childhood of the human race. It can clearly be seen that the possession of these ideas protects him in two directions--against the dangers of nature and fate, and against the injuries that threaten him from human society itself. Here is the gist of the matter. Life in this world serves a higher purpose; no doubt it is not easy to guess what the purpose is, but it certainly signifies a perfecting of man's nature. It is probably the spiritual part of man, the soul, which in the course of time has so slowly and unwillingly detached itself from the body, that is the object of this elevation and exaltation. Everything that happens in this world is an expression of the intentions of an intelligence superior to us, which in the end, though its ways and byways are difficult to follow, orders everything for the best--that is, to make it enjoyable for us. Over each one of us there watches a benevolent Providence, which is only seemingly stern and which will not suffer us to become a plaything of the over-mighty and pitiless forces of nature. Death itself is not extinction, is not a return to inorganic lifelessness, but the beginning of a new kind of existence which lies on the path of development to something higher. And, looking in the other direction, this view announces that the same moral laws which our civilizations have set up govern the whole universe as well, except that they are maintained by a supreme court of justice with incomparably more power and consistency. In the end all good is rewarded and all evil punished, if not actually in this form of life then in the later existences that begin after death. In this way all the terrors, the sufferings and the hardships of life are destined to be obliterated. Life after death, which continues life on earth, just as the invisible part of the spectrum joins onto the visible part, brings us all the perfection that we may perhaps have missed here. And the superior wisdom which directs this course of things, the infinite goodness that expresses itself in it, the justice that achieves its aim in it--these are the attributes of the divine beings who also created us and the world as a whole, or rather, of the one divine being into which, in our civilization, all the gods of antiquity have been condensed. The people which first succeeded in thus concentrating the divine attributes was not a little proud of the advance. It had laid open to view the father who had all along been hidden behind every divine figure as its nucleus. Fundamentally this was a return to the historical beginnings of the idea of God. Now that God was a single person, man's relations to him could recover the intimacy and intensity of the child's relation to his father. . . .

(Religious ideas) are given out as teachings, are not precipitates of experience or end-results of thinking: they are illusions, fulfilments of the oldest, strongest and most urgent wishes of mankind. The secret of their strength lies in the strength of those wishes. As we already know, the terrifying impression of helplessness in childhood aroused the need for protection--for protection through love--which was provided by the father; and the recognition that this helplessness lasts throughout life made it necessary to cling to the existence of a father, but this time a more powerful one. Thus the benevolent rule of a divine Providence allays our fear of the dangers of life; the establishment of a moral world-order ensures the fulfilment of the demands of justice, which have so often remained unfulfilled in human civilization; and the prolongation of earthly existence in a future life provides the local and temporal framework in which these wish-fulfilments shall take place. Answers to the riddles that tempt the curiosity of man, such as how the universe began or what the relation is between body and mind, are developed in conformity with the underlying assumptions of this system. It is an enormous relief to the individual psyche if the conflicts of its childhood arising from the father-complex--conflicts which it has never wholly overcome--are removed from it and brought to a solution which is universally accepted. . . .

(All religious doctrines) are illusions and insusceptible of proof. No one can be compelled to think them true, to believe in them. Some of them are so improbable, so incompatible with everything we have laboriously discovered about the reality of the world, that we may compare them--if we pay proper regard to the psychological differences-- to delusions. Of the reality value of most of them we cannot judge; just as they cannot be proved, so they cannot be refuted. We still know too little to make a critical approach to them. The riddles of the universe reveal themselves only slowly to our investigation; there are many questions to which science to-day can give no answer. But scientific work is the only road which can lead us to a knowledge of reality outside ourselves. . . .

But now the loud voice of our opponent brings us to a halt. We are called to account for our wrong-doing:

'Archaeological interests are no doubt most praiseworthy, but no one undertakes an excavation if by doing so he is going to undermine the habitations of the living so that they collapse and bury people under their ruins. The doctrines of religion are not a subject one can quibble about like any other. Our civilization is built up on them, and the maintenance of human society is based on the majority of men's believing in the truth of those doctrines. . . . And apart from the danger of the undertaking, it would be a purposeless cruelty. Countless people find their one consolation in religious doctrines, and can only bear life with their help. You would rob them of their support, without having anything better to give them in exchange. It is admitted that so far science has not achieved much, but even if it had advanced much further it would not suffice for man. Man has imperative needs of another sort, which can never be satisfied by cold science. . . '

On (one) point I agree with you unreservedly. It is certainly senseless to begin by trying to do away with religion by force and at a

217

single blow. Above all, because it would be hopeless. The believer will not let his belief be torn from him, either by arguments or by prohibitions. And even if this did succeed with some it would be cruelty. A man who has been taking sleeping draughts for tens of years is naturally unable to sleep if his sleeping draught is taken away from him. . . .

(But) I must contradict you when you go on to argue that men are completely unable to do without the consolation of the religious illusion, that without it they could not bear the troubles of life and the cruelties of reality. That is true, certainly, of the men into whom you have instilled the sweet--or bitter-sweet--poison from childhood onwards. But what of the other men, who have been sensibly brought up? Perhaps those who do not suffer from the neurosis will need no intoxicant to deaden it. They will, it is true, find themselves in a difficult situation. They will have to admit to themselves the full extent of their helplessness and their insignificance in the machinery of the universe; they can no longer be the centre of creation, no longer the object of tender care on the part of a beneficent Providence. They will be in the same position as a child who has left the parental house where he was so warm and comfortable. But surely infantilism is destined to be surmounted. Men cannot remain children for ever; they must in the end go out into 'hostile life'. We may call this 'education to reality'. Need I confess to you that the sole purpose of my book is to point out the necessity for this forward step?

WITHOUT GOD, LIFE MAY HAVE MEANING*

by Kurt Baier

As the natural sciences developed, . . . more and more things in the universe came to be explained without the assumption of a supernatural creator. Science, moreover, could explain them better, that is, more accurately and more reliably. The Christian hypothesis of a supernatural maker, whatever other needs it was capable of satisfying, was at any rate no longer indispensable for the purpose of explaining the existence or occurrence of anything. In fact, scientific explanations do not seem to leave any room for this hypothesis. The scientific approach demands that we look for a natural explanation of anything and everything. The scientific way of looking at and explaining things has yielded an immensely greater measure of understanding of, and control over, the universe than any other way. And when one looks at the world in this scientific way, there seems to be no room for a personal relationship between human beings and a supernatural perfect being ruling and guiding men. Hence many scientists and educated men have come to feel that the Christian attitudes towards the world and human existence are inappropriate. They have become convinced that the universe and human existence in it are without a purpose and therefore devoid of meaning. . . .

There are, however, two quite different senses of "purpose". Which one is meant? Has science deprived human life of purpose in both senses? And if not, is it a harmless sense, in which human existence has been robbed of purpose? Could human existence still have meaning if it did not have a purpose in that sense?

What are the two senses? In the first and basic sense, purpose is normally attributed only to persons or their behaviour as in "Did you have a purpose in leaving the ignition on?" In the second sense, purpose is normally attributed only to things, as in "What is the purpose of that gadget you installed in the workshop?" The two uses are intimately connected. We cannot attribute a purpose to a thing without implying that someone did something, in the doing of which he had some purpose, namely, to bring about the thing with the purpose. Of course, his purpose is not identical with its purpose. In hiring labourers and engineers and buying materials and a site for a factory and the like, the entrepreneur's purpose, let us say, is to manufacture cars, but the purpose of cars is to serve as a means of transportation.

There are many things that a man may do, such as buying and selling, hiring labourers, ploughing, felling trees, and the like, which it is foolish, pointless, silly, perhaps crazy, to do if one has no purpose in doing

*Excerpt from "The Meaning of Life," Inaugural Lecture at Canberra University College, 1957. Reprinted by permission of Kurt Baier.

them. A man who does these things without a purpose is engaging in inane, futile pursuits. Lives crammed full with such activities devoid of purpose are pointless, futile, worthless. Such lives may indeed be dismissed as meaningless. But it should also be perfectly clear that acceptance of the scientific world picture does not force us to regard our lives as being without a purpose in this sense. Science has not only not robbed us of any purpose which we had before, but it has furnished us with enormously greater power to achieve these purposes. Instead of praying for rain or a good harvest or offspring, we now use ice pellets, artificial manure, or artificial insemination.

By contrast, having or not having a purpose, in the other sense, is value neutral. We do not think more or less highly of a thing for having or not having a purpose. "Having a purpose", in this sense, confers no kudos, "being purposeless" carries no stigma. A row of trees growing near a farm may or may not have a purpose: it may or may not be a windbreak, may or may not have been planted or deliberately left standing there in order to prevent the wind from sweeping across the fields. We do not in any way disparage the trees if we say they have no purpose, but have just grown that way. They are as beautiful, made of as good wood, as valuable, as if they had a purpose. And, of course, they break the wind just as well. The same is true of living creatures. We do not disparage a dog when we say that it has no purpose, is not a sheep dog or a watch dog or a rabbiting dog, but just a dog that hangs around the house and is fed by us.

Man is in a different category, however. To attribute to a human being a purpose in that sense is not neutral, let alone complimentary: it is offensive. It is degrading for a man to be regarded as merely serving a purpose. If, at a garden party, I ask a man in livery, "What is your purpose?" I am insulting him. I might as well have asked, "What are you for?" Such questions reduce him to the level of a gadget, a domestic animal, or perhaps a slave. I imply that we allot to him the tasks, the goals, the aims which he is to pursue; that his wishes and desires and aspirations and purposes are to count for little or nothing. We are treating him, in Kant's phrase, merely as a means to our ends, not as an end in himself.

The Christian and the scientific world pictures do indeed differ fundamentally on this point. The latter robs man of a purpose in this sense. It sees him as a being with no purpose allotted to him by anyone but himself. It robs him of any goal, purpose, or destiny appointed for him by any outside agency. The Christian world picture, on the other hand, sees man as a creature, a divine artefact, something halfway between a robot (manufactured) and an animal (alive), a homunculus, or perhaps Frankenstein, made in God's laboratory, with a purpose or task assigned him by his Maker.

However, lack of purpose in this sense does not in any way detract from the meaningfulness of life. I suspect that many who reject the scientific outlook because it involves the loss of purpose of life, and therefore meaning, are guilty of a confusion between the two senses of "purpose" just distinguished. They confusedly think that if the scientific world picture is true, then their lives must be futile because that picture implies that man has no purpose given him from without. But this is muddled thinking, for, as has already been shown, pointlessness is implied only by purposelessness in the other sense, which is not at all implied by the scientific picture of the world. These people mistakenly conclude that there can be no purpose in life because there is no purpose of life; that men cannot themselves adopt and achieve purposes because man, unlike a robot or a watchdog, is not a creature with a purpose. . . .

It will perhaps be objected now that I have not really demonstrated that life has a meaning, but merely that it can be worthwhile or have value. It must be admitted that there is a perfectly natural interpretation of the question, "What is the meaning of life?" on which my view actually proves that life has no meaning. . . .: if we accept the explanations of natural science, we cannot believe that living organisms have appeared on earth in accordance with the deliberate plan of some intelligent being. Hence, on this view, life cannot be said to have a purpose, in the sense in which man-made things have a purpose. Hence it cannot be said to have a meaning or significance in that sense.

However, this conclusion is innocuous. People are disconcerted by the thought that life as such has no meaning in that sense only because they very naturally think it entails that no individual life can have meaning either. They naturally assume that this life or that can have meaning only if life as such has meaning. But it should be now be clear that your life and mine may or may not have meaning (in one sense) even if life as such as none (in the other). Of course, it follows from this that your life may have meaning while mine has not. The Christian view guarantees a meaning (in one sense) to every life, the scientific view does not (in any sense). By relating the question of the meaningfulness of life to the particular circumstances of an individual's existence, the scientific view leaves it an open question whether an individual's life has meaning or not. It is, however, clear that the latter is the important sense of "having a meaning". Christians, too, must feel that their life is wasted and meaningless if they have not achieved salvation. To know that even such lost lives have a meaning in another sense is no consolation to them. What matters is not that life should have a guaranteed meaning, whatever happens here or here-after, but that, by luck (Grace) or the right temperament and attitude (Faith) or a judicious life (Works) a person should make the most of his life.

STUDY QUESTIONS FOR CHAPTER VI

Questions for Review:

1.   Why must all purely human efforts to gain a good life end in failure, according to traditional theism?

2.   Why is naturalism unsatisfactory, according to theism?

3.   What is the connection between living rightly and living well as described in the editor's interpretation of theism?

4.   What is the meaning of kedushah?

5.   Review the stages of creation, as stated in Genesis 1:1-2:3. What authority is given by God to humans?

6.   What was the motive for disobeying God's will, in the Garden of Eden story?

7.   What punishments did God specify for the serpent, the woman, and the man for their disobedience?

8.   Why did God then drive Adam and Eve out of Eden?

9.   What was the covenant that God made with Abraham?

10.   What was God's purpose in commanding Abraham to sacrifice Isaac?

11.   What was the message conveyed to Moses by God out of the burning bush? What promises are made by God?

12.   Restate the Ten Commandments in your own words.

13.   Summarize in your own words the Great Commandment of Deuteronomy.

14.   What promises are made by God for those who follow God's commandments, in Deuteronomy?

15.   What blessings are promised for the person whose "delight is in the law of the Lord"?

16.   Psalm 8 marvels at the contrast between the apparent lowliness of humans, and the exalted state bestowed upon them by God. Restate this contrast in your own words.

17.   What are the blessings of those who obey God, according to Psalm 19?

18.   What are the kinds of support given by God to the narrator of the 23rd Psalm?

19.   What is the spirit or emotional tone of the 42nd Psalm?

20.   Which of the Psalms are primarily songs of joyful praise? Which are primarily reassurances of God's justice and mercy? Which are primarily earnest entreaties and pleas for succor?

21.   How do humans initially form the notion of deities, according to Freud?

22.   Restate in your own words Freud's summary account of the content of religious belief ("Here is the gist of the matter . . . ").

23.   What is Freud's reply to the critic who suggests that it is cruel to rob people of the support of religious faith?

24.   Restate Baier's two senses of "purpose." In what sense is it correct to say that the scientific world-view robs humans of a purpose in life? In what sense may humans still have a purpose in life, given the scientific world-view?

Questions for Reflection:

1. Do I believe that human efforts to achieve a good life must fail, without the support of belief in God?

2. Have I experienced anything resembling the sense of the sacredness of all of life (kedushah)? If so, under what conditions did my experience occur?

3. What meaning do I find in the creation story?

4. How do I feel about God's commandment to Abraham to sacrifice his son?

5. Do I accept the Ten Commandments as proper guides for my life?

6. (For those who believe in God:) How important is my belief in God, in my day-to-day life? If somehow I were no longer able to believe, what impact would such a loss of belief have upon my life?

7. How do I feel about my own religious tradition? Are my own beliefs consistent with the version of theism expressed in this chapter? If not, how do they differ?

Questions for Discussion:

1. Is it true that all efforts to achieve a good life that are not grounded in commitment to God must end in failure?

2. Is Freud's reconstruction of the origins of religious belief a plausible account?

3. Do you agree with Baier that human life may have satisfactory purpose or meaning, in the absence of a supreme being?

4. Is this world enough for a genuinely good life? Consider the following two views:

   a. "To project a supernatural realm and being is to demote the real in favor of an imagined ideal; it is to betray an unwillingness to accept one's humanness, one's morality and physical nature. Those who have not learned a full appreciation of this life may feel a need for another; and those who insist upon perfection will create for themselves a perfect fantasy. According to naturalism, such impulses are understandable but mistaken. For those who are alive to their own natural being, this world is enough." (Chapter 5, p. 154)

   b. ". . . without grounding in that which transcends this world, our lives are ultimately hollow and pointless, lacking in true meaning. We may find ways to enjoy ourselves; we may become wealthy and live comfortably; we may gain the admiration and respect of others; we may be regarded by most people as successful in everything we do. But without God, our lives will be like empty pantomimes, gestures without feeling. In itself, this world is not enough." (Chapter 6, p. 190)

   Which statement do you more nearly agree with? Why?

SUGGESTIONS FOR FURTHER READING

Peter Angeles, ed., Critiques of God: A Major Statement of the Case Against Belief in God (Prometheus, 1976)

Anthony Flew, God and Philosophy (Hutchinson, 1966)

Sigmund Freud, The Future of an Illusion (W. W. Norton, 1961)

John A. Hutchison, Paths of Faith, Chapters 11-14 (McGraw-Hill, 1969, 1975)

Huston Smith, The Religions of Man (Harper and Row, 1958)

Ways of Wisdom

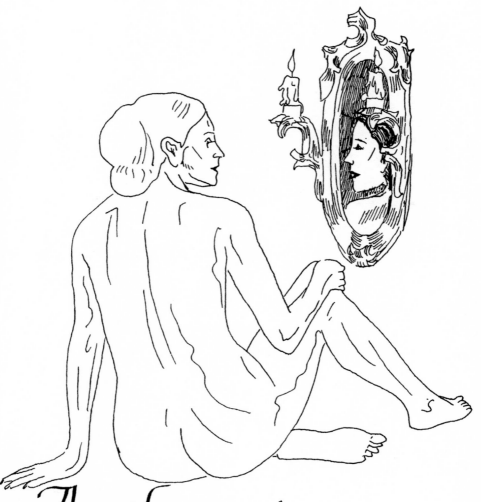

Chapter Seven:

Authentic Existence

Chapter VII: AUTHENTIC EXISTENCE

Introduction

God is dead!" cries Nietzsche's madman. His listeners laugh in derision. Like him, they no longer believe in God; but they fail to grasp, they choose not to see, how awful is their loss. And so they laugh and pretend; making light of the matter, they close their eyes to their own condition, taking refuge in comfortable complacency. They have evaded; only the madman is unflinching.

There are truths that are easy to hear: the sun is shining; I am welcome; the answer is yes. And there are truths that are hard to hear: he does not love me; I have failed; the answer is no. When we are told hard truths, our first defense is to deny: he loves me, after all; but I didn't really fail; surely the answer is yes. When this ruse is unsuccessful, a second defense pretends indifference: I don't care . . . it doesn't really matter . . . everything can go on as before. Both responses--simple denial, and feigned indifference--insulate us from reality and divide us within ourselves. Hiding from hard truths, we construct false worlds of comfortable illusion and hypocrisy. Thus we live our lives in havens of sweet poison, willing prisoners of our own elaborate lies. Dishonesty penetrates below the surface, into the core: our very existence, our way of being in the world, becomes inauthentic.

Atheistic existentialism challenges us to cease evading, and to confront the hard truths of our lives. Camus writes, "for a man who does not cheat, what he believes to be true must determine his action." If we would be in harmony with ourselves, there must come a time when we let go of self-deception, illusion, falseness; when we acknowledge the hard truths of our lives, and maintain those truths lucidly in our mind's eye. Such honesty cleanses our perception, washing away filters and distortions. If the resulting view seems stark and harsh, it also invigorates us with its immediacy, integrity and bite. Henceforth we will take responsibility for ourselves, without myths or excuses. Choosing to be honest, we gain honest being: authentic existence.

Evasion Through Abstraction

For millenia humans have projected upon the universe a comforting father figure, reassuring themselves thereby of their own special place and destiny. "Because God loves me, I am lovable; because God has a plan for me, my life has meaning." Such fantasies manifest the human temptation to evade by shifting from the concrete, particular fact to the abstract, the general and intangible. Like a man with a toothache, diverting himself by daydreaming, we evade by losing ourselves in abstractions and generalities--imagining another world that gives meaning and direction to this one. If we can believe that our present course is charted for us by a being of infinite wisdom, then we need only to surrender our autonomy and allow ourselves to be guided. But according to the atheistic existentialist, the world into which we are born is uncharted, and all the maps to guide us in it must be of our own making. "Right" and "wrong" are not signposts written on the heavens, but names invoked by humans to justify their own choices. To read morality into the nature of things is merely to disguise one's subjectivity by claiming for it a specious objectivity. Such intellectual games are a failure of authenticity, an example of what Sartre called "bad faith."

Without a divine blueprint, humans are no more--and no less--than what they make of themselves. There is no fixed human nature, only infinitely variable beings who are molded by their own decisions. The attempt to guide ourselves by an appeal to principles of right and wrong supposedly embedded in our nature is yet another attempt to flee our fearsome freedom: by shifting from the present, concrete moment of choice to an abstract theory about ourselves, we hide our responsibility for our actions behind rhetoric of the intangible. Human values are not discovered in the framework of the mind, nor are they part of the objective furniture of the universe; they are created only by human choices.

Anxiety and Creativity

An unblinking view of the human condition awakens in us a shuddering recognition of our underlying anxiety and despair. Without God, without any comforting illusions, we are forlorn--alien beings thrown into an indifferent universe. Transfixed by the death of God, Nietzsche's madman asks "Do we not stray, as through infinite nothingness?" Is there any point in continuing such a life? Why not simply end it all? Camus' startling assertion--"There is only one truly serious philosophical problem, and that is suicide"--here becomes understandable.

But the radical severance from old illusions is not only a death; it is also liberation to a new life, making way for fresh possibilities of creativity and courage. All that has ever been of truly authentic value to us is still available, recognized now as of our own making, dependent upon our own lives. Like one who at last acknowledges the death of one's parents and chooses henceforth to be one's own guide and judge, by divesting ourselves of illusions we gain a painful but exilarating freedom. Our head clears, our eyesight sharpens, the present moment emerges in bold detail out of the muddy chaos of persistent preoccupations. Without filters, both sorrow and joy intensify, and our experience gains a clean integrity of its own.

Maintaining lucidity requires vigilance. When we begin to dissemble, to slide away into abstract generalities and seductive absolutes, an act of will is required--a choice to cut through to the present moment, to the subjective and the personal, to the concrete, individual fact. In choosing this moment in all its detail, we choose ourselves, our own lives, our authentic existence.

The Good Life

For the existentialist, then, the good life as authentic existence is a life of radical honesty with oneself. It is a life of inner consistency and congruence, in which we feel the integrity of wholeness. We sense our own being as a substantial presence, encountering the immediacy of the world. Abjuring all subterfuge, we are liberated to the present, awakened as if for the first time to the texture and detail of our concrete existence. Accepting full responsibility for ourselves, we recognize unexpected possibilities available to us through lucid intention and courageous choice. We experience our own vitality, "the pure flame of life" that illumines and consumes. Morality is finally not a map handed to us by another, but a product of our own subjective choosing, reflecting that meaning we create. No formula can be given for living rightly or for living well; indeed, living according to formulas is not the solution, but the problem. Many disparate paths may be lived authentically. But it is necessary that we be wholly true to ourselves; that we not avert our eyes from what is before us; that we be unflinching.

The Selections

The three primary authors selected here--Friedrich Nietzsche (1844-1900), Albert Camus (1913-1960), and Jean Paul Sartre (1905-1980)--come from a loose, disparate group of thinkers known as existentialists. Resisting definition and categorization, existentialists are unified by few features save their common preference for attending to the immediate, concrete detail of lived experience, and their abhorrance of evasion through abstraction. Nietzsche, Camus and Sartre, together with Martin Heidegger (1889-1976) are the chief representatives of atheistic existentialism, for which the primary hard truth is the non-existence of God and the lack of other transcendent sources of value. Theistic existentialists such as Soren Kierkegaard (1813-1855) and Gabriel Marcel (1889-1973), while finding human meaning in a relation to the divine, see that relation as far more difficult and rare than is commonly supposed, and reject the human tendency to retreat from concrete experience into commonplace illusion, even when such illusion is given a religious name.

The brief selection from Nietzsche startles with its radical message. In proclaiming the death of God, the madman does not mean to imply that once there actually existed a real supreme being, a superhuman figure who was somehow killed by human action. Nietzsche's view is rather that the God of Judaism, Christianity and Islam has always been an illusion, a projection of human self-deception. As such, however, the imaginary God has been a powerful, life-guiding device by which we have created far-reaching value for ourselves, giving direction and meaning to our existence. When we begin to call into question this illusion, we at first suppose that God's existence can be cheaply denied, all else remaining much the same. We do not appreciate the degree to which our lives depend upon the framework of religious myth, nor do we grasp the enormity of the task of rebuilding, once that myth is abandoned. With the death of God, the sun is gone from our lives; we must light lanterns in the morning. We have sponged away our entire horizon, and now have no bearings, no direction. Drifting aimlessly into the void, we shiver from the chill. We are victims of our own crime, murderers of "the holiest and mightiest that the world has hitherto possessed." The death of God is a momentous event.

Sartre's essay summarizes straightforwardly the main themes of atheistic existentialism. The slogan that "existence precedes essence" reverses the traditional theistic view, according to which reality and human nature are patterned after a prior, transcendent blueprint, which specified the proper order and purpose of things. Instead, existentialism declares that "subjectivity must be the starting point": first I exist, and then I determine my own essence or nature by acts of self-definition. "Man is nothing else but what he makes of himself."

Because I must make myself through my choices, I am burdened in each choice with the anguish of creating human nature. I am responsible for the human project; in each moral decision that I make, I imply that "this is right," in effect speaking not only for myself but for all.

Forlornness also stems from the death of God. Without the comfort of absolute values, I am thrown back upon my own resources, condemned to find my own way. In the end, I bear full responsibility for what I become. I am the sum total of my choices, my concrete actions in the world: "What the existentialist says is that the coward makes himself cowardly, that the hero makes himself heroic." Authenticity permits no excuses; I have chosen what I am.

Writing at the outset of World War II, when his own world was collapsing about him, Albert Camus raises the question of suicide. "Judging whether life is or is not worth living amounts to answering the fundamental question of philosophy." In the absence of transcendent sources of value, the human condition reveals itself as absurd. Camus' compelling diagnosis identifies an "intellectual malady" whose key element is human frustration in an unresponsive universe. The absurd is not a property of human beings per se, nor of the world in itself, but a relation between the two, an incongruence, "born of this confrontation between the human need and the unreasonable silence of the world." Humans seek a rational understanding of things; the world does not yield to rational categories of explanation. Humans hunger for a synthesizing unity underlying the diversity of phenomena; the world reveals only a hopelessly disjointed plurality. Humans yearn for a higher reality, a source of transcendence; but no transcendence can be honestly discerned. And humans strive for continued life; yet their future confronts them with the inevitability of their own death.

As the logic of the absurd transforms our awareness, we experience moments of absurdity. Our meaningless activity is revealed as a charade: as Camus writes, "the stage sets collapse." The weariness of pointless effort is "tinged with amazement"; we wonder at our own lack of comprehension. The familiar becomes unfamiliar, and we realize that we are strangers. Life becomes "a ridiculous habit."

Does such a condition dictate suicide? Camus' answer is no. Honesty requires that rather than fleeing from the absurd, we confront it, hold it lucidly before us, and defy it. Suicide is an escape, a negation of the fundamental fact of our existence. Thus the first consequence of the absurd is revolt: "It is essential to die unreconciled, and not of one's own free will." Lucid recognition of the absurd yields two additional consequences: freedom and passion. Liberated from our slavery to false projects and hopes, we are freed to experience the present fully. "What does life mean in such a universe? Nothing else for the moment but indifference to the future and a desire to use up everything that is given." In the lucid struggle against insurmountable odds, human life gains dignity; "there is no fate that cannot be surmounted by scorn." A curious joy awakens. "One must imagine Sisyphus happy."

Ways of Wisdom

GOD IS DEAD*

by Friedrich Nietzsche

The Madman. -- Have you ever heard of the madman who on a bright morning lighted a lantern and ran to the market-place calling out unceasingly: "I seek God! I seek God!"--As there were many people standing about who did not believe in God, he caused a great deal of amusement. Why! is he lost? said one. Has he strayed away like a child? said another. Or does he keep himself hidden? Is he afraid of us? Has he taken a sea-voyage? Has he emigrated?--the people cried out laughingly, all in a hubbub. The insane man jumped into their midst and transfixed them with his glances. "Where is God gone?" he called out. "I mean to tell you! We have killed him,--you and I! We are all his murderers! But how have we done it? How were we able to drink up the sea? Who gave us the sponge to wipe away the whole horizon? What did we do when we loosened this earth from its sun? Whither does it now move? Whither do we move? Away from all suns? Do we not dash on unceasingly? Backwards, sideways, forewards, in all directions? Is there still an above and below? Do we not stray, as through infinite nothingness? Does not empty space breathe upon us? Has it not become colder? Does not night come on continually, darker and darker? Shall we not have to light lanterns in the morning? Do we not hear the noise of the grave-diggers who are burying God? Do we not smell the divine putrefaction?--for even Gods putrefy! God is dead! God remains dead! And we have killed him! How shall we console ourselves, the most murderous of all murderers? The holiest and the mightiest that the world has hitherto possessed, has bled to death under our knife,--who will wipe the blood from us? With what water could we cleanse ourselves? What lustrums, what sacred games shall we have to devise? Is not the magnitude of this deed too great for us? Shall we not ourselves have to become Gods, merely to seem worthy of it? There never was a greater event,--and on account of it, all who are born after us belong to a higher history than any history hitherto!"--Here the madman was silent and looked again at his hearers; they also were silent and looked at him in surprise. At last he threw his lantern on the ground, so that it broke in pieces and was extinguished. "I come too early," he then said, "I am not yet at the right time. This prodigious event is still on its way, and is travelling,--it has not yet reached men's ears. Lightning and thunder need time, the light of the stars needs time, deeds need time, even after they are done, to be seen and heard. This deed is as yet further from them than the furthest star,-- and yet they have done it!"--It is further stated that the madman made his way into different churches on the same day, and there intoned his Requiem aeternam deo. When led out and called to account, he always gave the reply: "What are these churches now, if they are not the tombs and monuments of God?"--

*From THE JOYFUL WISDOM, by Friedrich Nietzsche, translated by Thomas Common (London: George Allen & Unwin, 1919). Reprinted by permission of George Allen & Unwin Ltd.

EXISTENTIALISM*

by Jean-Paul Sartre

I should like on this occasion to defend existentialism against some charges which have been brought against it.

First, it has been charged with inviting people to remain in a kind of desperate quietism because, since no solutions are possible, we should have to consider action in this world as quite impossible. We should then end up in a philosophy of contemplation; and since contemplation is a luxury, we come in the end to a bourgeois philosophy. The communists in particular have made these charges.

On the other hand, we have been charged with dwelling on human degradation, with pointing up everywhere the sordid, shady, and slimy, and neglecting the gracious and beautiful, the bright side of human nature; for example, according to Mlle. Mercier, a Catholic critic, with forgetting the smile of the child. Both sides charge us with having ignored human solidarity, with considering man as an isolated being. The communists say that the main reason for this is that we take pure subjectivity, the Cartesian I think, as our starting point; in other words, the moment in which man becomes fully aware of what it means to him to be an isolated being; as a result, we are unable to return to a state of solidarity with the men who are not ourselves, a state which we can never reach in the cogito.

From the Christian standpoint, we are charged with denying the reality and seriousness of human undertakings, since, if we reject God's commandments and the eternal verities, there no longer remains anything but pure caprice, with everyone permitted to do as he pleases and incapable, from his own point of view, of condemning the points of view and acts of others.

I shall try today to answer these different charges. . . .

What is meant by the term existentialism?

Most people who use the word would be rather embarrassed if they had to explain it, since, now that the word is all the rage, even the work of a musician or painter is being called existentialist. A gossip columnist in Clartes signs himself The Existentialist, so that by this time the word has taken on so broad a meaning, that it no longer means anything at all. It seems that for want of an advance-guard doctrine analogous to surrealism, the kind of people who are eager for scandal and flurry turn to this philosophy which in other respects does not at all serve their purposes in this sphere.

*Abridged from Jean-Paul Sartre, EXISTENTIALISM, translated by Bernard Frechtman (New York: The Philosophical Library, 1947, 1974). Reprinted by permission of the publisher.

Actually, it is the least scandalous, the most austere of doctrines. It is intended strictly for specialists and philosophers. Yet it can be defined easily. What complicates matters is that there are two kinds of existentialist; first, those who are Christian, among whom I would include Jaspers and Gabriel Marcel, both Catholic; and on the other hand the atheistic existentialists, among whom I class Heidegger, and then the French existentialists and myself. What they have in common is that they think that existence precedes essence, or, if you prefer, that subjectivity must be the starting point.

Just what does that mean? Let us consider some object that is manufactured, for example, a book or a paper-cutter: here is an object which has been made by an artisan whose inspiration came from a concept. He referred to the concept of what a paper-cutter is and likewise to a known method of production, which is part of the concept, something which is, by and large, a routine. Thus, the paper-cutter is at once an object produced in a certain way and, on the other hand, one having a specific use; and one can not postulate a man who produces a paper-cutter but does not know what it is used for. Therefore, let us say that, for the paper-cutter, essence--that is, the ensemble of both the production routines and the properties which enable it to be both produced and defined--precedes existence. Thus, the presence of the paper-cutter or book in front of me is determined. Therefore, we have here a technical view of the world whereby it can be said that production precedes existence.

When we conceive God as the Creator, He is generally thought of as a superior sort of artisan. Whatever doctrine we may be considering, whether we like that of Descartes or that of Leibnitz, we always grant that will more or less follows understanding or, at the very least, accompanies it, and that when God creates He knows exactly what He is creating. Thus, the concept of man in the mind of God is comparable to the concept of paper-cutter in the mind of the manufacturer, and, following certain techniques and a conception, God produces man, just as the artisan, following a definition and a technique, makes a paper-cutter. Thus, the individual man is the realisation of a certain concept in the divine intelligence.

In the eighteenth century, the atheism of the philosophes discarded the idea of God, but not so much for the notion that essence precedes existence. To a certain extent, this idea is found everywhere; we find it in Diderot, in Voltaire, and even in Kant. Man has a human nature; this human nature, which is the concept of the human, is found in all men, which means that each man is a particular example of a universal concept, man. In Kant, the result of this universality is that the wild-man, the natural man, as well as the bourgeois, are circumscribed by the same definition and have the same basic qualities. Thus, here too the essence of man precedes the historical existence that we find in nature.

Atheistic existentialism, which I represent, is more coherent. It states that if God does not exist, there is at least one being in whom existence precedes essence, a being who exists before he can be defined by any concept, and that this being is man, or, as Heidegger says, human reality. What is meant here by saying that existence precedes essence? It means that, first of all, man exists, turns up, appears on the scene, and, only afterwards, defines himself. If man, as the existentialist conceives him, is indefinable, it is because at first he is nothing. Only afterward will he be something, and he himself will have made what he will be. Thus, there is no human nature, since there is no God to conceive it. Not only is man what he conceives himself to be, but he is also only what he wills himself to be after this thrust toward existence.

Man is nothing else but what he makes of himself. Such is the first principle of existentialism. It is also what is called subjectivity, the name we are labeled with when charges are brought against us. But what do we mean by this, if not that man has a greater dignity than a stone or table? For we mean that man first exists, that is, that man first of all is the being who hurls himself toward a future and who is conscious of imagining himself as being in the future. Man is at the start a plan which is aware of itself, rather than a patch of moss, a piece of garbage, or a cauliflower; nothing exists prior to this plan; there is nothing in heaven; man will be what he will have planned to be. Not what he will want to be. Because by the word "will" we generally mean a conscious decision, which is subsequent to what we have already made of ourselves. I may want to belong to a political party, write a book, get married; but all that is only a manifestation of an earlier, more spontaneous choice that is called "will." But if existence really does precede essence, man is responsible for what he is. Thus, existentialism's first move is to make every man aware of what he is and to make the full responsibility of his existence rest on him. And when we say that a man is responsible for himself, we do not only mean that he is responsible for his own individuality, but that he is responsible for all men.

The word subjectivism has two meanings, and our opponents play on the two. Subjectivism means, on the one hand, that an individual chooses and makes himself; and, on the other, that it is impossible for man to transcend human subjectivity. The second of these is the essential meaning of existentialism. When we say that man chooses his own self, we mean that every one of us does likewise; but we also mean by that that in making this choice he also chooses all men. In fact, in creating the man that we want to be, there is not a single one of our acts which does not at the same time create an image of man as we think he ought to be. To choose to be this or that is to affirm at the same time the value of what we choose, because we can never choose evil. We always choose the good, and nothing can be good for us without being good for all.

If, on the other hand, existence precedes essence, and if we grant that we exist and fashion our image at one and the same time, the image is valid for everybody and for our whole age. Thus, our responsibility is much greater than we might have supposed, because it involves all mankind. If I am a workingman and choose to join a Christian trade-union rather than be a communist, and if by being a member I want to show that the best thing for man is resignation, that the kingdom of man is not of this world, I am not only involving my own case--I want to be resigned for everyone. As a result, my action has involved all humanity. To take a more individual matter, if I want to marry, to have children; even if this marriage depends solely on my own circumstances or passion or wish, I am involving all humanity in monogamy and not merely myself. Therefore, I am responsible for myself and for everyone else. I am creating a certain image of man of my own choosing. In choosing myself, I choose man.

This helps us understand what the actual content is of such rather grandiloquent words as anguish, forlornness, despair. As you will see, it's all quite simple.

First, what is meant by anguish? The existentialists say at once that man is anguish. What that means is this: the man who involves himself and who realizes that he is not only the person he chooses to be, but also a law-maker who is, at the same time, choosing all mankind as well as himself, can not help escape the feeling of his total and deep responsibility. Of course, there are many people who are not anxious; but we claim that they are hiding their anxiety, that they are fleeing from it. Certainly, many people believe that when they do something, they themselves are the only ones involved, and when someone says to them, "What if everyone acted that way?" they shrug their shoulders and answer, "Everyone doesn't act that way." But really, one should always ask himself, "What would happen if everybody looked at things that way?" There is no escaping this disturbing thought except by a kind of double-dealing. A man who lies and makes excuses for himself by saying "not everybody does that," is someone with an uneasy conscience, because the act of lying implies that a universal value is conferred upon the lie.

Anguish is evident even when it conceals itself. This is the anguish that Kierkegaard called the anguish of Abraham. You know the story: an angel has ordered Abraham to sacrifice his son; if it really were an angel who has come and said, "You are Abraham, you shall sacrifice your son," everything would be all right. But everyone might first wonder, "Is it really an angel, and am I really Abraham? What proof do I have?"

There was a madwoman who had hallucinations; someone used to speak to her on the telephone and give her orders. Her doctor asked her, "Who is it who talks to you?" She answered, "He says it's God." What proof did she really have that it was God? If an angel comes to me, what proof is there that it's an angel? And if I hear voices, what proof is there that they come from heaven and not from hell, or from the subconscious, or a pathological condition? What proves that they are addressed to me? What proof is there that I have been appointed to impose my choice and my conception of man on humanity? I'll never find any proof or sign to convince me of that. If a voice addresses me, it is always for me to decide that this is the angel's voice; if I consider that such an act is a good one, it is I who will choose to say that it is good rather than bad.

Now, I'm not being singled out as an Abraham, and yet at every moment I'm obliged to perform exemplary acts. For every man, everything happens as if all mankind had its eyes fixed on him and were guiding itself by what he does. And every man ought to say to himself, "Am I really the kind of man who has the right to act in such a way that humanity might guide itself by my actions?" And if he does not say that to himself, he is masking his anguish.

There is no question here of the kind of anguish which would lead to quietism, to inaction. It is a matter of a simple sort of anguish that anybody who has had responsibilities is familiar with. For example, when a military officer takes the responsibility for an attack and sends a certain number of men to death, he chooses to do so, and in the main he alone makes the choice. Doubtless, orders come from above, but they are too broad; he interprets them, and on this interpretation depend the lives of ten or fourteen or twenty men. In making a decision he can not help having a certain anguish. All leaders know this anguish. That doesn't keep them from acting; on the contrary, it is the very condition of their action. For it implies that they envisage a number of possibilities, and when they choose one, they realize that it has value only because it is chosen. We shall see that this kind of anguish, which is the kind that existentialism describes, is explained, in addition, by a direct responsibility to the other men whom it involves. It is not a curtain separating us from action, but is part of action itself.

When we speak of forlornness, a term Heidegger was fond of, we mean only that God does not exist and that we have to face all the consequences of this. The existentialist is strongly opposed to a certain kind of secular ethics which would like to abolish God with the least possible expense. About 1880, some French teachers tried to set up a secular ethics which went something like this: God is a useless and costly hypothesis; we are discarding it; but, meanwhile, in order for there to be an ethics, a society, a civilization, it is essential that certain values be taken seriously and that they be considered as having an a priori existence. It must be obligatory, a priori, to be honest, not to lie, not to beat your wife, to have children, etc., etc. So we're going to try a little device which will make it possible to show that values exist all the same, inscribed in a heaven of ideas, though otherwise God does not exist. In other words--and this, I believe, is the tendency of everything called reformism in France--nothing will be changed if God does not exist. We shall find ourselves with the same norms of honesty, progress, and humanism, and we shall have made of God an outdated hypothesis which will peacefully die off by itself.

The existentialist, on the contrary, thinks it very distressing that God does not exist, because all possibility of finding values in a heaven of ideas disappears along with Him; there can no longer be an a priori Good, since there is no infinite and perfect consciousness to think it. Nowhere is it written that the Good exists, that we must be honest, that we must not lie; because the fact is we are on a plane where there are only men. Dostoievsky said, "If God didn't exist, everything would be possible." That is the very starting point of existentialism. Indeed, everything is permissible if God does not exist, and as a result man is forlorn, because neither within him nor without does he find anything to cling to. He can't start making excuses for himself.

If existence really does precede essence, there is no explaining things away by reference to a fixed and given human nature. In other words, there is no determinism, man is free, man is freedom. On the other hand, if God does not exist, we find no values or commands to turn to which legitimize our conduct. So, in the bright realm of values, we have no excuse behind us, nor justification before us. We are alone, with no excuses.

That is the idea I shall try to convey when I say that man is condemned to be free. Condemned, because he did not create himself, yet, in other respects is free; because, once thrown into the world, he is responsible for everything he does. The existentialist does not believe in the power of passion. He will never agree that a sweeping passion is a ravaging torrent which fatally leads a man to certain acts and is therefore an excuse. He thinks that man is responsible for his passion.

The existentialist does not think that man is going to help himself by finding in the world some omen by which to orient himself. Because he thinks that man will interpret the omen to suit himself. Therefore, he thinks that man, with no support and no aid, is condemned every moment to invent man. Ponge, in a very fine article, has said, "Man is the future of man." That's exactly it. But if it is taken to mean that this future is recorded in heaven, that God sees it, then it is false, because it would really no longer be a future. If it is taken to mean that, whatever a man may be, there is a future to be forged, a virgin future before him, then this remark is sound. But then we are forlorn.

To give you an example which will enable you to understand forlornness better, I shall cite the case of one of my students who came to see me under the following circumstances: his father was on bad terms with his mother, and, moreover, was inclined to be a collaborationist; his older brother had been killed in the German offensive of 1940, and the young man, with somewhat immature but generous feelings, wanted to avenge him. His mother lived alone with him, very much upset by the half-treason of her husband and the death of her older son; the boy was her only consolation.

The boy was faced with the choice of leaving for England and joining the Free French Forces--that is, leaving his mother behind--or remaining with his mother and helping her to carry on. He was fully aware that the woman lived only for him and that his going-off--and perhaps his death-- would plunge her into despair. He was also aware that every act that he did for his mother's sake was a sure thing, in the sense that it was helping her to carry on, whereas every effort he made toward going off and fighting was an uncertain move which might run aground and prove completely useless; for example, on his way to England he might, while passing through Spain, be detained indefinitely in a Spanish camp; he might reach England or Algiers and be stuck in an office at a desk job. As a result, he was faced with two very different kinds of action: one, concrete, immediate, but concerning only one individual; the other concerned an incomparably vaster group, a national collectivity, but for that very reason was dubious, and might be interrupted en route. And, at the same time, he was wavering between two kinds of ethics. On the one hand, an ethics of sympathy, of personal devotion; on the other, a broader ethics, but one whose efficacy was more dubious. He had to choose between the two.

Who could help him choose? Christian doctrine? No. Christian doctrine says, "Be charitable, love your neighbor, take the more rugged path, etc., etc." But which is the more rugged path? Whom should he love as a brother? The fighting man or his mother? Which does the greater good, the vague act of fighting in a group, or the concrete one of helping a particular human being to go on living? Who can decide a priori? Nobody. No book of ethics can tell him. The Kantian ethics says, "Never treat any person as a means, but as an end." Very well, if I stay with my mother, I'll treat her as an end and not as a means; but by virtue of this very fact, I'm running the risk of treating the people around me who are fighting, as means; and, conversely, if I go to join those who are fighting, I'll be treating them as an end, and, by doing that, I run the risk of treating my mother as a means.

If values are vague, and if they are always too broad for the concrete and specific case that we are considering, the only thing left for us is to trust our instincts. That's what this young man tried to do; and when I saw him, he said, "In the end, feeling is what counts. I ought to choose whichever pushes me in one direction. If I feel that I love my mother enough to sacrifice everything else for her--my desire for vengeance, for action, for adventure--then I'll stay with her. If, on the contrary, I feel that my love for my mother isn't enough, I'll leave."

240

But how is the value of a feeling determined? What gives his feeling for his mother value? Precisely the fact that he remained with her. I may say that I like so-and-so well enough to sacrifice a certain amount of money for him, but I may say so only if I've done it. I may say "I love my mother well enough to remain with her" if I have remained with her. The only way to determine the value of this affection is, precisely, to perform an act which confirms and defines it. But, since I require this affection to justify my act, I find myself caught in a vicious circle.

On the other hand, Gide has well said that a mock feeling and a true feeling are almost indistinguishable; to decide that I love my mother and will remain with her, or to remain with her by putting on an act, amount somewhat to the same thing. In other words, the feeling is formed by the acts one performs; so, I can not refer to it in order to act upon it. Which means that I can neither seek within myself the true condition which will impel me to act, nor apply to a system of ethics for concepts which will permit me to act. You will say, "At least, he did go to a teacher for advice." But if you seek advice from a priest, for example, you have chosen this priest; you already knew, more or less, just about what advice he was going to give you. In other words, choosing your adviser is involving yourself. The proof of this is that if you are a Christian, you will say, "Consult a priest." But some priests are collaborating, some are just marking time, some are resisting. Which to choose? If the young man chooses a priest who is resisting or collaborating, he has already decided on the kind of advice he's going to get. Therefore, in coming to see me he knew the answer I was going to give him, and I had only one answer to give: "You're free, choose, that is, invent." No general ethics can show you what is to be done; there are no omens in the world. The Catholics will reply, "But there are." Granted--but, in any case, I myself choose the meaning they have.

When I was a prisoner, I knew a rather remarkable young man who was a Jesuit. He had entered the Jesuit order in the following way: he had had a number of very bad breaks; in childhood, his father died, leaving him in poverty, and he was a scholarship student at a religious institution where he was constantly made to feel that he was being kept out of charity; then, he failed to get any of the honors and distinctions that children like; later on, at about eighteen, he bungled a love affair; finally, at twenty-two, he failed in military training, a childish enough matter, but it was the last straw.

This young fellow might well have felt that he had botched everything. It was a sign of something, but of what? He might have taken refuge in bitterness or despair. But he very wisely looked upon all this as a sign that he was not made for secular triumphs, and that only the triumphs of religion, holiness, and faith were open to him. He saw the hand of God in all this, and so he entered the order. Who can help seeing that he alone decided what the sign meant?

Some other interpretation might have been drawn from this series of setbacks; for example, that he might have done better to turn carpenter or revolutionist. Therefore, he is fully responsible for the interpretation. Forlornness implies that we ourselves choose our being. Forlornness and anguish go together. . . .

Actually, things will be as man will have decided they are to be. Does that mean that I should abandon myself to quietism? No. First, I should involve myself; then, act on the old saw, "Nothing ventured, nothing gained." Nor does it mean that I shouldn't belong to a party, but rather that I shall have no illusions and shall do what I can. For example, suppose I ask myself, "Will socialization, as such, ever come about?" I know nothing about it. All I know is that I'm going to do everything in my power to bring it about. Beyond that, I can't count on anything. Quietism is the attitude of people who say, "Let others do what I can't do." The doctrine I am presenting is the very opposite of quietism, since it declares, "There is no reality except in action." Moreover, it goes further, since it adds, "Man is nothing else than his plan; he exists only to the extent that he fulfills himself; he is therefore nothing else than the ensemble of his acts, nothing else than his life."

According to this, we can understand why our doctrine horrifies certain people. Because often the only way they can bear their wretchedness is to think, "Circumstances have been against me. What I've been and done doesn't show my true worth. To be sure, I've had no great love, no great friendship, but that's because I haven't met a man or woman who was worthy. The books I've written haven't been very good because I haven't had the proper leisure. I haven't had children to devote myself to because I didn't find a man with whom I could have spent my life. So there remains within me, unused and quite viable, a host of propensities, inclinations, possibilities, that one wouldn't guess from the mere series of things I've done."

Now, for the existentialist there is really no love other than one which manifests itself in a person's being in love. There is no genius other than one which is expressed in works of art; the genius of Proust is the sum of Proust's works; the genius of Racine is his series of tragedies. Outside of that, there is nothing. Why say that Racine could have written another tragedy, when he didn't write it? A man is involved in life, leaves his impress on it, and outside of that there is nothing. To be sure, this may seem a harsh thought to someone whose life hasn't been a success. But, on the other hand, it prompts people to understand that reality alone is what counts, that dreams, expectations, and hopes warrant no more than to define a man as a disappointed dream, as miscarried hopes, as vain expectatons. In other words, to define him negatively and not positively. However, when we say, "You are nothing else than your life," that does not imply that the artist will be judged solely on the basis of his works of art; a thousand other things will contribute toward summing him up. What we mean is that a man is nothing else than a series of undertakings, that he is the sum, the organization, the ensemble of the relationships which make up these undertakings.

When all is said and done, what we are accused of, at bottom, is not our pessimism, but an optimistic toughness. If people throw up to us our works of fiction in which we write about people who are soft, weak, cowardly, and sometimes even downright bad, it's not because these people are soft, weak, cowardly, or bad; because if we were to say, as Zola did, that they are that way because of heredity, the workings of environment, society, because of biological or psychological determinism, people would be reassured. They would say, "Well, that's what we're like, no one can do anything about it." But when the existentialist writes about a coward, he says that this coward is responsible for his cowardice. He's not like that because he has a cowardly heart or lung or brain; he's not like that on account of his physiological make-up; but he's like that because he has made himself a coward by his acts. There's no such thing as a cowardly constitution; there are nervous constitutions; there is poor blood, as the common people say, or strong constitutions. But the man whose blood is poor is not a coward on that account, for what makes cowardice is the act of renouncing or yielding. A constitution is not an act; the coward is defined on the basis of the acts he performs. People feel, in a vague sort of way, that this coward we're talking about is guilty of being a coward, and the thought frightens them. What people would like is that a coward or a hero be born that way. If you're born cowardly, you may set your mind perfectly at rest; there's nothing you can do about it; you'll be cowardly all your life, whatever you may do. If you're born a hero, you may set your mind just as much at rest; you'll be a hero all your life; you'll drink like a hero and eat like a hero. What the existentialist says is that the coward makes himself cowardly, that the hero makes himself heroic. There's always a possibility for the coward not to be cowardly any more and for the hero to stop being heroic. What counts is total involvement; some one particular action or set of circumstances is not total involvement.

Thus, I think we have answered a number of the charges concerning existentialism. You see that it can not be taken for a philosophy of quietism, since it defines man in terms of action; nor for a pessimistic description of man--there is no doctrine more optimistic, since man's destiny is within himself; nor for an attempt to discourage man from acting, since it tells him that the only hope is in his acting and that action is the only thing that enables a man to live. Consequently, we are dealing here with an ethics of action and involvement.

THE MYTH OF SISYPHUS*

by Albert Camus

There is but one truly serious philosophical problem, and that is suicide. Judging whether life is or is not worth living amounts to answering the fundamental question of philosophy. All the rest--whether or not the world has three dimensions, whether the mind has nine or twelve categories--comes afterwards. These are games; one must first answer. And if it is true, as Nietzsche claims, that a philosopher, to deserve our respect, must preach by example, you can appreciate the importance of that reply, for it will precede the definitive act. These are facts the heart can feel; yet they call for careful study before they become clear to the intellect.

If I ask myself how to judge that this question is more urgent than that, I reply that one judges by the actions it entails. I have never seen anyone die for the ontological argument. Galileo, who held a scientific truth of great importance, abjured it with the greatest ease as soon as it endangered his life. In a certain sense, he did right. That truth was not worth the stake. Whether the earth or the sun revolves around the other is a matter of profound indifference. To tell the truth, it is a futile question. On the other hand, I see many people die because they judge that life is not worth living. I see others paradoxically getting killed for the ideas or illusions that give them a reason for living (what is called a reason for living is also an excellent reason for dying). I therefore conclude that the meaning of life is the most urgent of questions. How to answer it? . . .

Living, naturally, is never easy. You continue making the gestures commanded by existence for many reasons, the first of which is habit. Dying voluntarily implies that you have recognized, even instinctively, the ridiculous character of that habit, the absence of any profound reason for living, the insane character of that daily agitation, and the uselessness of suffering.

What, then, is that incalculable feeling that deprives the mind of the sleep necessary to life? A world that can be explained even with bad reasons is a familiar world. But, on the other hand, in a universe suddenly divested of illusions and lights, man feels an alien, a stranger. His exile is without remedy since he is deprived of the memory of a lost home or the hope of a promised land. This divorce between man and his life, the actor and his setting, is properly the feeling of absurdity. All healthy men having thought of their own suicide, it can be seen, without further explanation, that there is a direct connection between this feeling and the longing for death.

The subject of this essay is precisely this relationship between the absurd and suicide, the exact degree to which suicide is a solution to the absurd. The principle can be established that for a man who does not cheat, what he believes to be true must determine his action. Belief in the absurdity of existence must then dictate his conduct. It is legitimate to wonder, clearly and without false pathos, whether a conclusion of this importance requires forsaking as rapidly as possible an incomprehensible condition. I am speaking, of course, of men inclined to be in harmony with themselves. . .

All great deeds and all great thoughts have a ridiculous beginning. Great works are often born on a street-corner or in a restaurant's revolving door. So it is with absurdity. The absurd world more than others derives its nobility from that abject birth. In certain situations, replying "nothing" when asked what one is thinking about may be pretense in a man. Those who are loved are well aware of this. But if that reply is sincere, if it symbolizes that odd state of soul in which the void becomes eloquent, in which the chain of daily gestures is broken, in which the heart vainly seeks the link that will connect it again, then it is as it were the first sign of absurdity.

It happens that the stage sets collapse. Rising, streetcar, four hours in the office or the factory, meal, streetcar, four hours of work, meal, sleep, and Monday Tuesday Wednesday Thursday Friday and Saturday according to the same rhythm--this path is easily followed most of the time. But one day the "why" arises and everything begins in that weariness tinged with amazement. . . .

Likewise and during every day of an unillustrious life, time carries us. But a moment always comes when we have to carry it. We live on the future: "tomorrow," "later on," "when you have made your way," "you will understand when you are old enough." Such irrelevancies are wonderful, for, after all, it's a matter of dying. Yet a day comes when a man notices or says that he is thirty. Thus he asserts his youth. But simultaneously he situates himself in relation to time. He takes his place in it. He admits that he stands at a certain point on a curve that he acknowledges having to travel to its end. He belongs to time, and by the horror that seizes him, he recognizes his worst enemy. Tomorrow, he was longing for tomorrow, whereas everything in him ought to reject it. That revolt of the flesh is the absurd.

A step lower and strangeness creeps in: perceiving that the world is "dense," sensing to what a degree a stone is foreign and irreducible to us, with what intensity nature or a landscape can negate us. At the heart of all beauty lies something inhuman, and these hills, the softness of the sky, the outline of these trees at this very minute lose the illusory meaning with which we had clothed them, henceforth more remote than a lost paradise. The primitive hostility of the world rises up to face us across

245

millennia. For a second we cease to understand it because for centuries we have understood in it solely the images and designs that we had attributed to it beforehand, because henceforth we lack the power to make use of that artifice. The world evades us because it becomes itself again. That stage scenery masked by habit becomes again what it is. It withdraws at a distance from us. Just as there are days when under the familiar face of a woman, we see as a stranger her we had loved months or years ago, perhaps we shall come even to desire what suddenly leaves us so alone. But the time has not yet come. Just one thing: that denseness and that strangeness of the world is the absurd.

Men, too, secrete the inhuman. At certain moments of lucidity, the mechanical aspect of their gestures, their meaningless pantomine makes silly everything that surrounds them. A man is talking on the telephone behind a glass partition; you cannot hear him, but you see his incomprehensible dumb show: you wonder why he is alive. This discomfort in the face of man's own inhumanity, this incalculable tumble before the image of what we are, this "nausea," as a writer of today calls it, is also the absurd. Likewise the stranger who at certain seconds comes to meet us in a mirror, the familiar and yet alarming brother we encounter in our own photographs is also the absurd.

I come at last to death and to the attitude we have toward it. On this point everything has been said and it is only proper to avoid pathos. Yet one will never be sufficiently surprised that everyone lives as if no one "knew." This is because in reality there is no experience of death. Properly speaking, nothing has been experienced but what has been lived and made conscious. Here, it is barely possible to speak of the experience of others' deaths. It is a substitute, an illusion, and it never quite convinces us. That melancholy convention cannot be persuasive. The horror comes in reality from the mathematical aspect of the event. If time frightens us, this is because it works out the problem and the solution comes afterward. All the pretty speeches about the soul will have their contrary convincingly proved, at least for a time. From this inert body on which a slap makes no mark the soul has disappeared. This elementary and definitive aspect of the adventure constitutes the absurd feeling. Under the fatal lighting of that destiny, its uselessness becomes evident. No code of ethics and no effort are justifiable a priori in the face of the cruel mathematics that command our condition. . . .

Whatever may be the plays on words and the acrobatics of logic, to understand is, above all, to unify. The mind's deepest desire, even in its most elaborate operations, parallels man's unconscious feeling in the face of his universe: it is an insistence upon familiarity, an appetite for clarity. Understanding the world for a man is reducing it to the human, stamping it with his seal. The cat's universe is not the universe of the anthill. The truism "All thought is anthropomorphic" has no other meaning. Likewise, the mind that aims to understand reality can consider itself satisfied only by reducing it to terms of thought. If man realized that the universe like him can love and suffer, he would be reconciled. If thought discovered in the shimmering mirrors of phenomena eternal relations capable of summing them up and summing themselves up in a single principle, then would be seen an intellectual joy of which the myth of the blessed would be but a ridiculous imitation. That nostalgia for unity, that appetite for the absolute illustrates the essential impulse of the human drama. But the fact of that nostalgia's existence does not imply that it is to be immediately satisfied. . . .

Of whom and of what indeed can I say: "I know that!" This heart within me I can feel, and I judge that it exists. This world I can touch, and I likewise judge that it exists. There ends all my knowledge, and the rest is construction. For if I try to seize this self of which I feel sure, if I try to define and to summarize it, it is nothing but water slipping through my fingers. I can sketch one by one all the aspects it is able to assume, all those likewise that have been attributed to it, this upbringing, this origin, this ardor or these silences, this nobility or this vileness. But aspects cannot be added up. This very heart which is mine will forever remain indefinable to me. Between the certainty I have of my existence and the content I try to give to that assurance, the gap will never be filled. Forever I shall be a stranger to myself. . . .

In this unintelligible and limited universe, man's fate henceforth assumes its meaning. A horde of irrationals has sprung up and surrounds him until his ultimate end. In his recovered and now studied lucidity, the feeling of the absurd becomes clear and definite. I said that the world is absurd, but I was too hasty. This world in itself is not reasonable, that is all that can be said. But what is absurd is the confrontation of this irrational and the wild longing for clarity whose call echoes in the human heart. The absurd depends as much on man as on the world. . .

I don't know whether this world has a meaning that transcends it. But I know that I do not know that meaning and that it is impossible for me just now to know it. What can a meaning outside my condition mean to me? I can understand only in human terms. What I touch, what resists me--that is what I understand. And these two certainties--my appetite for the absolute and for unity and the impossibility of reducing this world to a rational and reasonable principle--I also know that I cannot reconcile them. What other truth can I admit without lying, without bringing in a hope I lack and which means nothing within the limits of my condition?

If I were a tree among trees, a cat among animals, this life would have a meaning, or rather this problem would not arise, for I should belong to this world. I should be this world to which I am now opposed by my whole consciousness and my whole insistence upon familiarity. This ridiculous reason is what sets me in opposition to all creation. I cannot cross it out with a stroke of the pen. What I believe to be true I must therefore preserve. What seems to me so obvious, even against me, I must support. And what constitutes the basis of that conflict, of that break between the world and my mind, but the awareness of it? If therefore I want to preserve it, I can through a constant awareness, ever revived, ever alert. This is what, for the moment, I must remember. At this moment the absurd, so obvious and yet so hard to win, returns to a man's life and finds its home there. At this moment, too, the mind can leave the arid, dried-up path of lucid effort. That path now emerges in daily life. It encounters the world of the anonymous impersonal pronoun "one," but henceforth man enters in with his revolt and his lucidity. He has forgotten how to hope. This hell of the present is his Kingdom at last. All problems recover their sharp edge. Abstract evidence retreats before the poetry of forms and colors. Spiritual conflicts become embodied and return to the abject and magnificent shelter of man's heart. None of them is settled. But all are transfigured. Is one going to die, escape by the leap, rebuild a mansion of ideas and forms to one's own scale? Is one, on the contrary, going to take up the heart-rending and marvelous wager of the absurd? Let's make a final effort in this regard and draw all our conclusions. The body, affection, creation, action, human nobility will then resume their places in this mad world. At last man will again find there the wine of the absurd and the bread of indifference on which he feeds his greatness.

Let us insist again on the method: it is a matter of persisting. At a certain point on his path the absurd man is tempted. History is not lacking in either religions or prophets, even without gods. He is asked to leap. All he can reply is that he doesn't fully understand, that it is not obvious. Indeed, he does not want to do anything but what he fully understands. He is assured that this is the sin of pride, but he does not understand the notion of sin; that perhaps hell is in store, but he has not enough imagination to visualize that strange future; that he is losing immortal life, but that seems to him an idle consideration. An attempt is made to get him to admit his guilt. He feels innocent. To tell the truth, that is all he feels--his irreparable innocence. This is what allows him everything. Hence, what he demands of himself is to live solely with what he knows, to accommodate himself to what is, and to bring in nothing that is not certain. He is told that nothing is. But this at least is a certainty. And it is with this that he is concerned: he wants to find out if it is possible to live without appeal.

Now I can broach the notion of suicide. It has already been felt what solution might be given. At this point the problem is reversed. It was previously a question of finding out whether or not life had to have a meaning to be lived. It now becomes clear, on the contrary, that it will be lived all the better if it has no meaning. Living an experience, a particular fate, is accepting it fully. Now, no one will live this fate, knowing it to be absurd, unless he does everything to keep before him that absurd brought to light by consciousness. Negating one of the terms of the opposition on which he lives amounts to escaping it. To abolish conscious revolt is to elude the problem. The theme of permanent revolution is thus carried into individual experience. Living is keeping the absurd alive. Keeping it alive is, above all, contemplating it. Unlike Eurydice, the absurd dies only when we turn away from it. One of the only coherent philosophical positions is thus revolt. It is a constant confrontation between man and his own obscurity. It is an insistence upon an impossible transparency. It challenges the world anew every second. Just as danger provided man the unique opportunity of seizing awareness, so metaphysical revolt extends awareness to the whole of experience. It is that constant presence of man in his own eyes. It is not aspiration, for it is devoid of hope. That revolt is the certainty of a crushing fate, without the resignation that ought to accompany it.

This is where it is seen to what a degree absurd experience is remote from suicide. It may be thought that suicide follows revolt--but wrongly. For it does not represent the logical outcome of revolt. It is just the contrary by the consent it presupposes. Suicide, like the leap, is acceptance at its extreme. Everything is over and man returns to his essential history. His future, his unique and dreadful future--he sees and rushes toward it. In its way, suicide settles the absurd. It engulfs the absurd in the same death. But I know that in order to keep alive, the absurd cannot be settled. It escapes suicide to the extent that it is simultaneously awareness and rejection of death. It is, at the extreme limit of the condemned man's last thought, that shoelace that despite everything he sees a few yards away, on the very brink of his dizzying fall. The contrary of suicide, in fact, is the man condemned to death.

That revolt gives life its value. Spread out over the whole length of a life, it restores its majesty to that life. To a man devoid of blinders, there is no finer sight than that of the intelligence at grips with a reality that transcends it. The sight of human pride is unequaled. No disparagement is of any use. That discipline that the mind imposes on itself, that will conjured up out of nothing, that face-to-face struggle have something exceptional about them. To impoverish that reality whose inhumanity constitutes man's majesty is tantamount to impoverishing him himself. I understand then why the doctrines that explain everything to me also debilitate me at the same time. They relieve me of the weight of my own life, and yet I must carry it alone. At this juncture, I cannot conceive that a skeptical metaphysics can be joined to an ethics of renunciation.

Consciousness and revolt, these rejections are the contrary of renunciation. Everything that is indomitable and passionate in a human heart quickens them, on the contrary, with its own life. It is essential to die unreconciled and not of one's own free will. Suicide is a repudiation. The absurd man can only drain everything to the bitter end, and deplete himself. The absurd is his extreme tension, which he maintains constantly by solitary effort, for he knows that in that consciousness and in that day-to-day revolt he gives proof of his only truth, which is defiance. This is a first consequence. . . .

Before encountering the absurd, the everyday man lives with aims, a concern for the future or for justification (with regard to whom or what is not the question). He weighs his chances, he counts on "someday," his retirement or the labor of his sons. He still thinks that something in his life can be directed. In truth, he acts as if he were free, even if all the facts make a point of contradicting that liberty. But after the absurd, everything is upset. That idea that "I am," my way of acting as if everything has a meaning (even if, on occasion, I said that nothing has)--all that is given the lie in vertiginous fashion by the absurdity of a possible death. Thinking of the future, establishing aims for oneself, having preferences--all this presupposes a belief in freedom, even if one occasionally ascertains that one doesn't feel it. But at that moment I am well aware that that higher liberty, that freedom to be, which alone can serve as basis for a truth, does not exist. Death is there as the only reality. After death the chips are down. I am not even free, either, to perpetuate myself, but a slave, and, above all, a slave without hope of an eternal revolution, without recourse to contempt. And who without revolution and without contempt can remain a slave? What freedom can exist in the fullest sense without assurance of eternity?

But at the same time the absurd man realizes that hitherto he was bound to that postulate of freedom on the illusion of which he was living. In a certain sense, that hampered him. To the extent to which he imagined a purpose to his life, he adapted himself to the demands of a purpose to be achieved and became the slave of his liberty. Thus I could not act otherwise than as the father (or the engineer or the leader of a nation, or the post-office sub-clerk) that I am preparing to be. . . .

Thus the absurd man realizes that he was not really free. To speak clearly, to the extent to which I hope, to which I worry about a truth that might be individual to me, about a way of being or creating, to the extent to which I arrange my life and prove thereby that I accept its having a meaning, I create for myself barriers between which I confine my life. I do like so many bureaucrats of the mind and heart who only fill me with disgust and whose only vice, I now see clearly, is to take man's freedom seriously.

The absurd enlightens me on this point: there is no future. Henceforth this is the reason for my inner freedom. I shall use two comparisons here. Mystics, to begin with, find freedom in giving themselves. By losing themselves in their god, by accepting his rules, they become secretly freed. In spontaneously accepted slavery they recover a deeper independence. But what does that freedom mean? It may be said, above all, that they feel free with regard to themselves, and not so much free as liberated. Likewise, completely turned toward death (taken here as the most obvious absurdity), the absurd man feels released from everything outside that passionate attention crystallizing in him. He enjoys a freedom with regard to common rules. It can be seen at this point that the initial themes of existential philosophy keep their entire value. The return to consciousness, the escape from everyday sleep represent the first steps of absurd freedom. . . .

Losing oneself in that bottomless certainty, feeling henceforth sufficiently remote from one's own life to increase it and take a broad view of it--this involves the principle of a liberation. Such new independence has a definite time limit, like any freedom of action. It does not write a check on eternity. But it takes the place of the illusions of freedom, which all stopped with death. The divine availability of the condemned man before whom the prison doors open in a certain early dawn, that unbelievable disinterestedness with regard to everything except for the pure flame of life--it is clear that death and the absurd are here the principles of the only reasonable freedom: that which a human heart can experience and live. This is a second consequence. The absurd man thus catches sight of a burning and frigid, transparent and limited universe in which nothing is possible but everything is given, and beyond which all is collapse and nothingness. He can then decide to accept such a universe and draw from it his strength, his refusal to hope, and the unyielding evidence of a life without consolation.

But what does life mean in such a universe? Nothing else for the moment but indifference to the future and a desire to use up everything that is given. Belief in the meaning of life always implies a scale of values, a choice, our preferences. Belief in the absurd, according to our definitions, teaches the contrary. But this is worth examining.

Knowing whether or not one can live without appeal is all that interests me. I do not want to get out of my depth. This aspect of life being given me, can I adapt myself to it? Now, faced with this particular concern, belief in the absurd is tantamount to substituting the quantity of experiences for the quality. If I convince myself that this life has no other aspect than that of the absurd, if I feel that its whole equilibrium depends on that perpetual opposition between my conscious revolt and the darkness in which it struggles, if I admit that my freedom has no meaning except in relation to its limited fate, then I must say that what counts is not the best living but the most living. It is not up to me to wonder if this is vulgar or revolting, elegant or deplorable. Once and for all, value judgments are discarded here in favor of factual judgments. I have merely to draw the conclusions from what I can see and to risk nothing that is hypothetical. Supposing that living in this way were not honorable, then true propriety would command me to be dishonorable. . . .

Thus I draw from the absurd three consequences, which are my revolt, my freedom, and my passion. By the mere activity of consciousness I transform into a rule of life what was an invitation to death--and I refuse suicide. I know, to be sure, the dull resonance that vibrates throughout these days. Yet I have but a word to say: that it is necessary. When Nietzsche writes: "It clearly seems that the chief thing in heaven and on earth is to <u>obey</u> at length and in a single direction: in the long run there results something for which it is worth the trouble of living on this earth as, for example, virtue, art, music, the dance, reason, the mind--something that transfigures, something delicate, mad, or divine," he elucidates the rule of a really distinguished code of ethics. But he also points the way of the absurd man. Obeying the flame is both the easiest and the hardest thing to do. However, it is good for man to judge himself occasionally. He is alone in being able to do so.

"Prayer," says Alain, "is when night descends over thought." "But the mind must meet the night," reply the mystics and the existentials. Yes, indeed, but not that night that is born under closed eyelids and through the mere will of man--dark, impenetrable night that the mind calls up in order to plunge into it. If it must encounter a night, let it be rather that of despair, which remains lucid--polar night, vigil of the mind, whence will arise perhaps that white and virginal brightness which outlines every object in the light of the intelligence. At that degree, equivalence encounters passionate understanding. Then it is no longer even a question of judging the existential leap. It resumes its place amid the age-old fresco of human attitudes. For the spectator, if he is conscious, that leap is still absurd. In so far as it thinks it solves the paradox, it reinstates it intact. On this score, it is stirring. On this score, everything resumes its place and the absurd world is reborn in all its splendor and diversity.

But it is bad to stop, hard to be satisfied with a single way of seeing, to go without contradiction, perhaps the most subtle of all spiritual forces. The preceding merely defines a way of thinking. But the point is to live. . .

The Myth of Sisyphus

The gods had condemned Sisyphus to ceaselessly rolling a rock to the top of a mountain, whence the stone would fall back of its own weight. They had thought with some reason that there is no more dreadful punishment than futile and hopeless labor.

If one believes Homer, Sisyphus was the wisest and most prudent of mortals. According to another tradition, however, he was disposed to practice the profession of highwayman. I see no contradiction in this. Opinions differ as to the reasons why he became the futile laborer of the underworld. To begin with, he is accused of a certain levity in regard to the gods. He stole their secrets. AEgina, the daughter of AEsopus, was carried off by Jupiter. The father was shocked by that disappearance and complained to Sisyphus. He, who knew of the abduction, offered to tell about it on condition that AEsopus would give water to the citadel of Corinth. To the celestial thunderbolts he preferred the benediction of water. He was punished for this in the underworld. Homer tell us also that Sisyphus had put Death in chains. Pluto could not endure the sight of his deserted, silent empire. He dispatched the god of war, who liberated Death from the hands of her conqueror.

It is said also that Sisyphus, being near to death, rashly wanted to test his wife's love. He ordered her to cast his unburied body into the middle of the public square. Sisyphus woke up in the underworld. And there, annoyed by an obedience so contrary to human love, he obtained from Pluto permission to return to earth in order to chastise his wife. But when he had seen again the face of this world, enjoyed water and sun, warm stones and the sea, he no longer wanted to go back to the infernal darkness. Recalls, signs of anger, warnings were of no avail. Many years more he lived facing the curve of the gulf, the sparkling sea, and the smiles of earth. A decree of the gods was necessary. Mercury came and seized the impudent man by the collar and, snatching him from his joys, led him forcibly back to the underworld, where his rock was ready for him.

You have already grasped that Sisyphus is the absurd hero. He is, as much through his passions as through his torture. His scorn of the gods, his hatred of death, and his passion for life won him that unspeakable penalty in which the whole being is exerted toward accomplishing nothing. This is the price that must be paid for the passions of this earth. Nothing is told us about Sisyphus in the underworld. Myths are made for the imagination to breathe life into them. As for this myth, one sees merely the whole effort of a body straining to raise the huge stone, to roll it and push it up a slope a hundred times over; one sees the face screwed up, the cheek tight against the stone, the shoulder bracing the clay-covered mass, the foot wedging it, the fresh start with arms outstretched, the wholly human security of two earth-clotted hands. At the very end of his long effort measured by skyless space and time without depth, the purpose is achieved. Then Sisyphus watches the stone rush down in a few moments toward that lower world whence he will have to push it up again toward the summit. He goes back down to the plain.

It is during that return, that pause, that Sisyphus interests me. A face that toils so close to stones is already stone itself! I see that man going back down with a heavy yet measured step toward the torment of which he will never know the end. That hour like a breathing-space which returns as surely as his suffering, that is the hour of consciousness. At each of those moments when he leaves the heights and gradually sinks toward the lairs of the gods, he is superior to his fate. He is stronger than his rock.

If this myth is tragic, that is because its hero is conscious. Where would his torture be, indeed, if at every step the hope of succeeding upheld him? The workman of today works every day in his life at the same tasks, and this fate is no less absurd. But it is tragic only at the rare moments when it becomes conscious. Sisyphus, proletarian of the gods, powerless and rebellious, knows the whole extent of his wretched condition: it is what he thinks of during his descent. The lucidity that was to constitute his torture at the same time crowns his victory. There is no fate that cannot be surmounted by scorn.

If the descent is thus sometimes performed in sorrow, it can also take place in joy. This word is not too much. Again I fancy Sisyphus returning toward his rock, and the sorrow was in the beginning. When the images of earth cling too tightly to memory, when the call of happiness becomes too insistent, it happens that melancholy rises in man's heart: this is the rock's victory, this is the rock itself. The boundless grief is too heavy to bear. These are our nights of Gethsemane. But crushing truths perish from being acknowledged. Thus, Œeipus at the outset obeys fate without knowing it. But from the moment he knows, his tragedy begins. Yet at the same moment, blind and desperate, he realizes that the only bond linking him to the world is the cool hand of a girl. Then a tremendous remark rings out: "Despite so many ordeals, my advanced age and the nobility of my soul make me conclude that all is well." Sophocles' Œdipus, like Dostoevsky's Kirilov, thus gives the recipe for the absurd victory. Ancient wisdom confirms modern heroism.

One does not discover the absurd without being tempted to write a manual of happiness. "What! by such narrow ways--?" There is but one world, however. Happiness and the absurd are two sons of the same earth. They are inseparable. It would be a mistake to say that happiness necessarily springs from the absurd discovery. It happens as well that the feeling of the absurd springs from happiness. "I conclude that all is well," says Œdipus, and that remark is sacred. It echoes in the wild and limited universe of man. It teaches that all is not, has not been, exhausted. It drives out of this world a god who had come into it with dissatisfaction and a preference for futile sufferings. It makes of fate a human matter, which must be settled among men.

All Sisyphus' silent joy is contained therein. His fate belongs to him. His rock is his thing. Likewise, the absurd man, when he contemplates his torment, silences all the idols. In the universe suddenly restored to its silence, the myriad wondering little voices of the earth rise up. Unconscious, secret calls, invitations from all the faces, they are the necessary reverse and price of victory. There is no sun without shadow, and it is essential to know the night. The absurd man says yes and his effort will henceforth be unceasing. If there is a personal fate, there is no higher destiny, or at least there is but one which he concludes is inevitable and despicable. For the rest, he knows himself to be the master of his days. At that subtle moment when man glances backward over his life, Sisyphus returning toward his rock, in that slight pivoting he contemplates that series of unrelated actions which becomes his fate, created by him, combined under his memory's eye and soon sealed by his death. Thus, convinced of the wholly human origin of all that is human, a blind man eager to see who knows that the night has no end, he is still on the go. The rock is still rolling.

I leave Sisyphus at the foot of the mountain! One always finds one's burden again. But Sisyphus teaches the higher fidelity that negates the gods and raises rocks. He too concludes that all is well. This universe henceforth without a master seems to him neither sterile or futile. Each atom of that stone, each mineral flake of that night-filled mountain, in itself forms a world. The struggle itself toward the heights is enough to fill a man's heart. One must imagine Sisyphus happy.

CRITIQUE

J. von Rintelen charges existentialism with "the vigorous affirmation of senselessness," a kind of perverse delight in the absence of meaning. Camus' depiction of Sisyphus exemplifies this confusion, according to von Rintelen: Camus would have us believe that Sisyphus is happy, yet Sisyphus's fate "is the most melancholy imaginable"; suicide is in fact a reasonable response to such emptiness. Von Rintelen sees in the existentialist affirmation of meaninglessness a "creeping psychosis" which is "intent on ruining the very foundation of our life by rejecting all that is joyful and meaningful."

Mary Warnock subjects Sartre's views to sharp criticism, focussing especially upon Sartre's attempt to formulate an existentialist morality. Sartre's quasi-Kantian proposal that in choosing for myself, I choose for all is, she asserts, inconsistent with his earlier views--of morality as entirely individual and subjective--as expressed in his major work, Being and Nothingness; presumably for this reason, Sartre later repudiated the Kantian approach he advocates here, returning to the view of morality as a purely subjective and personal affair. Yet such radical individualism rules out a shared morality for the common good, and prevents general moral support for political ideals. According to Warnock, Sartre's analysis of existentialist ethics provides no answer to the question "How ought we to live?"

F. H. Heinemann advances a similar objection. In the existentialist emphasis upon pure subjectivity, radical aloneness--"Man for himself"--severs us from God and from one another. Such alienation in the last analysis puts us in conflict within ourselves; "the result is that existentialism becomes prevalently, though not exclusively, the philosophy of Man against himself." Heinemann suggests that the chief project of our age is to overcome this alienation and conflict, by achieving true community--both with one another and with the non-human world around us. Separation and conflict then yield to mutual interdependence and organic harmony.

SISYPHUS CANNOT BE HAPPY*

by J. von Rintelen

The endurance of meaninglessness. . . is the 'measure of willpower', which is the ultimate value both of Nietzsche and of our age. . . . The result is the vigorous affirmation of senselessness in order to see in this, paradoxically, a meaningful meaninglessness.

This we are told quite plainly in the Sisyphus myth of Camus. Throughout his life the 'absurd hero' tries quite senselessly to carry the piece of rock that always rolls down again to the top of a mountain. It would be more reasonable to commit suicide and to reject such an empty life. And yet: the senseless 'struggle for the summit suffices by itself to satisfy the heart of a man. Sisyphus must be accounted happy'--what we, however, refuse to admit. At the same time we are told that the whole universe, too, is utterly meaningless and worthless. But such a passive heroism is senseless and completely contradicts the aspirations of the human heart, especially as here--as against the ancient tale--man has become quite conscious of this meaninglessness. If this thought is fully realized it is the most melancholy imaginable. If not, it is yet another instance of the contemporary tendency to make astonishing statements which hide one's real thoughts. We meet again the completely irrational ambivalence which joyfully takes up the frightful and at the same time denies all higher meaning.

Thus we arrive at the strange conclusion that we possess an instinct which loves the unredeemed heart and is pleased to disappoint, to dissolve what brings happiness and to destroy hope. We might almost say: give me a new kind of distress so that I may continue to live and remain attached to life. Catastrophes and sufferings are the favourite experiences. Even Holderlin says: 'Life is nourished on suffering,' and Richard Wagner: 'Let contrition be my pleasure.' It looks as if we were in the grip of a creeping psychosis and were intent on ruining the very foundations of our life by rejecting all that is joyful and meaningful.

*From Beyond Existentialism, translated from the German by Hilda Graef (London: George Allen and Unwin, Ltd., 1961) Reprinted by permission of Humanities Press Inc., Atlantic Highlands, N.J. 07716, and George Allen and Unwin, Ltd.

SUBJECTIVITY AND ETHICS*

by Mary Warnock

There is . . . no question at all, in Sartre's view, of discovering any absolute values in the world. There just are no such things. If a man says that something is good or that it is bad, he is choosing it as a goal; he is not describing a property that it has. All moral philosophies tend, according to Sartre, to try to assert that something or other in the world has an absolute value, whether it is human happiness or some other thing. . . . To suppose that values are somehow given is just to fall into the kind of refusal to face his freedom which afflicts the bourgeois respectable man, whose duties all seem to be laid out for him, and who believes that he is completely bound by the rules which govern his life. And yet Sartre could not possibly deny that we must evaluate things somehow or other. Nor would he want to deny this, since evaluation is built into action. Value is, he says, 'simply lived' at the very heart of our life. We perceive things, evaluate them, and act upon them, all at the same time. But there can be no theory of values. All that a philosopher can do is to tell us what value is, and how it functions in our life. He cannot possibly presume to tell us what is and what is not valuable.

There is a real difficulty at this point in Sartre's philosophy which he did not in any way solve, at least until he abandoned Existentialism. In Being and Nothingness he seems to be saying that we must each decide for ourselves how to live, what is good and what is bad, and that this is a purely personal decision, which no one can take on behalf of another. But there is an element in genuine evaluation which will not submit to this analysis. If, for example, a man judges sincerely that tax evasion is wrong, then in some sense he has, whether he knows it or not, judged that it is wrong in general, and he may even believe, though without saying as much, that it is wrong necessarily, or absolutely. To say that something is wrong is certainly not merely to describe it. But neither is it merely to express one's own private feeling about it. 'Wrong' means 'wrong in general', unless special precautions are taken to ensure that it means less than this. . . .

And so Sartre has not said enough, when he insists that human beings cannot find absolute values in the world, they can only pretend to themselves to do so. He has not taken account of the facts of forming moral opinions. It is true that in one much publicized essay, frequently translated into English and, understandably, frequently taken to be the definitive statement of his moral views, he attempts a solution to the problem of how to construct an Existentialist morality. In this essay, Existentialism is a Humanism (1946), Sartre tries to defend Existentialism against the charge that it was a negative, gloomy, and depressing

*From Existentialism by Mary Warnock, (c) Oxford University Press 1970. Reprinted by permission of Oxford University Press.

258

philosophy. He argues that, far from being gloomy, Existentialism is an optimistic philosophy, since it inspires people to action by showing them the extent of their freedom to action; and it shows them that they are responsible not only for their own destinies but for other people's as well. For whatever a man chooses, he chooses for everyone and not only for himself; for the notion of choice entails the notion of a thing's being good, and 'good' means 'good for everyone'. Thus if a man chooses freedom for himself, he is thereby committed to choosing freedom for everyone.

There is a great deal that is confused and wrong-headed in this essay. It is worthy of mention for two reasons. First, it does meet the specific objection raised above, that there could be no such thing as an Existentialist morality, if all that a man must do is to evaluate the world for himself alone; but secondly, it must be mentioned simply because Sartre himself repudiated it later, and expressed a wish that it had not been published. It is easy to see that the superficially Kantian moral theory contained in the essay might seem at first attractive, and a way out of the negative conclusions of <u>Being and Nothingness</u>. But in fact, as Sartre came to see, it is quite impossible to envisage the true Existentialist man taking on responsibility for anyone's choice but his own, or adopting the Kantian view that rational beings are to be treated as ends in themselves. . . .

Sartre was faced with an <u>impasse</u>. Any attempt at an account of ethics that would have any generality was to be condemned as Bad Faith. The one established fact seemed to be that values were contingent, personal, and chosen, if they were genuine, by the individual, by himself, and for himself alone. There was no method by which he could hope permanently to establish a community of ends with other human beings, since he was locked in inevitable conflict with others, and could not argue that either he or they had any <u>natural</u> rights or duties towards each other. . . .

There was therefore <u>no</u> rational way open for Existentialism to order life in society. The only remaining rule appeared to be that each must save himself, by choosing his own life of freedom. Just as Authenticity, for Heidegger, consisted in each man launching himself freely towards his own destiny, which was death, so Sartre's Being-for-himself would redeem himself only by knowingly making his own decisions, for himself alone. But this must have seemed inadequate to Sartre who was and is, after all, an almost wholly political man. If any <u>political</u> policy is to be judged better than another, if there is ever any aspect of society of which one is to be able to say with certainty that it is wrong and must be eliminated, then there must be found some positive answer to the moralists' question 'How ought men to live?'

CONFLICT AND COMMUNITY*

by F. H. Heinemann

Man for himself; this seems to be a rather good characterization of contemporary man. He is man without God, the heir of Enlightenment and Positivism, of Schopenhauer, Marx, Feuerbach and Nietzsche. He wants to live without God, to be completely free in his choice, his life, his work and his thought. Is existentialism the philosophy of man for himself? At first sight it would seem so. Do not Heidegger's heroic defiance, Sartre's pour-soi and his absolute liberty, point to this fact? But if one looks deeper it becomes evident that this forms only the point of departure, and one of the ingredients of existentialism. There is at once the feeling that man is, with others, in a sphere of inter-subjectivity, within the world, in need of communication, and that the possibility of communicating with everyone and everything should be preserved. The uneasiness, created by man's separation from God, is the driving power which animates Kierkegaard and Jaspers as well as Heidegger and Sartre. The will to overcome this separation either from God or from others and from the world is there, but it is felt at once that a contradiction arises between being for oneself and communication with others. . . . The will to communication finds itself somehow frustrated. . . .

The result is that existentialism becomes prevalently, though not exclusively, the philosophy of Man against himself. It is the philosophy of an age where societies as well as individuals are in conflict with themselves. . . . What is needed is that the state of affairs characterized by the slogan Man against himself should be overcome. This is easy to say, but extremely difficult to achieve, because we are up against a human characteristic which, though prevalent in our age, is recurrent in all ages. "To be against oneself" is a specific human trait, nourished by the virtuosity and all the ingenuity of inner reflection, calculation and technology. It may be impossible to eradicate this attitude altogether; nevertheless the aim should be to go on to the stage of Man with himself, i.e. of Man with Man, Man with the World, and Man with God. Being with the world is not identical with being in the world, for I can be in the world and nevertheless be against it, or even reject it. This negative attitude prevailed in existentialism. It is most revealing that Heidegger discusses the mode of "being with others" as a modus deficiens of authentic existence, 'namely as the unauthentic mode of day-to-day co-existence. But it may be the other way round. It may be that we are in the world, because we are with the world. "Being with" implies, in this context, three elements: namely first, to be of the world, to be a part of it, to be co-natural with it; secondly, to respond to it unconsciously by taking part in it; and thirdly, on the level of consciousness, to accept it without eliminating the freedom of decision in each specific case.

*From Existentialism and the Modern Predicament (New York: Harper and Row, 1953, 1958), pp. 184-185, 188-189. Reproduced by permission from Existentialism and the Modern Predicament by F. D. Heinemann, published by A & C Black Ltd.

STUDY QUESTIONS FOR CHAPTER VII

Questions for Review:

1. According to the editor's introduction, what is the meaning of the saying "God is dead"?

2. How does existence become inauthentic, as described in the introduction?

3. What is the critique of religious belief by atheistic existentialism, as described in the introduction?

4. What is the source of human values, according to atheistic existentialism?

5. What is the good life as described in the introduction?

6. Why does Nietzsche's madman carry a lantern in the morning?

7. What is it necessary for humans to do, now that they have killed God, according to the madman?

8. What are the charges that have been brought against existentialism, according to Sartre?

9. What does Sartre mean by the slogan "existence precedes essence"?

10. In what sense do I choose for all humans, according to Sartre?

11. What does Sartre mean by "anguish"?

12. What does Sartre mean by "forlornness"?

13. What does Sartre mean by saying that "man is condemned to be free"?

14. What does Sartre mean by saying that "Man is nothing else . . . than the ensemble of his acts, nothing else than his life"?

15. Why does Camus assert that "There is but one truly serious philosophical problem, and that is suicide"?

16. What does Camus mean by saying that "the stage sets collapse"?

17. What does Camus mean by saying that "The world evades us because it becomes itself again"?

18. Why does Camus insist that the absurd is a relation?

19. What are the chief components of the relation of the absurd?

20. What are Camus' reasons for refusing a "leap" of faith?

21. Explain in your own words Camus' reasoning in rejection of suicide.

22. Summarize in your own words Camus' account of absurd revolt, freedom, and passion.

23. What was Sisyphus's crime?

24. In what respects is Sisyphus "the absurd hero"?

25. Summarize in your own words von Rintelen's critique of Camus' Sisyphus.

26. What is wrong with Sartre's efforts to establish an existentialist ethics, according to Warnock?

27. What does Heinemann mean by the phrases "Man for himself," "Man against himself," "Man with himself"?

28. What is the fundamental flaw of existentialist thought, according to Heinemann?

Questions for Reflection:

1. In what ways do I realize true authenticity in my life?
   In what ways is my life inauthentic?

2. What is my own experience like, when I drop my evasions and confront my hard truths?

3. In what ways do I experience absurdity in my life? How do I respond to such experiences?

4. What feelings are aroused in me as I read Nietzsche, Camus and Sartre?

5. Would it be possible for me to be happy, if I were in Sisyphus's position?

Questions for Discussion:

1. Has the madman accurately stated the significance of the death of God? Or does he overstate (or understate) the case?

2. Is authenticity always a good? Or is it desirable sometimes to be inauthentic? Clarify your terms.

3. If there is no God, is it true that we create ourselves and our own values?

4. Is it true that when I choose, I choose for all people?

5. Is it true that ultimately, I am nothing more than what I do with my life?

6. Has Camus accurately diagnosed the human condition, if one grants his premise that no supreme being can be discerned? Or does he overstate (or understate) the case?

7. Are Camus' reasons for rejecting suicide sound and persuasive?

8. Is it possible for Sisyphus to be happy?

9. Is Warnock's critique of Sartre correct?

10. Is Heinemann's critique of existentialism correct?

11. Does atheistic existentialism offer a view of the good life? Or does it merely indicate how to make the best of a bad thing?

12. Can life still be meaningful in a satisfying sense, from the point of view of atheistic existentialism?

SUGGESTIONS FOR FURTHER READING

William Barrett, Irrational Man: A Study in Existential Philosophy (Doubleday Anchor 1962)

H. J. Blackham, Six Existentialist Thinkers (Macmillan, 1952; Harper Torchbooks, 1959)

Albert Camus, The Stranger (Knopf, 1946; Random House, Vintage, 1954) A companion to The Myth of Sisyphus.

Fyodor Dostoyevsky, Notes From Underground (New American Library, 1961)

F. H. Heinemann, Existentialism and the Modern Predicament (Harper Torchbooks, 1958)

Walter Kaufmann, ed., Existentialism from Dostoyevsky to Sartre (Meridian, 1956)

Thomas Nagel, "The Absurd" in Mortal Questions (Cambridge University Press, 1979).

Jean-Paul Sartre, Existentialism and Human Emotions (Philosophical Library, 1957)

_____, Nausea (New Directions, 1964)

Philip Thody, ed., Albert Camus: Lyrical and Critical Essays (Knopf, 1968)

Mary Warnock, Existentialism (Oxford, 1970)

Chapter Eight:

Universe

Chapter VIII: UNIVERSE

Introduction

Be here now--that is all I need to know. For when I am fully open to this present moment, I see the beauty, light and joy that are inherent in myself and in all things. The ways of the Taoist sage and the Zen master, of Hindu and Western mystics, lead me not to a distant, unfamiliar land, but back to this world, to this place, to this moment--awakened to a new way of seeing.

Need and pain, evil and injustice continue to invite my compassionate response. Are there things I need to do? Then I will do them. Do others require my help? Then I will help them. But if I adopt the standpoint of this chapter, I will no longer put my happiness in hostage to another place and time; the time for happiness is now. Like a mother who, even while comforting her crying child, rejoices in the child's beauty, I may in the midst of suffering penetrate to a standpoint from which I see that in a deeper sense, all is well.

When I am wholly present in this moment, my awareness lightens, and I awaken to a new vision of the world. No facts are denied, yet all is transformed, and I realize that this world and this life are in themselves enough: complete, perfect, whole. I do not need to turn away from them toward an ideal otherworldly realm and a supernatural being. Nor must the absence of such a being throw me into anxiety, despair, forlornness. Anguished struggle against a recalcitrant universe, a universe that refuses to conform to my willful striving, insures only that I will alienate myself and sink deeper into misery. According to the view presented here, the good life requires not defiance and revolt, but a yielding trust and loving acknowledgement of what is true. In this spirit, Nietzsche writes,

> My formula for greatness in a human being is <u>amor fati</u> (love of fate): that one wants nothing to be other than it is, not in the future, not in the past, not in all eternity. Not merely to endure that which happens of necessity, still less to dissemble it--all idealism is untruthfulness in the face of necessity--but to <u>love</u> it.[1]

As I open myself to all that is true for me now--receptive, letting go, embracing my world--I feel myself settling into a larger, healing reality. The boundary that divides me from others and shuts me off from the world--the hard shell of my clutching fears--begins to soften and melt, and my separateness dissolves into a growing wholeness and union with all things. In heightened moments of total release, my sense of unity may become an ecstatic revelation of incomparable, transforming power. I realize in the depths of my being that I am one with the universe itself.

Such moments of enlightenment fade, and my world resumes its familiar hues--of suffering and hope, banality and struggle--but now seen in a new light. I am content to be engaged in the process of my life; I am fully present, without resistance. My awareness is no longer tight and divided, but unconstrained and whole--floating lightly upon the waves of my experience, like a lotus upon rippling water. I adapt fluidly to events as they occur, responding without strain, maintaining my balance and sense of place. I am deeply centered, trusting and transparent, wholly here now.

Strategies for Living in the Present

We readily recognize the value of such experience; but we are less clear about the conditions which produce it. Commonly we attempt to manipulate the external conditions of our lives, to induce in ourselves a sense of wholeness and satisfaction. "When I finally finish my education and get a good job, life will be good." "When I am married, I will at last be happy." "If I can increase my income, all will be well." But when the desired goal is reached, I find that satisfaction has again receded, like a carrot forever dangling a foot away--and my anxious quest resumes. According to the viewpoint of this chapter, the problem lies not in the world, but in myself. My unhappiness lies in refusing to be where I am: in drawing back from what is true for me now. My life may be rich by conventional standards; but if I judge it to be insufficient, to that degree I will be unhappy. When I regard this moment as not enough, I shrink from it, averting my awareness, closing off to what is--like a man who rejects his own face. What is needed is a transformation of consciousness, whereby I come to experience the beauty and joy of that which is present to me. As the French author, Marcel Proust declared, "The only real voyage of discovery . . . consists not in seeking new landscapes but in having new eyes . . ."[2]

Preventing such a transformation is my unwillingness to experience my own deficiency, loss and pain. Anxiously I stand guard over my perceptions, ready to shut down and turn away from any unpleasantness, hoping that my wary watchfulness will preserve a corner of consciousness where no shadow falls. When I encounter pain, I steel myself against it, retreating from my real experience into realms of fantasy and intellect. So long as I distance myself from my concrete, immediate experience, a genuine and deep appreciation of life will elude me. From the standpoint of the views of this chapter, what is needed is not clever control of circumstances so that only pleasant experiences filter through, nor a fortunate turn of fate that happens to bestow riches upon me--but self-discipline to permit myself to experience fully all of my life, the pain as well as the pleasure. Such self-discipline requires that I be willing to look squarely at what it is that I fear, to recognize those things I cling to, and to be willing to let go of my attachment to them, for the sake of fuller, freer experience. It requires that I yield to my emotions of grief and pain, rather than fighting them off. In letting go of my cramped and anxious conception of what life must be, I gain not only a richer experience of the world, but a deeper awareness of my own nature. The American psychologist and philosopher, William James regards such a shift as at the heart of religious experience. He writes

> The transition from tenseness, self-responsibility, and worry, to equanimity, receptivity, and peace, is the most wonderful of all those shiftings of equilibrium, those changes of the personal center of energy, which I have analyzed so often; and the chief wonder of it is that it so often comes about, not by doing, but by simply relaxing and throwing the burden down. This abandonment of self-responsibility seems to be the fundamental act in specifically religious, as distinguished from moral practice.[3]

The self-discipline to yield to all of one's experience is not a matter of gritting one's teeth and plunging into confrontation with distress, like a terrified soldier on the battlefield, determined to charge the enemy. Such an approach is not receptive but reactive, and remains caught within the struggle of aversions and attractions. Full awareness of the present moment may be cultivated by more effective and subtle means, among which are various forms of meditation as practiced in the great spiritual traditions of the West and especially the East, including Yoga and Zen. Through centuries of refinement in practice, precise techniques have been elaborated for cultivating a focussed awareness, centered and supple like a steady flame in quiet air.

Mystical Experience

The mastery of such discipline is no easy matter. A traditional Hindu analogy likens the process of training the mind to that of subduing a raging elephant; a similar metaphor in the Zen tradition speaks of domesticating a wild ox. But by all accounts, success in this process of self-cultivation is such as to justify all of one's efforts, beyond any possible doubt or reservation. The consummation of meditative practice is some form of enlightenment, or mystical experience: a state of awareness involving a profound recognition of oneness or community with all things; an unshakable conviction that one has at last broken through to acquaintance with the true nature of reality; an overwhelming feeling of satisfaction, joy and bliss; and realization that no description in words can begin to do justice to the experience. While accounts in various traditions differ widely, a common feature is the sense of loss of boundaries--the softening or dissolving of the narrow limits of one's private ego-self in the recognition of ultimate reality.

The achievement of such heightened moments of peak experience is not the only reason for meditative practice, however. According to the views presented here, the discipline of consciousness may enhance one's day-to-day experience in numerous ways, promoting buoyancy, vigor, directness, compassion, and many other desirable qualities of mind. The kind of awareness advocated in this chapter--an open, present-centered, dynamic emptiness--is a motif found in Taoism and to some degree in Hinduism; but it is most characteristic of Buddhism, and especially of Zen.

Morality and Goals

The advice to cultivate a complete acceptance of the present moment raises troubling ethical questions, however. There is much in the world around us that we not only want to change, but that we feel obliged to change. Acceptance of the present moment seems to undermine the motivation to achieve, to improve, to correct; for if the present moment is sufficient, why alter it? Shall I accept my own confusion and ignorance, my selfishness and lack of discipline? Shall I acquiesce in war and murder, racism and injustice, because "this moment is perfect"? Shall I advise the victims of exploitation and injustice to learn to love their lot? If we are committed to achievement and progress, to justice, compassion and other moral ideals, then it would seem necessary to say to much of our present world, "No! This will not do. Present conditions are unacceptable, and must be altered, for a better future."

But such a criticism is based upon a misinterpretation. The advice to live within the present moment has more to do with attitude than with external behavior. It is a call for a shift in consciousness, in perspective and frame of mind; it is not an invitation to passivity. According to the views of this chapter, those who are immersed in the present moment may also be fully engaged in bringing about desirable future goals. An analogy may be useful here: imagine two drivers, traveling an extended distance by car. One is so determined to arrive at his destination that he regards the trip itself as a nuisance. Straining forward, he pushes willfully ahead, fixed upon his goal, oblivious to the scenery along the way. He drives his car hard, curses any delay, and frequently becomes angry at other drivers. The second driver also makes good time, but while traveling, is happy to be within the process as it occurs. Her state of mind is open and receptive. She is attuned to the condition of her car and, while enjoying the passing view, engages in pleasant conversation with her passengers.

As such an example makes clear, it is possible to be both involved in a productive, goal-oriented activity and aware of the richness of one's present experience. Openness to the present is, in fact, often more productive of future goods than is single-minded attachment to one's image of those goods. To return to the above example: because he has closed himself off to much of his ongoing experience, the first driver may not notice, or may choose to ignore, a developing problem in his vehicle-- a tell-tale rattle, a bald tire--until the problem is serious enough to impose lengthy delays. Perhaps he will overlook important road markers, or exceed the speed limit and be stopped by police. The second driver, because she is aware of her immediate environment, will be less likely to encounter such difficulties, and more likely to arrive at her destination in a cheerful and constructive frame of mind.

Indeed, when one is fully present within a process, without uncertainty or strain, unified with one's own immediate activity, the result may be a level of performance that far exceeds usual levels. Examples of such consummate skill are especially evident in sport and other physical activities: A golfer is, on a particular day, so attuned to his game that his every stroke is effortless power and precision, and the ball "seems to have eyes." A tennis player realizes after an outstanding match that she has been playing "in the zone": she has been so fully released into her performance that she has transcended herself. Or a speaker is thoroughly caught up in his message, so that his words flow out with unconstrained eloquence, grace and power. Eastern traditions of the martial arts, of archery and swordplay, are explicitly directed to the cultivation of such a consummate union with performance; they can, in fact, be seen as forms of meditation in action.

According to the views presented here, full acceptance of the present moment, far from being advice to ignore moral requirements, conduces to greater responsiveness to those requirements. In yielding to the fullness of my own experience, I allow myself to become more sensitive to the needs of those around me. The openness of present-centered awareness is, in fact, a necessary condition for genuine compassion: an empathetic and nurturing response to the suffering of others. An accepting, present-centered awareness conduces to an interpersonal style that naturally gravitates away from conflict and strife, toward a harmonious equilibrium of the human community.

Morality often requires that we change present conditions in some way. But no moral end is served by denying or ignoring what is true. On the contrary, rejection of features of the present moment may well block a constructive moral response. Perhaps I am sometimes selfish or cruel. How shall I respond to that fact? To reject that part of me which is capable of selfish or cruel actions is to commit myself to an internal struggle from which there is likely to be no exit, only increasingly sophisticated styles of self-deception. But if I fully experience all that is within me, embracing what I am--that which seems evil as well as that which seems good--I am freed to do what I am capable of doing, and to grow beyond my present limits. Accepting all that I am does not mean that I act out every wayward impulse, however irrational--indeed, such reactive behavior is usually a willful ignoring of the larger picture--but that I acknowledge and accept, without judgment, all of my inner life. In penetrating to that place within me from which I can see that all is necessary, beautiful and good, I experience an overflowing of my own abundance and joy, which naturally expresses itself in acts of generosity and compassion.

The Selections

The first selection, from the Chinese philosopher Chuang Tzu (fourth century B.C.) depicts a Taoist sage, or fully realized person. Such a person is attuned to the natural course of events (The Tao, or Way), and thus lives in perfect harmony with all that occurs. Free from all attachment, without anxiety, the sage is imperturbable--not through living in a well-defended fortress, but by virtue of a fluid responsiveness to reality, like a strand of kelp that yields with the wash of the ocean. "The Man of the Way . . . to the most perfect degree . . . goes along with what has been allotted to him." According to the Taoist tradition, such adaptive responsiveness (wu-wei, or "inaction") is not merely a strategy for coping comfortably with life, but the key to skillful and wise management of all affairs, including the governance of states.

Deeply centered, the sage "breathes with his heels," living from an inner point of equilibrium that is perfectly accommodated to the Way. Mild, cheerful, relaxed and tolerant, the sage sees the relativity of all distinctions and judgments, and thus refrains from condemnation or praise. "It is impossible to establish any constant rule."

The sage is guided not by perceptual judgment nor by conscious deliberation, but by intuitive spontaneity, in identification with the Way. Chuang Tzu describes the consummate skill of a cook who cuts up an ox: "I go at it by spirit and don't look with my eyes. Perception and understanding have come to a stop and spirit moves where it wants." Such grace is possible only for one who is wholly unattached, and who thus freely accommodates the natural course of things. The self becomes transparent, a fluid openness through which pass the energies of life. The sage advises us: "Blend your spirit with the vastness . . . . Be empty, that is all."

A traditional Eastern tale, retold by Leo Tolstoy (1828-1910) dramatizes the human dilemma: caught between the beast of premature death and the dragon of death in old age, we see each day and night nibbling away at our precarious hold on life. Can we still savor the sweetness of this present moment? Zen's response to this question goes far beyond a desperate snatching for small pleasures, however. Disciplined Zen practice may so radically reorient us to our life and death that the most ordinary activities are experienced as miraculous; the Chinese sage Layman P'ang writes

> How wondrously supernatural!
> And how miraculous this!
> I draw water, I carry fuel![4]

In the Zen tradition, the opening of consciousness to such transfigured awareness is called satori. The eminent Zen scholar D. T. Suzuki (1870-1966) describes some of the characteristics of satori, though genuine understanding can be had "only through our once personally experiencing it." Suzuki's account represents the Rinzai or "sudden" school of Zen, which emphasizes a dramatic, "cataclysmic" transformation; in contrast, the Soto or "gradual" tradition of Zen understands enlightenment as the outcome of a gentler, incremental process.

The topic of enlightenment or mystical experience is also the subject of the essay by the contemporary philosopher Alan Watts (1915-1973). The heart of this experience is, Watts declares, "a vivid and overwhelming certainty that the universe, precisely as it is at this moment, as a whole and in every one of its parts, is so completely right as to need no explanation or justification beyond what it simply is." Watts explores the apparent dilemmas posed for this view by the existence of pain and suffering, evil and boredom, and concludes that at a deeper level, such phenomena are harmonious with the vision of reality as " 'right,' so right that our normal anxieties become ludicrous, that if only men could see it they would go wild with joy . . . ." Watts' discussion is lucid and engaging, and needs little comment here.

NOTES

1. Friedrich Nietzsche, Ecce Homo, translated by R. J. Hollingdale (Middlesex, England: Penguin, 1979), p 68.

2. The Maxims of Marcel Proust, ed. by Justin O'Brien (New York: Columbia University Press, 1948), p. 181.

3. The Varieties of Religious Experience, Foreword by Jacques Barzun (New York: Mentor, 1958, 1961), pp. 228f.

4. Quoted by D. T. Suzuki in Essays in Zen Buddhism, Third Series (London: Rider and Company, 1953), p. 83.

THE TAOIST SAGE*

by Chuang Tzu

Great understanding is broad and unhurried; little understanding is cramped and busy. Great words are clear and limpid; little words are shrill and quarrelsome. In sleep, men's spirits go visiting; in waking hours, their bodies hustle. With everything they meet they become entangled. Day after day they use their minds in strife, sometimes grandiose, sometimes sly, sometimes petty. Their little fears are mean and trembly; their great fears are stunned and overwhelming. They bound off like an arrow or a crossbow pellet, certain that they are the arbiters of right and wrong. They cling to their position as though they had sworn before the gods, sure that they are holding on to victory. They fade like fall and winter--such is the way they dwindle day by day. They drown in what they do--you cannot make them turn back. They grow dark, as though sealed with seals--such are the excesses of their old age. And when their minds draw near to death, nothing can restore them to the light.

Joy, anger, grief, delight, worry, regret, fickleness, inflexibility, modesty, willfulness, candor, insolence--music from empty holes, mushrooms springing up in dampness, day and night replacing each other before us, and no one knows where they sprout from. Let it be! Let it be! (It is enough that) morning and evening we have them, and they are the means by which we live. Without them we would not exist; without us they would have nothing to take hold of. This comes close to the matter. . .

II

Cook Ting was cutting up an ox for Lord Wen-hui. At every touch of his hand, every heave of his shoulder, every move of his feet, every thrust of his knee--zip! zoop! He slithered the knife along with a zing, and all was in perfect rhythm, as though he were performing the dance of the Mulberry Grove or keeping time to the Ching-shou music.

"Ah, this is marvelous!" said Lord Wen-hui. "Imagine skill reaching such heights!"

Cook Ting laid down his knife and replied, "What I care about is the Way, which goes beyond skill. When I first began cutting up oxen, all I could see was the ox itself. After three years I no longer saw the whole ox. And now--now I go at it by spirit and don't look with my eyes. Perception and understanding have come to a stop and spirit moves where it wants. I go along with the natural makeup, strike in the big hollows, guide the knife through the big openings, and follow things as they are. So I never touch the smallest ligament or tendon, much less a main joint.

*From Chuang Tzu: Basic Writings, Translated by Burton Watson (New York and London: Columbia University Press, 1964).

275

"A good cook changes his knife once a year--because he cuts. A mediocre cook changes his knife once a month--because he hacks. I've had this knife of mine for nineteen years and I've cut up thousands of oxen with it, and yet the blade is as good as though it had just come from the grindstone. There are spaces between the joints, and the blade of the knife has really no thickness. If you insert what has no thickness into such spaces, then there's plenty of room--more than enough for the blade to play about in. That's why after nineteen years the blade of my knife is still as good as when it first came from the grindstone.

"However, whenever I come to a complicated place, I size up the difficulties, tell myself to watch out and be careful, keep my eyes on what I'm doing, work very slowly, and move the knife with the greatest subtlety, until--flop! the whole thing comes apart like a clod of earth crumbling to the ground. I stand there holding the knife and look all around me, completely satisfied and reluctant to move on, and then I wipe off the knife and put it away."

"Excellent!" said Lord Wen-hui. "I have heard the words of Cook Ting and learned how to care for life!". . .

III

Confucius said,[1] "Life, death, preservation, loss, failure, success, poverty, riches, worthiness, unworthiness, slander, fame, hunger, thirst, cold, heat--these are the alternations of the world, the workings of fate. Day and night they change place before us and wisdom cannot spy out their source. Therefore, they should not be enough to destroy your harmony; they should not be allowed to enter the storehouse of spirit. If you can harmonize and delight in them, master them and never be at a loss for joy, if you can do this day and night without break and make it be spring with everything, mingling with all and creating the moment within your own mind--this is what I call being whole in power.". .

IV

There must first be a True Man[2] before there can be true knowledge.

What do I mean by a True Man? The True Man of ancient times did not rebel against want, did not grow proud in plenty, and did not plan his affairs. Being like this, he could commit an error and not regret it, could meet with success and not make a show. Being like this, he could climb the high places and not be frightened, could enter the water and not get

1. The Taoist views here attributed to Confucius by Chuang Tzu are not those of the historical Confucius. SAS
2. Another term for the Taoist sage, synonymous with the Perfect Man or the Holy Man.

wet, could enter the fire and not get burned. His knowledge was able to climb all the way up to the Way like this.

The True Man of ancient times slept without dreaming and woke without care; he ate without savoring and his breath came from deep inside. The True Man breathes with his heels; the mass of men breathe with their throats. Crushed and bound down, they gasp out their words as though they were retching. Deep in their passions and desires, they are shallow in the workings of Heaven.

The True Man of ancient times knew nothing of loving life, knew nothing of hating death. He emerged without delight; he went back in without a fuss. He came briskly, he went briskly, and that was all. He didn't forget where he began; he didn't try to find out where he would end. He received something and took pleasure in it; he forgot about it and handed it back again. This is what I call not using the mind to repel the Way, not using man to help out Heaven. This is what I call the True Man.

Since he is like this, his mind forgets; his face is calm; his forehead is broad. He is chilly like autumn, balmy like spring, and his joy and anger prevail through the four seasons. He goes along with what is right for things and no one knows his limit. . .

V

T'ien Ken was wandering on the sunny side of Yin Mountain. When he reached the banks of the Liao River, he happened to meet a Nameless Man. He questioned the man, saying, "Please may I ask how to rule the world?"

The Nameless Man said, "Get away from me, you peasant! What kind of a dreary question is that! I'm just about to set off with the Creator. And if I get bored with that, then I'll ride on the Light-and Lissome Bird out beyond the six directions, wandering in the village of Not-Even-Anything and living in the Broad-and-Borderless field. What business do you have coming with this talk of governing the world and disturbing my mind?"

But T'ien Ken repeated his question. The Nameless Man said, "Let your mind wander in simplicity, blend your spirit with the vastness, follow along with things the way they are, and make no room for personal views--then the world will be governed". . .

VI

Do not be an embodier of fame; do not be a storehouse of schemes; do not be an undertaker of projects; do not be a proprietor of wisdom. Embody to the fullest what has no end and wander where there is no trail.

Hold on to all that you have received from Heaven but do not think you have gotten anything. Be empty, that is all. The Perfect Man uses his mind like a mirror--going after nothing, welcoming nothing, responding but not storing. Therefore he can win out over things and not hurt himself. . .

VII

The Great Man in his actions will not harm others, but he makes no show of benevolence or charity. He will not move for the sake of profit, but he does not despise the porter at the gate. He will not wrangle for goods or wealth, but he makes no show of refusing or relinquishing them. He will not enlist the help of others in his work, but he makes no show of being self-supporting, and he does not despise the greedy and base. His actions differ from those of the mob, but he makes no show of uniqueness or eccentricity. He is content to stay behind with the crowd, but he does not despise those who run forward to flatter and fawn. All the titles and stipends of the age are not enough to stir him to exertion; all its penalties and censures are not enough to make him feel shame. He knows that no line can be drawn between right and wrong, no border can be fixed between great and small. I have heard it said, "The Man of the Way wins no fame, the highest virtue wins no gain, the Great Man has no self." To the most perfect degree, he goes along with what has been allotted to him."

The Lord of the River said, "Whether they are external to things or internal, I do not understand how we come to have these distinctions of noble and mean or of great and small."

Jo of the North Sea said, "From the point of view of the Way, things have no nobility or meanness. From the point of view of common opinion, nobility and meanness are not determined by the individual himself.

"From the point of view of differences, if we regard a thing as big because there is a certain bigness to it, then among all the ten thousand things there are none that are not big. If we regard a thing as small because there is a certain smallness to it, then among the ten thousand things there are none that are not small. If we know that heaven and earth are tiny grains and the tip of a hair is a range of mountains, then we have perceived the law of difference.

"From the point of view of function, if we regard a thing as useful because there is a certain usefulness to it, then among all the ten thousand things there are none that are not useful. If we regard a thing as useless because there is a certain uselessness to it, then among the ten thousand things there are none that are not useless. If we know that east and west are mutually opposed but that one cannot do without the other, then we can estimate the degree of function.

"From the point of view of preference, if we regard a thing as right because there is a certain right to it, then among the ten thousand things there are none that are not right. If we regard a thing as wrong because there is a certain wrong to it, then among the ten thousand things there are none that are not wrong. . . .

"Well then," said the Lord of the River, "what should I do and what should I not do? How am I to know in the end what to accept and what to reject, what to abide by and what to discard?"

Jo of the North Sea said, "From the point of view of the Way, what is noble or what is mean? These terms merely express excesses of contrast. Do not hobble your will, or you will be departing far from the Way! What is few, or what is many? These terms merely express states of fluctuation. Do not strive to unify your actions, or you will be at sixes and sevens with the Way! Be stern like the ruler of a state—he grants no private favor. Be benign and impartial like the god of the soil at the sacrifice—he grants no private blessing. Be broad and expansive like the endlessness of the four directions—they have nothing which bounds or hedges them. Embrace the ten thousand things universally—how could there be one you should give special support to? This is called being without bent. When the ten thousand things are unified and equal, then which is short and which is long?

"The Way is without beginning or end, but things have their life and death—you cannot rely upon their fulfillment. One moment empty, the next moment full—you cannot depend upon their form. The years cannot be held off; time cannot be stopped. Decay, growth, fullness, and emptiness end and then begin again. It is thus that we must describe the plan of the Great Meaning and discuss the principles of the ten thousand things. The life of things is a gallop, a headlong dash—with every movement they alter, with every moment they shift. What should you do and what should you not do? Everything will change of itself, that is certain!"

"If that is so," said the Lord of the River, "then what is there valuable about the Way?"

Jo of the North Sea said, "He who understands the Way is certain to have command of basic principles. He who has command of basic principles is certain to know how to deal with circumstances. And he who knows how to deal with circumstances will not allow things to do him harm. When a man has perfect virtue, fire cannot burn him, water cannot drown him, cold and heat cannot afflict him, birds and beasts cannot injure him. I do not say that he makes light of these things. I mean that he distinguishes between safety and danger, contents himself with fortune or misfortune, and is cautious in his comings and goings. Therefore nothing can harm him.

279

"Hence it is said: the Heavenly is on the inside, the human is on the outside. Virtue resides in the Heavenly. Understand the actions of Heaven and man, base yourself upon Heaven, take your stand in virtue, and then, although you hasten or hold back, bend or stretch, you may return to the essential and speak of the ultimate."

"What do you mean by the Heavenly and the human?"

Jo of the North Sea said, "Horses and oxen have four feet--this is what I mean by the Heavenly. Putting a halter on the horse's head, piercing the ox's nose--this is what I mean by the human. So I say: do not let what is human wipe out what is Heavenly; do not let what is purposeful wipe out what is fated; do not let (the desire for) gain lead you after fame. Be cautious, guard it, and do not lose it--this is what I mean by returning to the True.". .

LIVING IN THIS MOMENT*

by Leo Tolstoy

Long ago has been told the Eastern story about the traveller who in the steppe is overtaken by an infuriated beast. Trying to save himself from the animal, the traveller jumps into a waterless well, but at its bottom he sees a dragon who opens his jaws in order to swallow him. And the unfortunate man does not dare climb out, lest he perish from the infuriated beast, and does not dare jump down to the bottom of the well, lest he be devoured by the dragon, and so clutches the twig of a wild bush growing in a cleft of the well and holds on to it. His hands grow weak and he feels that soon he shall have to surrender to the peril which awaits him at either side; but he still holds on and sees two mice, one white, the other black, in even measure making a circle around the main trunk of the bush to which he is clinging, and nibbling at it on all sides. Now, at any moment, the bush will break and tear off, and he will fall into the dragon's jaws. The traveller sees that and knows that he will inevitably perish; but while he is still clinging, he sees some drops of honey hanging on the leaves of the bush, and so reaches out for them with his tongue and licks the leaves.

*From "My Confession" in The Complete Works of Count Tolstoy, Vol. 13, translated and edited by Leo Weiner (Boston: Dana Estes & Co., Publishers; Colonial Press, 1904), pp. 21f.

ON SATORI*

by D. T. Suzuki

The essence of Zen Buddhism consists in acquiring a new viewpoint of looking at life and things generally. By this I mean that if we want to get into the inmost life of Zen, we must forgo all our ordinary habits of thinking which control our everyday life, we must try to see if there is any other way of judging things, or rather if our ordinary way is always sufficient to give us the ultimate satisfaction of our spiritual needs. If we feel dissatisfied somehow with this life, if there is something in our ordinary way of living that deprives us of freedom in its most sanctified sense, we must endeavor to find a way somewhere which gives us a sense of finality and contentment. Zen proposes to do this for us and assures us of the acquirement of a new point of view in which life assumes a fresher, deeper, and more satisfying aspect. This acquirement, however, is really and naturally the greatest mental cataclysm one can go through with in life. It is no easy task, it is a kind of fiery baptism, and one has to go through the storm, the earthquake, the overthrowing of the mountains, and the breaking in pieces of the rocks.

This acquiring of a new point of view in our dealings with life and the world is popularly called by Japanese Zen students 'satori' (wu in Chinese). It is really another name for Enlightenment (annuttara-samyak-sambodhi), which is the word used by the Buddha and his Indian followers ever since his realization under the Bodhi-tree. . .

Satori may be defined as an intuitive looking into the nature of things in contradistinction to the analytical or logical understanding of it. Practically, it means the unfolding of a new world hitherto unperceived in the confusion of a dualistically-trained mind. Or we may say that with satori our entire surroundings are viewed from quite an unexpected angle of perception. Whatever this is, the world for those who have gained a satori is no more the old world as it used to be; even with all its flowing streams and burning fires, it is never the same one again. Logically stated, all its opposites and contradictions are united and harmonized into a consistent organic whole. This is a mystery and a miracle, but according to the Zen masters such is being performed every day. Satori can thus be had only through our once personally experiencing it.

Its semblance or analogy in a more or less feeble and fragmentary way is gained when a difficult mathematical problem is solved, or when a great discovery is made, or when a sudden means of escape is realized in the midst of most desperate complications; in short, when one exclaims 'Eureka! Eureka!' But this refers only to the intellectual aspect of satori, which is therefore necessarily partial and incomplete and does not touch

*From D. T. Suzuki, ESSAYS IN ZEN BUDDHISM, First Series (New York: Grove Press, 1961), pp. 229-231. Copyright 1961 by Grove Press, Inc. Reprinted by permission of Grove Press, Inc.

the very foundations of life considered one indivisible whole. Satori as the Zen experience must be concerned with the entirety of life. For what Zen proposes to do is the revolution, and the revaluation as well, of oneself as a spiritual unity. The solving of a mathematical problem ends with the solution, it does not affect one's whole life. So with all other particular questions, practical or scientific, they do not enter the basic life-tone of the individual concerned. But the opening of satori is the remaking of life itself. When it is genuine--for there are many simulacra of it--its effects on one's moral and spiritual life are revolutionary, and they are so enhancing, purifying, as well as exacting. When a master was asked what constituted Buddhahood, he answered, 'The bottom of a pail is broken through.' From this we can see what a complete revolution is produced by this spiritual experience. The birth of a new man is really cataclysmic. . .

THIS IS IT*

by Alan Watts

The most impressive fact in man's spiritual, intellectual, and poetic experience has always been, for me, the universal prevalence of those astonishing moments of insight which Richard Bucke called "cosmic consciousness." There is no really satisfactory name for this type of experience. To call it mystical is to confuse it with visions of another world, or of gods and angels. To call it spiritual or metaphysical is to suggest that it is not also extremely concrete and physical, while the term "cosmic consciousness" itself has the unpoetic flavor of occultist jargon. But from all historical times and cultures we have reports of this same unmistakable sensation emerging, as a rule, quite suddenly and unexpectedly and from no clearly understood cause.

To the individual thus enlightened it appears as a vivid and overwhelming certainty that the universe, precisely as it is at this moment, as a whole and in every one of its parts, is so completely right as to need no explanation or justification beyond what it simply is. Existence not only ceases to be a problem; the mind is so wonder-struck at the self-evident and self-sufficient fitness of things as they are, including what would ordinarily be thought the very worst, that it cannot find any word strong enough to express the perfection and beauty of the experience. Its clarity sometimes gives the sensation that the world has become transparent or luminous, and its simplicity the sensation that it is pervaded and ordered by a supreme intelligence. At the same time it is usual for the individual to feel that the whole world has become his own body, and that whatever he is has not only become, but always has been, what everything else is. It is not that he loses his identity to the point of feeling that he actually looks out through all other eyes, becoming literally omniscient, but rather that his individual consciousness and existence is a point of view temporarily adopted by something immeasurably greater than himself.

The central core of the experience seems to be the conviction, or insight, that the immediate now, whatever its nature, is the goal and fulfillment of all living. Surrounding and flowing from this insight is an emotional ecstasy, a sense of intense relief, freedom, and lightness, and often of almost unbearable love for the world, which is, however, secondary. Often, the pleasure of the experience is confused with the experience and the insight lost in the ecstasy, so that in trying to retain the secondary effects of the experience the individual misses its point--that the immediate now is complete even when it is not ecstatic. For ecstasy is a necessarily impermanent contrast in the constant fluctuation

*Condensed by permission of Pantheon Books, a Division of Random House, Inc. from THIS IS IT AND OTHER ESSAYS ON ZEN AND SPIRITUAL EXPERIENCE, by Alan Watts. Copyright (c) 1958, 1960 by Alan Watts.

of our feelings. But insight, when clear enough, persists; having once understood a particular skill, the facility tends to remain.

The terms in which a man interprets this experience are naturally drawn from the religious and philosophical ideas of his culture, and their differences often conceal its basic identity. As water seeks the course of least resistance, so the emotions clothe themselves in the symbols that lie most readily to hand, and the association is so swift and automatic that the symbol may appear to be the very heart of the experience. Clarity--the disappearance of problems--suggests light, and in moments of such acute clarity there may be the physical sensation of light penetrating everything. To a theist this will naturally seem to be a glimpse of the presence of God, as in the celebrated testimony of Pascal:

> The year of grace 1654,
> Monday the 23rd of November, St. Clement's day. . . .
> From about half past ten in the evening
> until about half past twelve, midnight,
>
> FIRE
>
> God of Abraham. God of Isaac. God of Jacob
>   not of the philosophers and the wise.
> Certainty, joy, certainty, feeling, joy, peace.

Or in a case quoted by William James:

> The very heavens seemed to open and pour down rays of light and glory. Not for a moment only, but all day and night, floods of light and glory seemed to pour through my soul, and oh, how I was changed, and everything became new. My horses and hogs and everybody seemed changed.

But clarity may also suggest transparency, or the sense that the world confronting us is no longer an obstacle and the body no longer a burden, and to a Buddhist this will just as naturally call to mind the doctrine of reality as the ungraspable, indefinable Void (sunyata).

> I came back into the hall and was about to go to my seat when the whole outlook changed. A broad expanse opened, and the ground appeared as if all caved in. . . . As I looked around and up and down, the whole universe with its multitudinous sense-objects now appeared quite different; what was loathsome before, together with ignorance and passions, was now seen to be nothing else but the outflow of my own inmost nature which in itself remained bright, true, and transparent.[1]

1.   Yüan-chou (d. 1287), quoted by Suzuki, Essays in Zen Buddhism, vol. 2, p. 92.

As one and the same pain may be described either as a hot pang or as a cold sting, so the descriptions of this experience may take forms that seem to be completely opposed. One person may say that he has found the answer to the whole mystery of life, but somehow cannot put it into words. Another will say that there never was a mystery and thus no answer to it, for what the experience made clear to him was the irrelevance and artificiality of all our questions. One declares himself convinced that there is no death, his true self being as eternal as the universe. Another states that death has simply ceased to matter, because the present moment is so complete that it requires no future. One feels himself taken up and united with a life infinitely other than his own. But as the beating of the heart may be regarded as something that <u>happens</u> to you or something that you <u>do</u>, depending on the point of view, so another will feel that he has experienced, not a transcendent God, but his own inmost nature. One will get the sense that his ego or self has expanded to become the entire universe, whereas another will feel that he has lost himself altogether and that what he called his ego was never anything but an abstraction. One will describe himself as infinitely enriched, while another will speak of being brought to such absolute poverty that he owns not even his mind and body, and has not a care in the world.

Rarely is the experience described without metaphors that might be misleading if taken literally. But in reading Bernard Berenson's <u>Sketch for a Self-Portrait</u> I came across a passage which is one of the simplest and "cleanest" accounts of it I have ever seen.

> It was a morning in early summer. A silver haze shimmered and trembled over the lime trees. The air was laden with their fragrance. The temperature was like a caress. I remember--I need not recall--that I climbed up a tree stump and felt suddenly immersed in Itness. I did not call it by that name. I had no need for words. It and I were one.[2]

Just "It"--as when we use the word to denote the superlative, or the exact point, or intense reality, or what we were always looking for. Not the neuter sense of the mere object, but something still more alive and far wider than the personal, and for which we use this simplest of words because we have no word for it. . .

Such experiences imply, then, that our normal perception and valuation of the world is a subjective but collective nightmare. They suggest that our ordinary sense of practical reality--of the world as seen on Monday morning--is a construct of socialized conditioning and repression, a system of selective inattention whereby we are taught to screen out aspects and relations within nature which do not accord with the rules of the game of civilized life. Yet the vision almost invariably includes the realization that this very restriction of consciousness is also

2.   Bernard Berenson, <u>Sketch for a Self-Portrait</u>, p. 18. Pantheon Books, New York, 1949.

part of the eternal fitness of things. In the words of the Zen master Gensha:

> If you understand, things are such as they are;
> If you do not understand, things are such as they are--

this "such as they are" being the utterly unproblematic and self-sufficient character of this eternal now in which, as Chuang-tzu said,

> A duck's legs, though short, cannot be lengthened without discomfort to the duck; a crane's legs, though long, cannot be shortened without discomfort to the crane.

For in some way the vision seems to come about through accepting the rightness of the fact that one does not have it, through being willing to be as imperfect as one is--perfectly imperfect. . .

Even though it may be exploited for this purpose, the experience itself is in no sense a philosophy designed to justify or to desensitize oneself to the inequalities of life. Like falling in love, it has a minimal connection with any particular cultural background or economic position. It descends upon the rich and the poor, the moral and the immoral, the happy and the miserable without distinction. It carries with it the overwhelming conviction that the world is in every respect a miracle of glory, and though this might logically exclude the necessity to share the vision with others and awaken them from their nightmare the usual reaction is a sense, not of duty, but of sheer delight in communicating the experience by word or deed.

From this new perspective the crimes and follies of man's ordinary nightmare life seem neither evil nor stupid but simply pitiable. One has the extraordinarily odd sensation of seeing people in their mean or malicious pursuits looking, at the same time, like gods--as if they were supremely happy without knowing it. As Kirillov puts it in Dostoyevsky's The Possessed,

> "Man is unhappy because he doesn't know he's happy. It's only that. That's all, that's all! If anyone finds out he'll become happy at once, that minute. . . . It's all good. I discovered it all of a sudden."
>
> "And if anyone dies of hunger," (asks Stavrogin), "and if anyone insults and outrages the little girl, is that good?"
>
> "Yes! And if anyone blows his brains out for the baby, that's good too. And if anyone doesn't, that's good too. It's all good, all. It's good for all those who know that it's all good. If they knew that it was good for them, it would be

287

good for them,but as long as they don't know it's good for them, it will be bad for them. That's the whole idea, the whole of it! . . . They're bad because they don't know they're good. When they find out, they won't outrage a little girl. They'll find out that they're good and they'll all become good, every one of them."[3]

Ordinarily one might feel that there is a shocking contrast between the marvellous structure of the human organism and its brain, on the one hand, and the uses to which most people put it, on the other. Yet there could perhaps be a point of view from which the natural wonder of the organism simply outshines the degrading performances of its superficial consciousness. In a somewhat similar way this strange opening of vision does not permit attention to remain focussed narrowly upon the details of evil; they become subordinate to the all-pervading intelligence and beauty of the total design.

Such insight has not the slightest connection with "shallow optimism" nor with grasping the meaning of the universe in terms of some neat philosophical simplification. Beside it, all philosophical opinions and disputations sound like somewhat sophisticated versions of children yelling back and forth--"'Tis!" "'Tisn't!' "'Tis!" "'Tisn't!"--until (if only the philosophers would do likewise) they catch the nonsense of it and roll over backwards with hoots of laughter. Furthermore, so far from being the smug rationalization of a Mr. Pangloss, the experience has a tendency to arise in situations of total extremity or despair, when the individual finds himself without any alternative but to surrender himself entirely.

Something of this kind came to me in a dream when I was about eight years old. I was sick at the time and almost delirious with fever, and in the dream I found myself attached face-downward and spread-eagled to an immense ball of steel which was spinning about the earth. I knew in this dream with complete certainty that I was doomed to be spun in this sickening and terrifying whirl forever and ever, and the conviction was so intense that there was nothing for it but to give up--for this was hell itself and nothing lay before me but a literal everlastingness of pain. But in the moment when I surrendered, the ball seemed to strike against a mountain and disintegrate, and the next thing I knew was that I was sitting on a stretch of warm sand with nothing left of the ball except crumpled fragments of sheet-metal scattered around me. This was not, of course, the experience of "cosmic consciousness," but simply of the fact that release in extremity lies through and not away from the problem.

That other experience came much later, twice with intensity, and other times with what might be called more of a glow than a brilliant flash. Shortly after I had first begun to study Indian and Chinese

3. Dostoyevsky, The Possessed, pp. 240-41. Trans. Constance Garnett. Modern Library, New York, 1936.

philosophy, I was sitting one night by the fire, trying to make out what was the right attitude of mind for meditation as it is practiced in Hindu and Buddhist disciplines. It seemed to me that several attitudes were possible, but as they appeared mutually exclusive and contradictory I was trying to fit them into one--all to no purpose. Finally, in sheer disgust, I decided to reject them all and to have no special attitude of mind whatsoever. In the force of throwing them away it seemed that I threw myself away as well, for quite suddenly the weight of my own body disappeared. I felt that I owned nothing, not even a self, and that nothing owned me. The whole world became as transparent and unobstructed as my own mind; the "problem of life" simply ceased to exist, and for about eighteen hours I and everything around me felt like the wind blowing leaves across a field on an autumn day.

The second time, a few years later, came after a period when I had been attempting to practice what Buddhists call "recollection" (smriti) or constant awareness of the immediate present, as distinct from the usual distracted rambling of reminiscence and anticipation. But, in discussing it one evening, someone said to me, "But why try to live in the present? Surely we are always completely in the present even when we're thinking about the past or the future?" This, actually quite obvious, remark again brought on the sudden sensation of having no weight. At the same time, the present seemed to become a kind of moving stillness, an eternal stream from which neither I nor anything could deviate. I saw that everything, just as it is now, is IT--is the whole point of there being life and a universe. I saw that when the Upanishads said, "That art thou!" or "All this world is Brahman," they meant just exactly what they said. Each thing, each event, each experience in its inescapable nowness and in all its own particular individuality was precisely what it should be, and so much so that it acquired a divine authority and originality. It struck me with the fullest clarity that none of this depended on my seeing it to be so; that was the way things were, whether I understood it or not, and if I did not understand, that was IT too. Furthermore, I felt that I now understood what Christianity might mean by the love of God--namely, that despite the commonsensical imperfection of things, they were nonetheless loved by God just as they are, and that this loving of them was at the same time the godding of them. This time the vivid sensation of lightness and clarity lasted a full week.

These experiences, reinforced by others that have followed, have been the enlivening force of all my work in writing and in philosophy since that time, though I have come to realize that how I feel, whether the actual sensation of freedom and clarity is present or not, is not the point--for, again, to feel heavy or restricted is also IT. . . .

Human purposes are pursued within an immense circling universe which does not seem to me to have purpose, in our sense, at all. Nature is much more playful than purposeful, and the probability that it has no special goals for the future need not strike one as a defect. On the contrary, the processes of nature as we see them both in the surrounding world and in the involuntary aspects of our own organisms are much more like art than like business, politics, or religion. They are especially like the arts of music and dancing, which unfold themselves without aiming at future destinations. No one imagines that a symphony is supposed to improve in quality as it goes along, or that the whole object of playing it is to reach the finale. The point of music is discovered in every moment of playing and listening to it. It is the same, I feel, with the greater part of our lives, and if we are unduly absorbed in improving them we may forget altogether to live them. The musician whose chief concern is to make every performance better than the last may so fail to participate and delight in his own music that he will impress his audience only with the anxious rigor of his technique.

Thus it is by no means the main work of a philosopher to be classed with the moralists and reformers. There is such a thing as philosophy, the love of wisdom, in the spirit of the artist. Such philosophy will not preach or advocate practices leading to improvement. As I understand it, the work of the philosopher as artist is to reveal and celebrate the eternal and purposeless background of human life. Out of simple exuberance or wonder he wants to tell others of the point of view from which the world is unimaginably good as it is, with people just as they are. No matter how difficult it may be to express this point of view without sounding smug or appearing to be a wishful dreamer, some hint of it may be suggested if the philosopher has had the good fortune to have experienced it himself. . .

"Cosmic" consciousness is a release from self-consciousness, that is to say from the fixed belief and feeling that one's organism is an absolute and separate thing, as distinct from a convenient unit of perception. For if it becomes clear that our use of the lines and surfaces of nature to divide the world into units is only a matter of convenience, then all that I have called myself is actually inseparable from everything. This is exactly what one experiences in these extraordinary moments. It is not that the outlines and shapes which we <u>call</u> things and use to delineate things disappear into some sort of lum<del></del>inous void. It simply becomes obvious that though they may be used as divisions they do not really divide. However much I may be impressed by the difference between a star and the dark space around it, I must not forget that I can see the two only in relation to each other, and that this relation is inseparable.

The most astonishing feature of this experience is, however, the conviction that this entire unspeakable world is "right," so right that our normal anxieties become ludicrous, that if only men could see it they would go wild with joy,

> And the king by cutting capers,
> And the priest be picking flowers. . .

The experience makes it perfectly clear that the whole universe is through and through the playing of love in every shade of the word's use, from animal lust to divine charity. Somehow this includes even the holocaust of the biological world, where every creature lives by feeding on others. Our usual picture of this world is reversed so that every victim is seen as offering itself in sacrifice. . . .

Toward the vast and all-encompassing background of human life, with which the philosopher as artist is concerned, there must be total affirmation and acceptance. Otherwise there is no basis at all for caution and control with respect to details in the foreground. But it is all too easy to become so absorbed in these details that all sense of proportion is lost, and for man to make himself mad by trying to bring everything under his control. We become insane, unsound, and without foundation when we lose consciousness of and faith in the uncontrolled and ungraspable background world which is ultimately what we ourselves are. And there is a very slight distinction, if any, between complete, conscious faith and love.

291

CRITIQUE

Both critique selections treat with respect the point of view expressed in this chapter, while criticizing its account of moral distinctions. The eminent English philosopher Bertrand Russell (1872-1970) addresses the paradox of asserting both that (1) evil exists, and (2) "all Reality is good." Russell notes the explanation usually given by mystics: that ordinary good and evil belong only to the appearance of things, while recognition that all is good sees deeper into the nature of reality. Russell offers an alternative account that he regards as more plausible: judgments of good and evil reflect merely subjective states of mind; they are not descriptions of the objective conditions of the world. The transformation of consciousness in mystic experience, while it "is of supreme importance for the conduct and happiness of life," "does not reveal anything about the nature of the universe in general." A truly objective view of reality would not judge things as either good or bad.

The critique by the American philosopher, Arthur Danto (1924-   ) attacks the other horn of the dilemma: if one holds that the world is indeed perfect and complete as it is, one cannot distinguish between torture and compassion, between evil and good. Spontaneous, consummate skill may be exercised not only in the performance of acceptable but also of unacceptable actions such as the Nazi "final solution," according to Danto. Ultimately the advice to live fully in the present, to cultivate our own salvation, fails as a morality because it does not tell us how to treat one another.

GOOD AND EVIL ARE SUBJECTIVE*

by Bertrand Russell

Mysticism maintains that all evil is illusory, and sometimes maintains the same view as regards good, but more often holds that all Reality is good. Both views are to be found in Heraclitus: "Good and ill are one," he says, but again, "To God all things are fair and good and right, but men hold some things wrong and some right.". . . Some such distinction, I think is necessary in order to understand the ethical outlook of mysticism: there is a lower mundane kind of good and evil, which divides the world of appearance into what seem to be conflicting parts; but there is also a higher, mystical kind of good, which belongs to Reality and is not opposed by any correlative kind of evil.

It is difficult to give a logically tenable account of this position without recognising that good and evil are subjective, that what is good is merely that towards which we have one kind of feeling, and what is evil is merely that towards which we have another kind of feeling. In our active life, where we have to exercise choice, and to prefer this to that of two possible acts, it is necessary to have a distinction of good and evil, or at least of better and worse. But this distinction, like everything pertaining to action, belongs to what mysticism regards as the world of illusion, if only because it is essentially concerned with time. In our contemplative life, where action is not called for, it is possible to be impartial, and to overcome the ethical dualism which action requires. So long as we remain merely impartial, we may be content to say that both the good and the evil of action are illusions. But if, as we must do if we have the mystic vision, we find the whole world worthy of love and worship, if we see

> "The earth, and every common sight. . . .
> Apparell'd in celestial light,"

we shall say that there is a higher good than that of action, and that this higher good belongs to the whole world as it is in reality. In this way the twofold attitude and the apparent vacillation of mysticism are explained and justified.

The possibility of this universal love and joy in all that exists is of supreme importance for the conduct and happiness of life, and gives inestimable value to the mystic emotion, apart from any creeds which may be built upon it. But if we are not to be led into false beliefs, it is necessary to realise exactly what the mystic emotion reveals. It reveals a possibility of human nature--a possibility of a nobler, happier, freer life than any that can be otherwise achieved. But it does not reveal anything

*From Bertrand Russell, "Mysticism and Logic" in MYSTICISM AND LOGIC AND OTHER ESSAYS. Permission granted by Barnes & Noble Books, Totowa, N.J.

about the non-human, or about the nature of the universe in general. Good and bad, and even the higher good that mysticism finds everywhere, are the reflections of our own emotions on other things, not part of the substance of things as they are in themselves. And therefore an impartial contemplation, freed from all pre-occupation from Self, will not judge things good or bad, although it is very easily combined with that feeling of universal love which leads the mystic to say that the whole world is good.

'ALL IS GOOD' IS AMORAL*

by Arthur Danto

It is the high Vedantic teaching that the world is <u>Brahma</u> so that one's flight from the world to <u>Brahma</u> is in the end a flight to the world, but to the world seen in a different light and under a different perspective. In this perspective, one at the same time lives in the world and does not. Buddhism, too, comes to teach that the <u>Samsara</u> world, thought to be distinct from Nirvana, is really Nirvana. Nirvana is here. It is in this spirit that a Zen monk, reprimanded for spitting upon a statue of the Buddha, replied that since Buddha was everywhere, it is impossible to spit and not spit on Buddha. When the <u>Samsara</u> world is made Nirvana, it is equally impossible not to be saved whatever one does: even if one just eats and sleeps. This teaching I should like to discuss, for it brings us to an aspect of Oriental thought that is distinctive and important to our purpose.

When the distinction between the <u>samsara</u> world, the perpetual cycle of rebirth, and Nirvana is collapsed, our daily life is stained with religious significance. The entirety of life is religious, rather than a restricted portion of it reserved for ritual and specific observances marked out as "religious." Everything we do becomes a religious act, even, to use the example cited a moment ago, eating and sleeping. Can religion be that simple? In one sense, yes; in another, no. For most of us do not eat and sleep in the consciousness of them as religious acts. A religious act is not one of a special class of acts, but an act performed with a certain attitude and through a certain perspective. So we need not change our practices in any way, only the spirit in which we pursue them. It is instructive to think in this connection of a distinction that has very recently been blurred, the distinction between art works and ordinary objects: it has been found that ordinary objects can be art works without undergoing any internal modification—that art works and ordinary objects are the same things, though grouped in different ways and appreciated in a different spirit. The whole world can become aestheticized without there being any change in the world at all.

In a way, one can think of Nietzsche's <u>amor fati</u> ("love of fate") doctrine in this connection. <u>Amor fati</u> is the key to a release from the bondage of one's destiny, for by affirming what one does, by endorsing it, one makes it one's own. The content of our actions has not changed. Only the light in which we perform acts has altered making the difference between freedom and bondage. In one way, nothing is changed. But in another way, everything is changed. It is in this way that the <u>samsara</u> world becomes the nirvana world without any alteration. To do what we

*From MYSTICISM AND MORALITY: ORIENTAL THOUGHT AND MORAL PHILOSOPHY by Arthur C. Danto. (c) 1972 by Basic Books, Inc. By permission of Basic Books, Inc., Publishers, New York.

Ways of Wisdom

always do in this way is at once to be within the world and without the world: to be in and beyond the world at once.

Whether or not this is a formula for salvation, it is not bad as a formula for attaining happiness. According to it, this world is the only world, salvation not consisting in the transcendence of this world into a world beyond, but in accepting this world as sanctified. What is called for, is not a transformation of the world, but a transformation of the vision of ourselves and our relation to the world. So in doing our "thing," as it has become fashionable to say, we each attain the salvation we seek.

This is a teaching it is difficult not to respect. But I do not believe it will do as a moral philosophy. Since it permits the ritualization of everything, every act can be interpreted as a religious discipline, such as the manufacture of instruments of torture, the skills involved in bringing the maximum of exquisite agony to one's victim. One of the great logical insights of Socrates was that every skill, every "thing" can be used or abused, the same skills that enable one to win a race enable one, as a positive achievement, to lose a race as well. It was this insight that led him to seek a moral knowledge that could not be reduced to the various sorts of knowledge in which the possession of skills consists. Nor will the doing of one's "thing" selflessly and impersonally make an act "good": for it was the boast of such figures as Adolf Eichmann, for example, that he was only doing his thing. Finally, if the samsara world is the Nirvana world, whatever exists in one exists in the other, and the conditions that occasioned us to relinquish desire and repress craving in order to surmount suffering could only assert themselves in the same way as before. And some way has to be found for rationalizing evil.

Ethics has to do with how we should treat one another, not merely with how we are to treat ourselves alone. Devotion to our dharma, appropriate and selfless execution of our tasks, while it may promote or even constitute salvation, is neither sufficient nor even necessary as a minimal ethical requirement. To be sure, Buddhism as a religion is concerned with salvation. But we can see that the demands of salvation and the demands of morality are not automatically and simultaneously fulfilled, and they may even be antithetical. Morality cannot be a technique of salvation, even if the same acts that are moral are the same ones that entail salvation. The fact that they lead to salvation cannot constitute a moral justification.

STUDY QUESTIONS FOR CHAPTER VIII

Questions for Review:

1. Summarize Nietzsche's notion of amor fati in your own words.

2. What strategies are appropriate for living in the present, according to the introduction?

3. What are the characteristics of mystical experience as described in the introduction?

4. Is living in the present consistent with productive, goal-seeking behavior? Summarize the arguments of the introduction on this question.

5. Summarize in your own words Chuang Tzu's criticism of ordinary consciousness and behavior, in Section I.

6. How does Cook Ting go about cutting up an ox?

7. What does Confucius mean by "being whole in power"?

8. Summarize in your own words the characteristics of the "True Man" as described in Section IV.

9. What is the secret of ruling the world, according to T'ien Ken?

10. What does Chuang Tzu mean by the statement that "The Perfect Man uses his mind like a mirror"?

11. Summarize Chuang Tzu's arguments in Section VII for the claim that "It is impossible to establish any constant rule."

12. What is the distinction between the Heavenly and the human, as stated by Jo of the North Sea?

13. What is the editor's interpretation of the "Eastern tale, retold by Leo Tolstoy"?

14. What problem with human life does Zen propose to solve, according to Suzuki?

15. What are the chief characteristics of satori, as described by Suzuki?

16. What are the chief characteristics of moments of "cosmic consciousness" as described by Alan Watts?

17. Why is it that different traditions describe the experience of "cosmic consciousness" in different ways, according to Watts?

18. How does one see the evil in the world, from the point of view of the goodness of all things, according to Watts?

19. Watts describes three remarkable experiences of his own. Among the events leading up to and precipitating each experience, are there any common features?

20. What is the usual account of good and evil given by mystics, according to Russell? What is Russell's alternative account?

21. What does the mystical experience reveal, according to Russell?

22. Explain Danto's analogy of "Samsara is Nirvana" to a new kind of art form.

23. What is the problem with "the ritualization of everything," according to Danto?

24. Why is it true, according to Danto, that "Morality cannot be a technique of salvation"?

Questions for Reflection:

1. Have I at times had experiences of the kind described in this chapter, in which the world seemed to be wholly right and good? If so, what circumstances surrounded my experiences? What seemed to precipitate them?

2. How do I feel about the advice "to love that which happens of necessity"?

3. For those who have some experience with meditation: How have my experiences in meditation compared with the kind of shift of consciousness described in the introduction?

4. What ideas from this chapter, if any, would I like to incorporate into my own outlook on life?

Questions for Discussion:

1. Does living in the present pose any serious problems for the conduct of life? Are there times when one should <u>not</u> live in the present?

2. Is the attitude of acceptance, of embracing the present, as described in the introduction, consistent with constructive and morally responsible behavior? Or does it tend to promote passive quiescence, in your opinion?

3. Do you agree with Russell's critique of the mystic account of good and bad?

4. Do you agree with Danto that "Morality cannot be a technique of salvation"?

5. Are the views expressed in this chapter of value for large numbers of people? Or are they relevant only to a small minority who have had certain very rare experiences?

6. Are there similarities between the central ideals of this chapter, and themes that appear in previous chapters? If so, what commonalities and similarities can you discern?

7. It has been sometimes argued that Western culture is predominently oriented toward control, manipulation, and active change, while Eastern culture and tradition are more oriented toward an intuitive appreciation of things as they are. Do the readings of this chapter lend any credibility to such generalizations?

SUGGESTIONS FOR FURTHER READING

Arthur Danto, Mysticism and Morality: Oriental Thought and Moral Philosophy (Basic Books, 1972)

John A. Hutchison, Paths of Faith, Chapters 5, 6, 8 (McGraw-Hill, 1969, 1975)

Abraham Maslow, Religions, Values, and Peak Experiences (Penguin, 1976)

Baba Ram Dass, Be Here Now (The Lama Foundation, 1971; distributed by Crown Publishing)

Paul Reps, Zen Flesh, Zen Bones: A Collection of Zen and Pre-Zen Writings (Doubleday Anchor)

Nancy Wilson Ross, ed., The World of Zen: An East-West Anthology (Random House, Vintage, 1960)

Bertrand Russell, Mysticism and Logic and Other Essays (George Allen and Unwin, 1917)

Fredrick J. Streng, Emptiness: A Study in Religious Meaning (Abingdon, 1967)

D. T. Suzuki, Essays in Zen Buddhism, Second Series, esp. Essay IV, "Passivity in the Buddhist Life" (Luzac, 1933)

Shunryu Suzuki, Zen Mind, Beginner's Mind (Weatherhill, 1970)

Alan Watts, This Is It and Other Essays on Zen and Spiritual Experience (Random House, Vintage, 1973)

About the Author

Steve Smith was born in 1939 near What Cheer, Iowa. In 1961 he received his B.A. in philosophy and German from Earlham College, having spent one year at the Free University in West Berlin. He held Woodrow Wilson and Danforth Graduate Fellowships at Harvard University, from which he received his M.A. in 1963 and Ph.D. in 1972. Since 1968 he has been teaching at Claremont McKenna College (formerly Claremont Men's College) in Claremont, California, where he is currently Associate Professor of Philosophy. He is the author of Satisfaction of Interest and the Concept of Morality (Bucknell University Press, 1974) and several articles on moral theory. He is married to Daryl Goldgraben Smith and has a son, David.